COLORADO
PROFILES

July 1993

Lisa

Hope you have some good
Colorado memories to take
back with you.

I'm glad we are friends!
Love Jim and
Jag

COLORADO PROFILES

MEN AND WOMEN WHO SHAPED THE
CENTENNIAL STATE

John H. Monnett
&
Michael McCarthy

CORDILLERA PRESS, INC.

Publishers in the Rockies

Library of Congress Cataloging-in-Publication Data

Monnett, John H.
  Colorado profiles.

  Bibliography: p.
  Includes index.
    1. Colorado — History.   2. Colorado — Biography.
  I. McCarthy, Michael, 1940-   II. Title.
  F776.M65   1987   978.8   87-22262
  ISBN 0-917895-19-3

About the Cover

"Denver From the Highlands." Water color painting by Paul Frenzeny and Jules Tavernier, 1874. Courtesy of the Western History Department, Denver Public Library.

In fall 1873, *Harper's Weekly* commissioned two young French artists, Paul Frenzeny and Jules Tavernier, to journey west and make sketches. They spent the winter in Denver, and their work included this beautiful but inaccurate water color which later appeared in *Harper's*. The *Rocky Mountain Herald* remarked, "Everybody who examines that painting of Denver, in Richards and Co.'s windows, comes at once to the conclusion that the artist must have been cross-eyed to have located the city between the Platte river and the mountains and near sighted to have the foot hills appear to be immediately joining the suburbs, when they are fully ten miles distant."

First Edition
    3 4 5 6 7 8 9
Printed in the United States of America
ISBN: 0-917895-19-3

Cordillera Press, Inc., P.O. Box 3699, Evergreen, Colorado 80439
(303) 670-3010

Contents

To Pete and Kelly, Kevin and Susan, and Jeff —
the best family a guy could have

For Linda

Preface

*O*n September 5, 1881, silver king Horace Tabor opened his ornate Grand Opera House in Denver. It was built of pressed brick from Ohio and cherry wood from Honduras. Tabor himself decorated the interior with expensive pieces of fine art from Europe. It seated 1,500 people, and was undoubtedly one of the finest theaters in America. On opening night Emma Abbott sang the mad aria from *Lucia*. The proper Victorian audience applauded enthusiastically, and the next day, Eugene Field, the irreverent young editor of the *Denver Tribune*, wrote a poem for his newspaper to commemorate the event. The first stanza read:

> "The Opera House — a union grand
> Of capital and labor —
> Long will the stately structure stand
> A monument to Tabor."

Tabor and Field were fortunate. When they died, they left something behind for society to remember them. For Tabor it was a structure made of cherry wood and pressed brick. It was tangible and visible, and for a generation and more it kept his memory alive. Eugene Field, "The Poet Laureate of Childhood," left his famous verses that included "A Dutch Lullaby" and "Little Boy Blue."

There were many others, of course, who passed through Colorado's history like Tabor and Field. But most people left no monument behind, and so they are largely forgotten.

The history of Colorado is filled with monument builders, and every school child knows who they are. But the past is also filled with a mass of faceless people unknown to anyone. Some were rich and some were poor. Some were good and some were evil. Some were men and women of consummate talent who made their way on wits and skill. Others were opportunists who preyed on the land, on its resources, and on other people. Some were lucky and some were not.

But all left stories behind them. The tales of some were written in marble and paint, as well as in literature. The stories of others were simply their unusual lives embroiled in turbulent times. Some, like Alexander Majors, Poker Alice Tubbs, Alferd Packer, Otto Mears, Tom Horn, Soapy Smith, Jack Dempsey, and Wayne Aspinall, are known to all. But others, like Susan Shelby Magoffin, Jack Stillwell, Sig Schlesinger, Chin Lin Sou, Lewis Price, and Preston Porter, are known to few. In retrospect, they were all as varied as the state they shaped. And they are all a part of Colorado's human tapestry.

It must be remembered that the portraits in this book are only representative; yet they all share a common theme. All of them carried bright visions of the future, and those visions they planted in the rich soil of the new land they called Colorado. In pursuit of their dreams, they built a world that lasted generations beyond them.

This is their story.

This book would not have been completed without the assistance of many others. The fine staff of the Colorado Historical Society directed us to much unused material, as did the many librarians in the Western History Department of the Denver Public Library, the Boulder Public Library, the Auraria Library, and the Norlin Library at the University of Colorado, Boulder. The National Archives provided much needed material. Special thanks goes to western historian Fred Lee of Kansas City, Missouri, who reviewed portions of the manuscript and made valuable suggestions.

John H. Monnett
  Boulder, Colorado

Michael McCarthy
  Denver, Colorado

Juan Bautista de Anza

*T*he morning sunrise gleamed off a gossamer coat of early frost on the bunch grass which spread endlessly away toward the hazy eastern horizon. Then the shadows began to define the gorges and talus slopes of the massive Sangre de Cristo Range. The great Comanche chief spread his arms and gestured defiantly at the approaching formation of soldiers partially concealed by a rising cloud of dust. The warriors heard the faint sound of a drum cadence. Then the ranks of men brightly clad in blue and red tunics and tricorn hats began to divide into two columns. Quickly they flanked the Indians on both sides. The chief looked around in confusion, shouting orders to his lieutenants and their impatient warriors. The situation had become desperate. The flanking movement had cut off the chief and about fifty of his ablest fighting men from the main camp.

With frosty breath, the chief shouted encouraging words to his young warriors as they mounted their swift ponies. His great medicine hat, fashioned from the hide of a mighty buffalo bull and gracefully winged by the beast's tremendous green-dyed horns, would protect them in battle. They were invincible! Seemingly at once, the painted war ponies attained full-gait. Astride their bare backs rode some of the greatest horsemen on the high plains. Screaming insults at the approaching troops, the confident warriors began releasing a barrage of deadly arrows from under the necks of their speeding ponies.

Then within yards of the enemy, the fifty warriors heard the devastating sound of musketry. Blue puffs of smoke billowed rhythmically down a line of 300 guns, then rose lazily and dissipated into the early autumn air. Instantly, a lead ball struck the chief in the chest. He was thrown back so forcefully that he plunged head-first over the animal's flanks and hit the ground with such an impact that he rolled several yards before coming to rest face down at the edge of a snaking arroyo. The buffalo headdress, his divine assurance of immortality, had separated from his head upon impact. It now lay against a jutting boulder, one chartreuse horn cracked and broken at the tip. The great Comanche chief, Cuerno Verde ("Greenhorn"), was mortally wounded.

Immediately, the Comanches wheeled around and began a frantic retreat. In a running battle, many more were slain, including Cuerno Verde's first-born son. The fight was over.

The next day, Comanche emissaries prudently entered the soldiers' camp for council with the Spanish leader. The man to whom they spoke talked with extreme assurance in his voice. He promised them farming implements and instruction from his people in the way of agriculture. Ornamented in full military dress, his elegantly groomed beard and long-flowing locks of hair radiated an image of confidence and power befitting his noble station in life. He was Juan Bautista de Anza, Governor of all New Mexico. The Indians promised to make peace, take up the plow share, and pledge their allegiance to the man who had defeated them at the base of Greenhorn Mountain.

The defeat of the Comanches on September 2, 1779, some thirty miles south of the Arkansas River, climaxed one of the most extraordinary military expeditions ever conducted in Colorado. The eventual peace with these Indians led to the establishment of San Carlos in the vicinity of present-day Pueblo; and it became Spain's northernmost outpost along the Rocky Mountain cordillera.

Juan Bautista de Anza was principally responsible for this first and last attempt by the Spanish to establish a settlement within the borders of present-day Colorado. In retrospect, his expedition of 1779 and the eventual settlement of a colony in southern Colorado are even more remarkable when later generations consider that during the waning years of the eighteenth century, Spain was futilely attempting to administer a decaying empire in the New World.

For God, glory, and gold the Spanish had come to the Americas. Since the conquest of the Aztecs deep in Mexico in 1520, they had pushed their frontiers steadily northward. Rumors of gold had led the daring Coronado close to present-day Colorado in 1541 in search of the legendary Quivera. The founding of Santa Fe in 1610 by Pedro de Peralta gave New Spain a base of operations in the northern extremities of the colonies. From that crude adobe outpost the Spanish eventually sent out expeditions to all quarters of the compass.

Although they fully exploited the wealth of Mexico and Peru, the Spanish made only sparse inroads in most of North America. Settlements were few. Instead, the absolute rule of the monarchy dictated that a progression of soldiers and priests would serve tours of duty in the Western Hemisphere with the sole purpose of enhancing Spanish wealth and prestige among the European powers. Far-flung colonies on the northern borders of the Spanish dominions were consequently underpopulated and heavily dependent upon forced Indian labor centered around the ever-present evangelical mission church. In the settlements adjacent to Santa Fe, the Spanish masters found themselves outnumbered by their Native American laborers. Consequently, they spent most of the time trying to preserve order among their subjects.

Control of Santa Fe meant the domination of what eventually became the American Southwest, but there were many rivals. From the east came the French, ever determined to infiltrate the northern corridors to Mexico. From the north, along the Pacific coast, came Russian fur hunters determined to claim their share of the wealth of the New World. The continuous policy of the Spanish was to keep the foreigners out of their widely dispersed colonies.

This policy kept the civil authorities constantly busy marching out to expel foreigners whenever rumors of their presence reached Santa Fe. These expeditions, however, were frequently attacked by the Comanches and their occasional allies, the Utes, who sought to keep the Spanish intruders off the great buffalo ranges. In addition, the artificial structure of the economy which depended heavily upon forced Indian labor meant that frequent military expeditions were needed to track down escaped slaves who sought refuge with the plains tribes.

So it was that Juan Bautista de Anza, a Spaniard born in Sonora, launched his punitive expedition against Cuerno Verde in 1779. Peace with the Comanches, it was believed, would bring tranquility to the northern provinces and end the damaging raids by these Indians conducted in Santa Fe's hinterland or at the Taos fairs where Pueblo Indian slaves escaped their Spanish masters to seek refuge with the lords of the southern plains.

Anza's ventures in the Southwest won him acclaim which led to his appointment as Governor of New Mexico in 1778. By making peace with the Comanches and establishing a northern citadel on the plains, Anza believed he could stabilize the sparse frontier colony which he loved so dearly.

Determined to move straight up the Rio Grande Valley, Anza led a fighting force of 600 strong north from the capital at Santa Fe on August 15, 1779. Marching at night to avoid detection, he traveled into the San Luis Valley, crossed Poncha Pass, and entered the upper Arkansas Valley in the vicinity of present-day Salida. This journey was the first documented penetration of this vast mountain stronghold by Spaniards.

Eventually, the force turned east, crossed Trout Creek Pass, and entered South Park. They passed near Pikes Peak and the vicinity of what a century later would become the mining camp of Cripple Creek. Once on the plains, the army surprised and defeated Cuerno Verde's Comanches in the dawn battle of September 2, 1779. About the same time, another beleaguered commander by the name of George Washington was preparing to go into winter quarters at Morristown, New Jersey, after five years of bitter, though inconclusive, warfare with the British.

With the death of Cuerno Verde, the Comanches never again posed a serious threat to the settlements of northern New

Mexico. On the return trip to Santa Fe, Anza crossed Sangre de Cristo Pass and descended the San Luis Valley once again. Not only had this most formidable Spanish force discovered two important mountain passes in the southern Rockies (Poncha Pass and Trout Creek Pass), but they also had circled the northern Sangre de Cristo Range, opening a new, more direct route through the mountains.

Keeping his promise to the Comanches, Governor Anza pacified the Utes in 1786 and established the meager settlement of San Carlos the following year in hope of transforming the Comanches into an agrarian people under Spanish authority. But the community failed almost immediately. During the first year the untimely death of a respected Comanche woman alarmed the Indians, who viewed the incident as an ill omen. They scattered from the village, and the Spanish lacked sufficient manpower to force their return. Thus ended Spain's only attempt to establish a permanent settlement in the mysterious north that is today the State of Colorado.

Juan Bautista de Anza remained Governor of New Mexico until the end of 1787, but within thirty-four years the seeds of revolution would come to fruition within the Spanish dominions. Mexico won its independence in 1821, and with the peace treaty Spain's domination of the Southwest ceased.

By that time, a host of new, more numerous invaders were slowly penetrating what would become Colorado. Men with the names of Pike, Long, Bent, and Becknell replaced those with names like Anza. Gaining access to the old Spanish borderlands via the Santa Fe Trail and the Rocky Mountain fur trade, these vanguards of an on-rushing America broke down the forbidden boundary at the Arkansas River and led the way to the overt annexation of the Southwest in 1848. In less than half a century from the time Spain's empire in North America disintegrated, these newcomers would discover the gold and silver that the Spanish had failed to find in the Rocky Mountains.

Despite the political wedding of the Southwest to the United States, the cultural heritage of Spain became forever engrained throughout southern Colorado. In 1851, three years after annexation, Hispanic migrants from New Mexico settled the town of

San Luis, now Colorado's oldest, continuously inhabited community. Spanish customs, Spanish place names (including the name Colorado), and Spanish architecture are still richly prevalent throughout the southern portion of the state. Spanish land grants and boundary lines surveyed in the eighteenth century continue to affect land ownership and water rights. The Spanish put their boots down in Colorado over two centuries ago, and their descendants continue to help shape Colorado's development with the same tenacity and zeal as the bold adventurer, Juan Bautista de Anza, who came before them.

Susan Shelby Magoffin

As the heat vapors rose to blur the vision of the dogged travelers, the caravan slowly rounded a sharp bend in the Arkansas River. The attractive young bride of eight months grew more excited as she caught the first glimpse of the strange golden castle rising abruptly above the scorched plains. For over a month, the party had laboriously plied the endless, rutted trail from Independence, Missouri, toward this rude way station on the great route of the Santa Fe traders. Susan Shelby Magoffin, age eighteen, and in all likelihood the first white woman to traverse the legendary trail, had finally arrived at Bent's Fort. It was July 26, 1846.

Throughout the middle decades of the nineteenth century, a quarter of a million Americans crossed the continent in response to free land, new opportunity, adventure, and profit. Collectively, these journeys comprise one of the great human migrations in history. The lure of the West with its unbounded wilderness inspired the pens as well as the souls of many travelers. With the one exception of the Civil War, no other event elicited so many personal chronicles than these overland journeys. The great majority of the diarists were women.

Undoubtedly, one of the most remarkable daily records of the trek across the parched western prairie on the road to Santa Fe was compiled by this energetic young woman, Susan Shelby

Susan Shelby Magoffin.
*Western History Department,
Denver Public Library.*

Magoffin. Born to a wealthy Kentucky family, she married Samuel Magoffin, her senior by twenty-seven years and one of the most successful men to engage in what Josiah Gregg called "The Commerce of the Prairies." She was making the journey at a time when the Santa Fe trade was at its zenith. That year, American traders hauled merchandise valued at well over one million dollars a thousand miles to the northern Mexican provinces. In addition, the young Susan was very fortunate to go west during the year of decision when a zealous wave of American expansionism spread across the plains in the spirit of Manifest Destiny, a movement destined to wrest forcibly from Mexico lands that would almost double the size of the United States.

By the standards of the Santa Fe Trail, Susan Magoffin traveled in luxury. Her husband provided her with a private carriage, a small "tent house," a maid, and at least two servant boys. No wonder she found time to write during an age of travel when a few blankets spread in a hard-board wagon provided standard overnight accommodation for the weary.

Despite this comparative comfort, the rigors of the trail became evident as the caravan traversed the short-grass prairies of western Kansas and southeastern Colorado. On the evening of June 30, 1846, they camped along the swampy banks of the little Arkansas River, whereupon they gave battle to overwhelming legions of mosquitoes. From the security of her carriage, Susan vividly described the vexatious engagement so typical of the discomfort associated with overland travel during the mid-nineteenth century.

"Millions upon millions [of mosquitos] were swarming around me, and their knocking against the carriage reminded me of a hard rain," she wrote. "It was equal to any of the plagues of Egypt. I lay almost in a perfect stupor, the heat and stings made me perfectly sick, till Magoffin came to the carriage and told me to run if I could, with my shawl, bonnet and shoes on (and without opening my mouth, Jane said, for they would choke me) straight to bed. When I got there they pushed me straight in under the mosquito bar, which had been tied up in some kind of a fashion, and oh, dear, what a relief it was to breathe again. There I sat in my cage, like an imprisoned creature frightened half to death."

Overcoming such obstacles, the Magoffin party pushed on. By the last week of July, Susan sighted famed Bent's Fort. Growing weary from the trials of pregnancy, she spent the better part of the summer in one of the fort's rooms overlooking the plains. As was typical of so many nineteenth-century women making the overland journey, Susan did not write much about her physical condition. Taboos of the times prevented not only open discussion but also written references. In the end, the strain of travel took its toll and she lost her baby. She made only brief mention of the tragedy in her diary.

One significant legacy of Mrs. Magoffin's journey was her

striking description of Bent's Fort. Built in 1832 by brothers William and Charles Bent and their partner Ceran St. Vrain, this adobe trading post had become a venerable institution on the southern plains. An important fur trade center, it supported a wide range of commerce while playing host to some of the era's best known frontiersmen.

Situated as the last bastion of American civilization before the great trail crossed the Arkansas River and descended into northern Mexico, Bent's Fort was fortified with six-foot-thick walls and equipped with a watchtower and cannon. From even a short distance the structure reminded travelers of a medieval castle. Susan Shelby Magoffin became one of the first chroniclers to describe it, and she did so in vibrant detail:

"The outside exactly fills my idea of an ancient castle," she wrote. "It is built of adobes, unburnt brick, and Mexican style so far. The walls are very high and very thick with rounding corners. There is but one entrance, this is to the East rather."

"Inside is a large space some ninety or an hundred feet square, all around this and next the wall are rooms, some twenty-five in number. They have dirt floors — which are sprinkled with water several times during the day to prevent dust. Standing in the center of some of them is a large wooden post as a firmer prop to the ceiling which is made of logs. Some of these rooms are occupied by boarders as bed chambers. One is a dining room — another a kitchen — a little store, a blacksmith's shop, a barber's, and an ice house, which receives perhaps more customers than any other. . . ."

"They have one large room as a parlor; there are no chairs but a cushion next to the wall on two sides, so the company set all round in a circle. There is no other furniture than a table on which stands a bucket of water, free to all. Any water that may be left in the cup after drinking is unceremoniously tossed onto the floor."

One significant effect of the thousands of American traders crossing the prairies to Santa Fe between 1821 and 1846 was the impression they planted in the minds of Americans back east about the perceived inadequacy of the Mexican people. As relations between the two nations worsened, the traders described the Mexicans as an indolent people who managed their government and economy ineffectively and therefore had no right to possess the rich lands they governed.

While convalescing at Bent's Fort, however, Susan Shelby Magoffin formulated a different opinion of Hispanics. Learning Spanish, she made many friends among the Mexican people whom she found charming and delightful. Even when the Magoffin party was under severe threat of attack later in the year, and even when her brother-in-law was jailed in Mexico for espionage, she retained her esteem for her country's enemies in time of war. It seems clear from her writing that the prevailing attitudes of the Americans were indeed incorrect. "What a polite people these Mexicans are," she wrote, "altho' they are looked upon as a half-barbarous set by the generality of people. . . . What a strange people this. They are not to be called cowards; take them in mass they are brave. . . . Take them one by one and they will not flinch from danger."

Despite these impressions, Susan could not escape the reality of Manifest Destiny set in motion by Stephen Watts Kearny's Army of the West. The federal government had designated Bent's Fort as the advance base for Kearny's planned invasion of New Mexico. Acting under secret orders, the general's objective was to seize Santa Fe and then drive across the desert to link up with John C. Fremont's "Bear Flag" army in California so that the United States would possess the coveted northern provinces before the great Mexican Army of Antonio Lopez de Santa Anna could take the field.

The Magoffins entertained Kearny and Colonel Alexander Doniphan's Missouri volunteers while at Bent's Fort and afterwards in Santa Fe. If the army presented the young woman with a sense of security once the caravan crossed the Arkansas River, the daily reminder of her country's invasion must have bothered her to some extent as she continued to make friends throughout New Mexico. When the caravan at long last entered the ancient provincial capital, Susan's admiration for the Mexican women grew. While in Santa Fe she was especially impressed by the social liberation of Mexican women in terms of fashion and dress. Smoking "cigaretos" at the numerous fandangos in the plaza and in the homes of wealthy hidalgos was quite foreign to the value system she had known in ante-bellum Kentucky.

Ironically, Susan Shelby Magoffin's very presence in Santa Fe, which had spurred her admiration for the New Mexicans, was made possible through a secret mission of political intrigue surrounding her family. President James K. Polk himself had requested Susan's brother-in-law, James Magoffin, to accompany the traders to Santa Fe. While the party was resting at Bent's Fort, James Magoffin pushed on and persuaded the governor of New Mexico, Manuel Armijo, to vacate the city for American troops. This bloodless coup enabled the Army of the West to accomplish its objectives and secured the allegiance of many New Mexicans, who had long felt an economic affinity with the Missouri traders.

This act paved the way for the annexation of the Southwest to the United States once the guns of Chapultepec were silenced in Mexico City in 1848. By the terms of the Treaty of Guadalupe Hidalgo, the lands immediately south of the Arkansas River passed into the hands of the United States. They would eventually become portions of the State of Colorado.

Susan Shelby Magoffin eventually journeyed deep into Mexico with her husband, gave birth to a son in 1847, then returned by ship to the United States. She died prematurely in 1852 shortly after giving birth to a fourth child. She was buried in Bell-Fontaine Cemetery in St. Louis.

The chronicles of her journey give us perhaps the most unbiased assessment of the Mexican culture as it evolved from its Spanish roots through the era of Manifest Destiny to become an integral part of Colorado's heritage. It is the responsibility of present and future generations to recognize and utilize the elements of that rich culture for the betterment of the state and its people.

Alexander Majors

*T*he advent of the Pikes Peak Gold Rush in 1858 brought out the worst in people. The fact that gold strikes in Colorado and throughout the West did not occur in an orderly fashion, progressing logically and steadily from eastern states bordering the frontier to the next nearest western territory, upset the entire balance of communication and transportation from "the states." As historians Martin Ridge and Ray Allen Billington have written: "How could the widely scattered camps be supplied with the essentials of life? And more important, how could the miners be reunited with their government in the 'states' and the separatist tendencies usual on isolated frontiers be defeated. Not only the welfare of the miners but the perpetuation of a united nation depended on forging links connecting the Far West with the Mississippi Valley." The use of private enterprise to forge supply lines across the plains to the Rocky Mountains and beyond would exhaust the resources of the most affluent private concerns.

Fortunately, there were precedents from the early days of turnpikes and canals in the mid-Atlantic states and the first development of railroad networks through the country's heartland. Government subsidy! To win a coveted government contract, however, entrepreneurs who sought fame and fortune uniting East and West had to convince Congress that the security

Alexander Majors.
Western History Department,
Denver Public Library.

and welfare of the entire nation was at stake. Those who sought to compete with government contractors usually regretted it financially.

Among those enterprising souls who learned this fact of economics the hard way was a representative frontiersman by the name of Alexander Majors. His subsequent ruination, along with that of his partners, William H. Russell and William B. Waddell, demonstrated to many that opportunity based on frontier exploitation was highly speculative, at best.

Living on the edge of the frontier along the rough Missouri border, Majors became familiar with the West at an early age. The tales of mountain men and Santa Fe traders spurred his imagination. Having learned the ropes from experienced wagoneers along the Missouri River landings, Majors incorporated a freighting business along with Russell and Waddell on March 27, 1855. In its early years, the young firm received a government contract for hauling military supplies to the isolated army posts along the Santa Fe Trail. For a time it held a virtual freighting monopoly along the Great Plains corridor. By 1858, it is estimated that the firm had 4,000 men and 3,500 wagons. The company flourished.

The Missouri River landings at Atchison, Council Bluffs, and St. Joseph were major shipping points. Ox-drawn Murphy wagons would ply their way across the rolling plains carrying gunpowder, manufactured goods, food, and mining equipment. Alexander Majors, who was always happier on the plains than counting his profits in an office, accompanied many of the trains in the early years. Reminiscing many years later, he recalled: "Oxen proved to be the cheapest and most reliable teams for long trips, where they had to live upon the grass." That was usually the case. "They did good daily work," wrote Majors, "gathered their own living, and if properly driven would travel 2,000 miles in a season, or during the months from April to November; traveling from 1,000 to 1,200 miles with the loaded wagons, and with plenty of good grass and water, would make the return trip with the empty wagons in the same season. However, the distance traveled depended much upon the skill of the wagonmasters who had them in charge. . . . "

Alexander Majors was very selective in choosing his wagonmasters and bullwhackers. Often, these men came from the lowest classes of frontier society. Alexander Majors supplied each man with a Bible and a hymn book and required new employees to pledge: "While I am in the employ of A. Majors, I agree not to use profane language, not to get drunk, not to gamble, not to treat animals cruelly, and not to do anything else that is incompatible with the conduct of a gentleman."

Although profits from the freighting business poured into the company's coffers, the discovery of gold at the confluence of Cherry Creek and the South Platte River in 1858 set Alexander Majors and his partners on a course of self-destruction from which they never recovered. As fifty-niners rolled into Denver City, then a part of Kansas Territory, demands for communications and supplies reverberated through the Missouri River landings. The only way the community could stay alive was through a 600-mile-long supply line across the dusty plains.

Alexander Major's partner, William H. Russell, could not resist the temptation. Estimating huge profits, Russell saw the Pikes Peak Gold Rush as an opportunity to haul passengers, mail, and supplies to the new gold camps of the Rocky Mountains. He was sure that no government subsidy would be needed. When Alexander Majors tried to counsel his partner on the financial dangers inherent in such an operation unsupported by a government contract, Russell borrowed money to the hilt and took on a less conservative partner by the name of John S. Jones.

The result was the formation of the Leavenworth and Pikes Peak Express Company. The first stage rolled out of Leavenworth for Denver City with the advent of warm weather in 1859. Along the way the stagecoach drivers must have grumbled as they saw more than a few returning argonauts whose wagons were aptly labeled, "Busted."

Not much gold had been discovered on the banks of Cherry Creek. The rich strike made in May by John Gregory in the foothills west of Denver City, however, assured at least a temporary resurgence of the Denver community, and coaches continued to roll toward the Rocky Mountains. Of course, freight was also hauled along the Smoky Hill Route between Leavenworth and Denver City. On one occasion, much to the delight of awaiting Denverites, a flock of over 500 turkeys ambled across the plains, subsisting on prairie vegetation along the way. Over the dusty miles the bullwhackers composed a little ditty that they sang to the tune of "Sweet Betsy of Pike":

"We arrived at Denver City on the
Twenty-first of June,
The people were surprised to
See us there so soon.
But we are all good bullwhackers,

On whom you may rely,
We go it on the principle
of root hog or die."

Denverites rejoiced at the establishment of the new lifeline.
Alexander Majors did not. The Pikes Peak Express, as predicted,
was a financial disaster from the beginning. Within two months
he and his associates shifted the operation from the Smoky Hill
Route north to the Platte River through Nebraska and then up
the South Platte River to Denver City. The operation cost the
company in excess of $1,000 a day, a sum that could be effectively
borne only with a government subsidy. Russell's answer was
to continue a branch line to Denver City while extending the
main line into Salt Lake City, where a California company could
provide connections on to San Francisco. Alexander Majors and
his partner William Waddell were sucked into the whirlpool.
Fearful that their partner's exploits might ruin the freighting
line, they agreed to subsidize the stage line with profits from
freighting until they could secure a government mail contract.

The company reorganized as the Central Overland, California,
and Pikes Peak Express or simply (as the initials over the coaches
read), the C.O.C. & P.P. The name was against the partners as
were the financial odds. Cynics said the initials meant "Clean
Out of Cash and Poor Pay." The tri-weekly service to California
impaired the partners' credit beyond salvation.

There was only one hope. If the partners could convince the
government that the Central Route along the Platte River, where
their coaches were traveling, was superior and faster than the
so-called Ox Bow Route through the Southwest where the Butterfield Overland Stage was currently operating (with a government mail contract of $600,000 annually), then Uncle Sam might
award the firm its long sought-after subsidy. The result was the
inception of one of the most romanticized institutions in Western
history — the Pony Express.

The Pony Express was never intended to be anything more
than an elaborate advertising device. Its purpose was to pub-
licize the advantages of the Central Route and lead to a coveted
federal mail contract. But it was an anachronism from the very

start. All during 1861, the Pacific Telegraph Company was building its lines across the plains toward the Pacific.

Nevertheless, the partners constructed 190 stations between St. Joseph, Missouri, and Sacramento, California, and stocked them with 500 swift ponies. They hired young riders like William F. Cody and others who became romantic legends as they set new speed records across the plains. When service commenced on April 3, 1860, the rate for sending a letter to California was five dollars an ounce. The mail was delivered within ten days.

Within a year and a half the Pony Express was dead! Telegraph service across the country began on October 24, 1861. The Pony Express did get Alexander Majors and his partners favorable publicity for the Central Route, but unfortunately, they were not awarded a government contract.

In late 1861, Alexander Majors and his partners slid into bankruptcy, ruined by the exploits of William H. Russell. Even worse, in a desperate attempt to save the company, Russell stooped to appropriating federal securities with the complicity of a corrupt Interior Department clerk who was not above embezzlement to help his friend out of a jam. Ironically, the outbreak of the Civil War forced the government to shift to the Central Route, but Russell, Majors, and Waddell were denied the contract. It remained with the Butterfield Overland Mail, whose operations simply moved north.

The remaining assets of Russell, Majors, and Waddell went to the public auction block on March 21, 1862. The "C.O.C. & P.P." was purchased by Benjamin Holladay, and this empire builder dominated the express business until 1866, when he sold out to Wells Fargo & Company.

In May 1869, the Union Pacific and Central Pacific railroads linked up at a nondescript spot known as Promontory, Utah. It was the nation's first transcontinental line. Then in June 1870, the first Union Pacific locomotive steamed from Cheyenne to Denver followed two months later by the first train of the Kansas Pacific Railroad. From that point forward, overland stagecoaches and freight wagons became obsolete as lifelines to the Queen City.

Alexander Majors and his partners died penniless, but despite their disastrous business practices, and perhaps unbeknownst to them at their unfortunate ends, their efforts helped to keep Denver alive during its earliest, most critical years. Nevertheless, the experiences of Alexander Majors brought to light a critical point regarding financial ventures on the untested frontier and provided Andrew Carnegie's famous adage that "pioneering don't pay."

Black Kettle
of the Cheyenne

*B*lack Kettle was worried as he rode silently across the treeless prairie toward his new village. It was a crisp autumn day in 1864. He knew that after a summer of raiding in eastern Colorado and western Kansas by roving bands of young Cheyenne and Arapahoe warriors, the citizens of Colorado Territory had taken measures to remedy the so-called "Indian Problem." With the coming of the Civil War, federal troops had largely been withdrawn from the western territories. Settlers of eastern Colorado were left to deal with the Native Americans on their own. After a period of journalistic hysteria lambasting the government for the troop withdrawal and subsequent lack of protection, the influential press began to call for the ultimate extinction of the Cheyenne. In the wake of this general paranoia, Colorado Governor John Evans had issued orders for all Cheyennes and Arapahoes to lay down their arms, give up their captives, and return to their lands agreed upon in 1861. To enforce this order, the governor called for the organization of citizen militia companies to annihilate those Indians who disobeyed.

From previous dealings with the white people, Black Kettle knew that many times the would-be enforcers could not or would not distinguish between what the white man called "hostiles" and those Indians who truly sought peace.

Black Kettle.
Western History Department,
Denver Public Library.

Black Kettle, who was born around 1801, was widely respected as a fierce adversary of the Pawnee and Kiowa, but he stood for peace with the white man. In 1861, he had signed the Treaty of Fort Wise, promising to remain in the vicinity of the Arkansas River and not to molest settlers and emigrants on the Smoky Hill Trail. In 1863, he and Lean Bear had traveled to Washington, D.C. to "see the might of the Great Father." Perhaps it was during this visit that Black Kettle's astute pragmatic sense convinced him that all-out warfare with the whites would reap nothing less than genocide for his proud people.

The Cheyenne were truly a proud people. Having emigrated to the High Plains from the Great Lakes region around the seventeenth century along with their Arapahoe allies, and acquiring the horse about 1750, by 1830 they had become one of the great nomadic hunting cultures of North America. The Sioux whom they befriended called them "Sahiyela," the "alien speakers." They called themselves "Tsistsista," meaning simply, "The

People." By 1833, the Cheyenne had divided into two major groups with Black Kettle's people living between the South Platte and Arkansas rivers. To the north, their brethren remained with the Sioux hunting buffalo in western Montana, eastern Wyoming, and northwestern Nebraska. People of later generations would recognize that contact with the white man's superior technological weaponry transformed Black Kettle's warriors into some of the greatest light cavalry in military history.

The settlers of Colorado Territory had the chance to witness the martial skills of the Southern Cheyenne and Arapahoe during the summer of 1864. During the initial gold strikes in Colorado, emigrants passed through the Indian land mostly unmolested, exacting little more than curiosity. After the Treaty of Fort Wise in 1861, however, the prime buffalo hunting grounds near the foothills of the Front Range were ceded by the peace chiefs Black Kettle and his close ally, seventy-five-year-old White Antelope. During the subsequent three years, the Indians began to complain that the remaining dry lands north of the Arkansas supported too little game and that white settlers depleted the timber resources along the watercourses. In essence, the Cheyenne and Arapahoe faced not only a wave of miners, but also an ever-increasing number of farmer homesteaders as boosters like William Byers of the *Rocky Mountain News* attempted to stimulate agricultural development east of Denver. By 1862, many of the young Cheyenne men comprising the warrior societies adamantly refused to obey the policies of the treaty.

During the spring and summer of 1864, raiding parties struck throughout the Arkansas Valley, running off livestock and terrorizing the few settlers in the region. By August the raiders had killed several dozen settlers including the Nathan Hungate family on their ranch a mere thirty miles from Denver. Equally bad, war parties had cut the mail route across the plains, put freighters out of business, and threatened merchants in Denver with bankruptcy because they could not resupply themselves with merchandise from the East.

These events frustrated and angered a generation of Denverites categorically disposed to hating the American Indian. When a search party brought in the badly mutilated bodies of the

Hungate family and displayed the corpses in a city theater, the anger turned rapidly to mass hysteria. The press broadcast edicts calling for the extermination of the Cheyenne.

Territorial Governor John Evans responded in kind. Concerned by the withdrawal of federal troops during the Civil War, Evans had been unsuccessful in his attempts to secure reinforcements from General Samuel R. Curtis. Finally, he obtained permission from Washington to authorize the muster of the Third Regiment of Colorado Volunteer Militia for 100-day terms in order to defend the inflamed Colorado frontier.

On June 27, Evans issued a general proclamation carried to the Indian camps by runners, ordering all Indian groups desiring peace and protection of the military to assemble immediately at Fort Lyon, Colorado Territory, or at Fort Larned, which was across the border in Kansas. Those Indians who did not comply with the order would be killed. By August 11, the same day the governor received permission to raise the regiment, Evans issued a second proclamation to all citizens of Colorado. The order authorized them individually or in organized parties to "go in pursuit of all hostile Indians on the plains" and "kill and destroy, as enemies of the country, wherever they may be found, all such hostile Indians."

Due to the vast distances involved, it is not known whether or not all of the Cheyenne and Arapahoe groups actually received word from Evans to assemble at Fort Lyon. The ability of the various chiefs to round up all of their followers on the plains was likewise logistically difficult in such a short period of time. Consequently, the exact intentions of Black Kettle during midsummer 1864 is a subject of some controversy. What is known, however, is that by August 29, the chief and his band, though still considered to be in violation of Evans' order and therefore "hostile," desired to make peace with the white people of Colorado Territory.

On the morning of September 4, four troopers on their way from Fort Lyon to Denver had a startling experience. Three Cheyennes rode into their midst and presented the soldiers with a crumpled piece of paper containing a message addressed to Major Colley, the agent for the Cheyennes. The letter was written in the hand of George Bent, the mixed-blood son of William Bent and his Cheyenne wife, Owl Woman. The Indians had once traded at Bent's Fort on the Arkansas and trusted Bent completely. The letter was addressed from the Cheyenne Village, August 29, 1864, and expressed a sincere desire to make peace.

The message was signed "Black Kettle & Other Chieves [sic]." Although under orders to kill all Indians not camping at one of the forts, the soldiers delivered the Indian messengers to major Edward W. Wynkoop, the commander at Fort Lyon. Skeptical, but nevertheless desirous of bringing peace to the plains, Wynkoop mustered 127 volunteers and on September 6 set off for the Cheyenne camp on the Smoky Hill River along with the Indian prisoners and two twelve-pound howitzers.

At a place the Indians called "Bunch of Timbers," Wynkoop's command was confronted by over 600 Cheyenne and Arapahoe warriors including Black Kettle and White Antelope, technically still at war with the United States. A council ensued. Wynkoop told the chiefs that although he had no authority to make peace, if the Indians would deliver their white prisoners to Fort Lyon, he would take the chiefs to Denver to discuss a lasting peace with Governor Evans.

The gamble paid off. Two days later the chiefs began delivering their captives to the fort and shortly thereafter Black Kettle, White Antelope, and Bull Bear of the Cheyennes, along with Neva, Heap of Buffalo, Bosse, and Nonantee, who were relatives of the great Arapahoe chief Left Hand, left for Denver with Major Wynkoop.

The conference with Evans was generally inconclusive and subject to much controversy. Nevertheless, Wynkoop and the chiefs understood that if they were truly desirous of peace, they could put themselves in Wynkoop's protection and move to the vicinity of Fort Lyon. Believing that he had at least brought about an uncertain truce, pending a more lasting peace, Wynkoop returned to the Arkansas. However, General Samuel R. Curtis soon removed him of command, for leaving his post to journey to Denver and because of rumors that he was illegally issuing rations to the Indians camped at the fort. Wynkoop's successor, Major Scott J. Anthony. who was inexperienced and irresolute in shouldering responsibility in delicate situations, allowed the vague truce to continue. Anthony instructed Black Kettle and White Antelope to move their camp to Sand Creek, a small waste reserve some forty miles from the fort. Anthony told the Cheyennes and Arapahoes that they would be safe there and their young men could better hunt for food. According to more than one witness, Anthony presented Black Kettle with a small white flag to show his intentions of protecting the Indians while acknowledging their resolution to live in peace.

The change in command at Fort Lyon, the vagueness of Governor Evans, and the attitudes of the people he had seen in Denver, must have worried Black Kettle as he rode out to Sand Creek on the day that Anthony gave him the flag. Would he be able to control his young warriors? Would there be enough game on Sand Creek? Most of all, Black Kettle must have considered whether or not the peace would be lasting. The council with Evans had been vague, and Evans' principal military commander, Colonel John M. Chivington, had seemed pompous, untrustworthy, and inconsiderate of Indian ways. What would Chivington ultimately do? What would the coming winter bring to the windswept plains at Sand Creek? Black Kettle stoically rode on.

An ordained Methodist minister, Chivington had preferred a fighting commission at the outset of the Civil War. Through a series of brilliant tactical maneuvers, he had been victorious against Sibley's Confederate invaders at the Battle of La Glorieta Pass in New Mexico during 1862. In possibly saving the Colorado gold country from the rebels, Chivington had instantly elevated himself to the imposing position of war hero. Boastful, vociferous, and politically ambitious, Chivington firmly believed that the Cheyenne and Arapahoe should be punished severely for their summer raids. He also recognized that a resounding victory against the Indians would not hurt his political ambitions in Colorado Territory.

After recruiting the Third Regiment of Colorado Volunteers and training them to the extent possible at Camp Chambers, Chivington took his command on a long march east across the plains in November 1864. There is strong evidence that once he rendezvoused with Anthony, the major urged him to strike the Cheyenne and Arapahoe camp at Sand Creek. Certainly, Anthony pointed the way to the village. No doubt he must have felt intimidated by the huge Chivington and his zealous, almost addictive, obsession to exterminate the Indians, in the name of the public good.

Accompanied by three scouts — Robert Bent, the aged and almost blind mountain man Jim Beckwourth, and the half-breed captive Jack Smith — Chivington's troops slipped silently into position in front of the Indian camp just as the first pink rays of dawn ascended over the rolling hills above Sand Creek on November 29. Chivington had between 675 and 700 troops that day. Approximately 450 untried men comprised the so-called "Bloodless Third" regiment whose 100-day enlistments were about to expire, and who wanted to see action before being mustered out of service. Another 100 to 125 men belonged to the Colorado First Regiment, which accompanied Chivington on his march, and they were joined by 125 troops of the First Regiment from Fort Lyon under Major Anthony. In addition, the command had four twelve-pound mountain howitzers. The Indian camp consisted of approximately 100 lodges with 500 to 600 souls, mostly women and children. From west to east along the creek were the respective lodges of the bands led by War Bonnet, White Antelope, Lone Bear, Black Kettle, Left Hand, and Sand Hill.

The attack came at dawn. When the troops fired their first volleys into the quiet camp, the warriors present began fleeing up the creek bed and digging hasty rifle pits to establish a line of defense. Their meager weaponry, however, was no match for the mountain howitzers. The deadly artillery broke the Indian ranks and drove them steadily back throughout the day. Meanwhile, the soldiers rushed into the camp where they began mercilessly slaughtering the women and small children who had not escaped during the first fusillade. George Bent, along with several white traders in the Indian camp, remembered the peaceful intentions of the Indians. According to Bent, Black Kettle evacuated his lodge dumbfounded by the firing. After realizing what was happening, he tied a large American flag, given to him in 1860, to the end of a tall lodge pole, added a white flag, and hoisted the banners over his teepee. Bent later wrote: "When I looked toward the chief's lodge, I saw that Black Kettle had a large American flag up on a long lodge pole as a signal to the troop that the camp was friendly. Part of the people were rushing about the camp in great fear. All the time Black Kettle kept calling out not to be frightened; that the camp was under protection and there was no danger. Then suddenly the troops opened fire on this mass of men, women, and children, and all began to scatter and run." Bent went on: "At the beginning of the attack Black Kettle, with his wife and White Antelope, took their position before Black Kettle's lodge and remained there after all others had left the camp. At last Black Kettle, seeing that it was useless to stay longer, started to run. . . ."

White Antelope, who had been counseling his people as to the peaceful intention of the whites, decided to die when he comprehended the true nature of the attack. Accordingly, he folded his arms, stood erect before his lodge, and sang his death song. A moment later he lay dead, shot to pieces by the soldiers. After the battle his body was found scalped and his ears, nose, and sex organs cut off.

According to both Indian and white accounts, the mutilation of Indian corpses by the Colorado troopers was rampant. One eyewitness described a Cheyenne woman wandering aimlessly around the battlefield: "Her whole scalp had been taken off and the blood was running down into her eyes so that she could not see where to go." The testimony of white soldiers, like the officer's account that follows, at a government investigation after the battle vividly brought out further atrocities and the proclivity of the troops to exterminate the Indians without taking prisoners: "There was one little child, probably three years old, just big enough to walk through the sand. The Indians had gone ahead, and this little child was behind following after them. The little fellow was naked, travelling on the sand. I saw one man get off his horse, at a distance of about seventy-five yards, and draw up his rifle and fire — he missed the child. Another man came up and said, "Let me try the son of a bitch; I can hit him." He got down off his horse, kneeled down, and fired at the little child, but he missed him. A third man came up and made a similar remark, and fired, and the little fellow dropped."

During the massacre Black Kettle aparently remained in the camp until most of his people had escaped or were killed. Eventually, he started upstream with his wife. Shots rang out in their direction and his wife fell. Thinking she was dead, Black Kettle continued up the creek to where his people were fighting furiously in the rifle pits. After the engagement, he descended the stream and found his wife still alive, although nine bullet wounds riddled her body. Carrying her back to the rifle pits on his shoulders, Black Kettle extracted the slugs and his wife survived.

By afternoon the Sand Creek Massacre was over. The next day, scattered along the little streambed and in the burning camp lay the corpses of between 150 and 200 men, women, and children, mutilated and left unburied. The lust to avenge the Hungate family was complete, and John M. Chivington was given a hero's welcome when he returned to Denver.

During the spring and summer of 1865 many of the Cheyenne and Arapahoe who had survived the Sand Creek disaster joined with other bands to wreak havoc throughout the Smoky Hill and South Platte valleys. Black Kettle, however, was not among them. Though blamed and despised by many young Cheyenne for the Sand Creek Massacre, he continued his peaceful approach and persuaded many Indian people not to participate in the raids of revenge.

Three years later Congress appointed a formal commission to investigate the Sand Creek affair. After hearing numerous participants testify for seventy-two days about the atrocities, the government repudiated Chivington's actions in the Indian camp and labeled the episode a massacre that "scarcely had its parallel in the records of Indian barbarity." General Nelson A. Miles, in writing his memoirs, characterized the event as "perhaps the foulest and most unjustifiable crime in the annals of America."

In 1867, Black Kettle signed the Treaty of Medicine Lodge. It promised peace, but the Indians gave up their last tribal lands along the Arkansas River in exchange for a reservation in the Indian Territory, today the State of Oklahoma. Many young Cheyenne warriors, however, refused to recognize Black Kettle's capitulation to the whites; they defied the treaty, and throughout the summer of 1868 continued their raids despite dogged pursuit from federal troops.

By autumn of that year, at least 2,000 warriors with their families and captives established their winter villages extending for a distance of ten miles through the valley of the Washita River in Indian Territory. Black Kettle's village consisted of a few hundred people continuing to try to live at peace with the whites. In mid-November, the Cheyenne chief met with General William B. Hazen at Fort Cobb and received a promise that the army would attempt to contact troops already in the field and inform them that Black Kettle's camp, at least, was friendly.

During that fateful month of November 1868, General Philip Sheridan, disgusted by his failure to subjugate the Cheyennes during the summer, decided to inaugurate a grand winter campaign to strike terror into the camps hidden away in the Indian Territory and force the inhabitants back to the reservation. He reasoned that during the cold time of the year, the Indians would be less suspecting of attack and practically immobile. The officer assigned the task of conducting the operation was the flamboyant Civil War veteran George Armstrong Custer of the 7th Cavalry, which was then operating in western Kansas.

Guided by Indian scouts, Custer picked up a fresh trail in the snow near Camp Supply on November 26, 1868. Ironically, the trail led to the camp of the peaceful Black Kettle. In a characteristic maneuver Custer divided his command into four detachments and surrounded the Indian camp in the bitter cold pre-dawn hours of November 27. At the first sign of morning's light, a bugle sounded the charge and the 7th Cavalry rode into the doomed village from all directions. A woman reputedly emerged from her lodge shouting, "Soldiers! Soldiers!" Then the slaughter ensued. By 10 a.m., it was over. Except for the funeral chants of Cheyenne squaws mourning dead warriors, a smoky pall of silence and destruction lay in the village.

Always boastful and usually overestimating his successes,

Custer later reported that he had killed over 100 Indians (including many women and children), captured fifty-three squaws and children, destroyed more than a thousand buffalo robes, five hundred pounds of lead, an equal amount of gunpowder, burned all of the lodges, and slaughtered seven hundred Indian ponies. Among the slain were Black Kettle and his wife Maiyuna.

According to the Cheyenne brave Red Shin, Black Kettle's wife had brought up his horse. They mounted the animal, rode off, and were shot dead along the banks of the river. It was almost four years to the day after the Sand Creek Massacre in Colorado. Shortly after the engagement, Black Kettle's followers buried him on a sandy knoll. His body was discovered in 1934 by a group of WPA workers. The bones were donated to a local newspaper office where they were displayed in a window.

Thus ended the tragic life of Black Kettle. He had always perceived the consequences of not living at peace with the white man, and ironically, he had ultimately been struck down by the people with whom he sought so persistently to coexist. No longer do the Cheyenne camp on the banks of the Arkansas. More than a century of cultural assimilation and poverty on the reservation has all but relegated the Great Plains Indian culture to a fleeting memory in the collective conscience of America.

"Nothing lives long, only the earth and the mountains"

—*Death Song of White Antelope, Cheyenne Camp,
Sand Creek, Colorado Territory, November 29, 1864*

Jack Stillwell and
Sig Schlesinger

*F*ar out on the windswept plains of east-central Colorado near the small prairie town of Wray stands a lonely monument adjacent to the Arikaree Fork of the Republican River. The simple memorial commemorates a bitterly fought battle between a force of about fifty plainsmen under the command of Major George A. Forsyth and approximately 1,000 Southern Cheyenne Indians, led by chiefs Roman Nose, Pawnee Killer, and others. Pursued from Fort Wallace, Kansas, the Indians attacked the troops on September 16, 1868. Surrounded and cut off, the men entrenched themselves on a small sand bar in the middle of the Arikaree Fork. There, for nine consecutive days, eating the flesh of their dead horses for sustenance, the plainsmen held off one suicidal charge after another by the proud Cheyenne. During the siege, Major Forsyth sent scouts through enemy lines to obtain relief at Fort Wallace, 125 miles to the east. When reinforcements finally arrived on September 24, one-half of Forsyth's command had been killed or wounded. The dead included Lieutenant Frederick W. Beecher, after whom the battle came to be named. Major Forsyth was wounded four times during the battle. The Indian dead, which perhaps extended into the hundreds, included the giant Chief Roman Nose, a seven-foot-tall warrior whom the Cheyenne called "Bat."

Jack Stillwell.
Western History Department,
Denver Public Library.

The island of death has long since disappeared due to the shifting nature of the river channels. Little is left to remind the modern traveler of this bloody and important event in the annals of the Indians wars on the Colorado plains. Yet, here in this forbidding sea of prairie grass, two forgotten teenage boys grew up and became heroes during late September 1868 — in one of the most harrowing events ever played out on the wild Colorado frontier.

The teenagers' names were Jack Stillwell, age nineteen, and Sigmund Schlesinger, age eighteen. They had little in common. Scant evidence reveals little about their early lives. Jack was probably born on the rolling prairie of western Kansas and undoubtedly grew up around the rough-hewn buffalo hunters and plains scouts whom he admired. Sig, on the other hand, was a cultured Jewish immigrant from New York City who had come west after his eighteenth birthday to seek action and adventure. During the late summer of 1868 their paths crossed and a lifelong friendship began.

After the infamous Sand Creek Massacre of November 29, 1864, the Plains Indians had devastated western Kansas and eastern Colorado with raids of revenge. On one occasion in 1865, they sacked the infant town of Julesburg. No settler or emigrant was safe from their depredations. Throughout the Saline, Platte, and Smoky Hill valleys, the Southern Plains tribes spread a path of death in defiance of recent treaties. During the autumn of 1867, the Cheyenne and Arapahoe had agreed at Medicine Lodge, Kansas, to accept a 4.3-million-acre reservation in the Indian Territory, today's Oklahoma. They promised to walk the white man's road. Most of the peace chiefs who signed the Treaty of Medicine Lodge, however, did not speak for the young warriors who throughout the spring and summer of 1868 witnessed the daily slaughter of buffalo to supply meat for railroad track crews pushing their iron rails westward toward the Pacific. In addition, the outrage of Sand Creek still smarted in the memories of the more militant warriors who had lost women and children during the attack. Consequently, large groups of Indians returned to raiding during the summer of 1868.

The situation became so critical by August that General Philip Sheridan, commander of the Department of the Missouri, took the field in person. He quickly realized the futility of trying to track the swift Cheyenne over the vast prairie with inexperienced recruits who were heavily dependent upon the army's slow-moving supply trains. About this time, Major Forsyth suggested that Sheridan allow him to recruit fifty experienced plainsmen as a freelance column. The men were familiar with the country and could be self-sufficient in the field. In this fashion the Indians could be effectively tracked and forced back to the reservation agreed upon at Medicine Lodge. Sheridan approved the plan and instructed Forsyth to raise the company.

There was no shortage of volunteers for the unit. Bronzed and rugged plainsmen from throughout western Kansas and eastern Colorado hurried to enlist. Buffalo hunters, Civil War veterans, and old trappers signed up with the confidence that singlehandedly, they could whip any number of Indians they would encounter.

The morning of September 10, 1868 dawned warm and clear. Only a few puffy white clouds gave perspective to the vast panorama of sky and plains as the motley band of rugged frontiersmen rode out of Fort Wallace, Kansas, to the strains of "Hail Columbia," ineptly played by the post's brass band. According to one historian, the "cock-sure handful of hard-bitten fighters" rode out of Fort Wallace with "Spencer seven-shooter carbines slung on their backs, holstered revolvers slapping their thighs, dressed in buckskin or nondescript uniforms — the most careless, irresponsible, hard-riding, straight-shooting company of scapegoats that ever set out under the United States flag." Among their ranks were the two teenagers, Jack Stillwell and Sig Schlesinger.

Being the youngest in the company, the two boys "hit it off" from the start. An expert shot, the tobacco-chewing Stillwell tutored Sig in the art of the plainsman while he learned about life in the urbanized East. Almost from the start Schlesinger became the butt of crude jokes from the ranks of the command. "Greenhorn," he was labeled. "A Jew can't shoot straight" was perhaps one of the milder remarks made in reference to his ancestry. Even Forsyth was unsure of the ability of the eastern youth if the going got rough. The commander had only let him come along after incessant pleading by the half-hysterical Schlesinger, eager to see action on the western plains. Nevertheless, each night the youth would walk out on the prairie and practice his marksmanship under the tutelage of the suresighted Stillwell.

For several days the command scouted westward under the blistering sun. Finally, they struck a big trail of many Indians, and Forsyth followed it. The trail had been made by the combined war parties of Pawnee Killer, Tall Bull, White Horse, and Roman Nose. Almost immediately, the Indians detected the pitifully small command and laid plans for an ambush.

Reaching the Arikaree Fork, within the boundaries of Colorado Territory, Forsyth ordered his men to make camp on the north bank of the shallow stream on the night of September

16. For some, it would be their last night.

As dawn came to the river bottom, the plainsmen heard a yell nearby. "Indians!" shouted one of the men. Almost immediately the river bottom was seething with hundreds of warriors. One experienced plainsman noted that in addition to Cheyenne, a smattering of Brule Sioux and Arapahoe warriors were breathing down their necks. Seven of the horses in the command were run off by the warriors and captured. Instantly, with the first volleys, Forsyth ordered his command to retreat to the small sand island located in the middle of the river. With rifle butts and bare hands they began digging rifle pits in the loose sand and took up a defensive position on the island against the overwhelming force of Indians.

As a mass collection of squaws and children watched from the top of a nearby hill, the warriors began their first charge. The frontiersmen clenched their teeth and waited as a thundering drone of hoofbeats could be heard moving rapidly toward their position. Finally came the command to "fire," and the repeating carbines proved their worth. The Indians recoiled and retreated after riding into a stream of lead.

Undaunted, the warriors circled the island defenses. Creeping into willow bushes along the stream bed, they unleashed a steady and deadly barrage into Forsyth's defenses for the remainder of the day. At nightfall Forsyth counted his losses. Out of a total command of fifty-one officers and men, twenty-three lay dead or wounded. Included in that number were Lieutenant Beecher, second in command, who died later that evening, and Surgeon Moorhead, who died three days later. Major Forsyth had three wounds himself.

During the night, Forsyth, who was still able to walk, ordered the wounded horses and mules shot to serve as barricades for the besieged men. Young Sig Schlesinger noticed a wounded army mule near his position with several arrows sticking in him. Sig decided to shoot the mule to serve as a breastwork. A few days later, Sig noted that the mule "served the double purpose of food and barricade."

Under the cover of darkness, Forsyth called his men together. He pointed out their desperate situation. Someone had to go for help and the nearest help was at Fort Wallace, nearly 125 miles away. The volunteer would have to move only at night and on foot. It was an impossible mission. To Forsyth's surprise, every man able to travel volunteered, including young Jack Stillwell and Sig Schlesinger. Jack was selected to go along with old Henry Trudeau, a veteran fur trapper.

At midnight the man and the boy slipped out of camp and into the river bed. Wrapped in blankets, the pair removed their boots, slung them over their shoulders, and walked backwards in the sand to make the Indians believe their tracks were made by moccasined warriors sneaking up on the troops' position. They only made a few miles the first night, crawling on their hands and knees once they left the river bed. During the next day they lay concealed in soap weed, listening to the battle in the river, a few miles away. All day long they sat under the broiling sun, unable to move lest they be detected by the Indians.

As darkness fell they started out again, making faster progress than the night before. Indians were everywhere. At one point the two had to hide beside the rotting carcass of a buffalo to escape the attention of a passing war party. By the third night they were traveling in a straight line toward Fort Wallace. At dawn they took refuge in a shallow buffalo wallow flanked by a few high weeds and went to sleep.

As the sun rose over the plains, a war party of Cheyennes rode up and dismounted within a few hundred yards of where they were hiding. Amazingly, at almost the same time that the Indians rode up, a large rattlesnake came wriggling through the grass near the spot where Jack lay hidden. To kill the snake would mean sudden detection from the Cheyennes. The pair lay perfectly still, and waited.

It was at this point that the disgusting habits Stillwell had acquired in the company of his crude plains mentors, saved his life. Jack chewed tobacco. As the snake drew closer, the Kansan slung a giant spat of tobacco fluid in the face of the loathsome reptile. Whether through expert practice or sheer luck, the dose hit home, and the snake beat a hasty retreat. Soon, the Indians rode off, never knowing the life and death drama that had been acted out only a few hundred yards away.

When night fell, Stillwell and Trudeau started out once again, making good time. By the next day, however, Trudeau's age began to catch up with him and he could not walk. Undaunted, the young Jack Stillwell put his arm around the old trapper and literally dragged him the rest of the way to Fort Wallace, Kansas.

The soldiers at Fort Wallace were in awe of Jack Stillwell's feat. he had covered 125 miles on foot in the midst of a determined enemy, dragging a helpless comrade over about a third of the distance. A large force of cavalry was dispatched from the fort to join another column that had taken the field the previous day in search of the missing Forsyth command.

Young Jack Stillwell joined the soldiers leaving Fort Wallace. He wondered if his friend Sig Schlesinger was still alive back on the Arikaree.

Indeed, Sig Schlesinger was still alive. During the previous days' fighting Sig had stayed close to his wounded commander, Major George Forsyth. At one point when Forsyth attempted to rally his men he stood up in the face of the Indians' volley, receiving a fourth wound. Sig stood up with him, drawing the Indians' fire so that the major could accomplish his task. Forsyth noted the teenager's bravery, as did all the other men still alive on the island. He was no longer a naive greenhorn from the East. Sig Schlesinger had become a hero.

After the first day or two on the island the rations became exhausted. So the men began eating horse flesh. Sig Schlesinger later recorded his experiences with hunger: "My horse was securely tethered to the underbrush on the island, and later that day I saw the poor beast rearing and plunging in a death struggle, having been shot and killed like the rest of our horses and mules. He furnished me with several meals during the siege, even after he began to putrefy. There was little to choose between horse and mule meat under such circumstances — both were abominable."

By the fifth day on the island even generous doses of acrid gunpowder could not hide the putrid taste of the tainted meat and the men found themselves with nothing to eat. Many felt that if the Indians did not get them, starvation would.

By the sixth day the Indians began to disperse. Still tied to their wounded and without horses, however, Forsyth's men could not leave their position. They found some prickly pear cactus fruit and killed a coyote for food. Sig recalled receiving a rib and the brains as his share of the rations.

A day after Stillwell and Trudeau had been dispatched to Fort Wallace, Forsyth sent out two more scouts just in case Jack and the old trapper had not made it through to the post. This second party succeeded in discovering the troop of cavalry that had been sent from Fort Wallace the day before Jack's arrival. On the ninth day of the siege, this command under Colonel Carpenter arrived at the scene. Forsyth's plainsmen had been rescued by a detachment of the 10th United States Cavalry, one of the famous units of black cavalry to see service in the West under white officers. The Indians called the 10th the "Buffalo Soldiers" in reference to the heavy buffalo-hide coats they wore on the plains during the winter months.

The next day the second relief command arrived from Kansas and Jack Stillwell was with them. A pervasive sense of security swept through the beleaguered, emaciated ranks of Forsyth's troops. According to Sig Schlesinger, Jack jumped from his horse, "and in his joy to see so many of us alive again, he permitted his tears free flow down his good honest cheeks." The two friends embraced. Jack Stillwell and Sigmund Schlesinger had survived the bloody island of death.

The publicity over the Battle of Beecher's Island prompted General Sheridan to inaugurate a winter campaign to punish the Cheyenne during the cold months when they were least mobile. The campaign ended with Colonel George Armstrong Custer's attack on Black Kettle's village on the Washita River in Indian Territory, now Oklahoma. The days of the free-roaming Cheyenne on the Colorado plains were over, forever.

George A. Forsyth was given a brevet rank of colonel and went on to distinguish himself in the Apache Wars in Arizona. Jack Stillwell received much acclaim for his remarkable journey to Fort Wallace. He came to know General Nelson A. Miles, Colonel George Armstrong Custer, and Wild Bill Hickock. He eventually studied law and became a judge in Texas, where he lived to an old age. He died early in this century. Jack Stillwell and Sig Schlesinger corresponded for many years.

Little is known about Schlesinger's later life except that he lived to an old age. He was all but forgotten. When General James B. Fry wrote a narrative titled *Army Sacrifices* at the end of the nineteenth century, however, he noted that a little eighteen-year-old Jewish boy by the name of Sig Schlesinger had proven himself perhaps the bravest of all on that long ago island of death where every man was a hero.

Ceran St. Vrain

*T*he Louisiana Purchase of 1803 doubled the size of the
United States overnight. The lands west of the great Mississippi
River and east of the Continental Divide, north of Spanish Texas,
passed into the hands of the infant American nation for the
resounding price of four cents per acre, the "slickest deal in the
history of real estate."

Then, exploration began. Coinciding with the official explorations of that vast wilderness which encompassed the Great
Plains and the mighty cordillera of the Rocky Mountains, free-
roaming trappers began an assault of this mysterious land in
search of beaver pelts. They sold the furs to Missouri merchants
and eventually satisfied the fashion-conscious desires of both
Eastern and European noblesse.

By the time the industry finally declined in the middle of the
nineteenth century, these mountain men had set their traps in
almost every creek and stream of the Far West. They blazed
trails that later became lifelines for overland emigrants. They
discovered passes through the mountains and into fertile valleys
beyond which spawned new dreams for farmer and herdsman.
If it were not for the unofficial explorations of these hearty men,
Colorado and the great West would have remained unexplored
wilderness for years to come. Collectively, their wanderings

Ceran St. Vrain.
Western History Department,
Denver Public Library.

were far more significant than the expeditions of Lewis and Clark, Pike, and Long, combined.

Ascending to the very headwaters of the Missouri River and beyond, the mountain men helped strengthen the American claim to the Oregon Country. While trapping (illegally) in the southern Rockies before 1821, the beaver hunters broke down the weak Spanish barrier south of the Arkansas River. In doing so, they helped spark the belief that the glorious American free enterprise system was sanctioned by almighty God and was destined to extend its influence beyond the borders of the growing nation to "less fortunate" peoples in nearby lands.

One of the most influential men to assert the American cause in the Southwest was a portly, pock-marked trapper by the name of Ceran St. Vrain. His exploits in Colorado and New Mexico between 1824 and 1870 reflected the conflict of cultures and the resulting dichotomous lifestyles experienced by the early trappers on the border.

Ceran St. Vrain was born to Jacques Marcellin Ceran de Hault de Lassus de St. Vrain and Marie Felicite Dubreuil St. Vrain on May 5, 1802, in what is today St. Louis County, Missouri. The family, loyal to King Louis XVI, had originally migrated to America at the time of the French Revolution. Ceran was the second son in a family of ten children. Upon the death of his father in 1818, sixteen-year-old Ceran entered the trading firm of Bernard Pratte, where he remained until age twenty-two. During his apprenticeship with Pratte, the young St. Vrain came in contact with numerous Rocky Mountain trappers who brought their furs downriver to the St. Louis markets. The yarns they spun of survival on the frontier gave the young man a practical, if not exactly formal, education. And, they instilled in him a burning desire to abandon familiar surroundings to explore the mysteries of the West.

In 1824, Ceran left the employ of Bernard Pratte and hired on with an early trading caravan to Santa Fe. The expedition was led by none other than William Becknell, the man who had first opened trade between New Mexico and Missouri in the months following Mexican independence from Spain, three years previous. During that summer of 1824, Ceran St. Vrain first wandered onto the dusty prairies of Colorado, a region upon which he would leave his mark and his name. Although his first impression of the landscape was negative, the young adventurer eventually became enamored with western life. During the seven years following 1824, he formed several partnerships and made the 775-mile trek between the Missouri River landings and Santa Fe almost annually, using credit supplied by St. Louis merchants. He also trapped the elusive beaver as far south as Mexico's Gila River and as far north as the Green River.

During this time he came to know old Bill Williams, Jedediah

Smith, the illustrious Kit Carson, who became his lifelong friend, and perhaps most importantly, brothers Charles and William Bent. It is quite possible that St. Vrain and the Bents first discussed the idea of a partnership as early as 1828 while suffering through a freezing winter in the valley of Wyoming's Green River. In any case, the firm of Bent, St. Vrain and Company commenced operations in 1831; for the next eighteen years the affairs of the company dominated the interest of Ceran St. Vrain.

The partners cast their lot with Mexico, a good business decision. By the end of 1832, St. Vrain and Charles Bent had opened a business house in Taos while William Bent supervised (with St. Vrain's help) the construction of Fort William, or Bent's Fort, on the north bank of the Arkansas River, the border between the United States and Mexico. For the next decade and a half this "Adobe Empire," as historian David Lavender called it, dominated a multi-directional trade in furs, buffalo robes, and manufactured goods throughout Missouri, New Mexico, and the southern plains. It brought tremendous, though temporary, success to the firm of Bent, St. Vrain and Company.

By 1838, the company had established a second trading post to the north at the confluence of the South Platte River and the charming Front Range stream which today bears the name St. Vrain Creek. The post was commonly known as Fort St. Vrain. It was located along the old Trappers' Trail about halfway between Fort Laramie and the Arkansas River. During the six and one-half years it existed, the post saw an enormous amount of trade. By 1844, it was abandoned as the demand for furs declined and excessive competition north of the Platte increased. Together, Bent's Fort and Fort St. Vrain were two of the earliest, semi-permanent American settlements in Colorado.

During the years of the Bent, St. Vrain trade, it became shrewd business practice to form marriage alliances with the native peoples of the plains and Mexico. William Bent eventually married Owl Woman, the daughter of a powerful Southern Cheyenne chief. The union virtually assured that the company would dominate the trade in buffalo hides with the Indians living on the eastern Colorado prairies. Likewise, both Charles

Bent and Ceran St. Vrain married Mexican women of status.

St. Vrain left us little record of his marriages, which eventually numbered four. He married — or lived with — Maria Dolores de Luna in Taos and was blessed with the first of four children, Vincente, in 1827. Rumor has it that he married the daughter of Charles Beaubien in 1843. Nevertheless, at that very time, he loved and resided with Maria Ignacia Trujillo, who bore him another son, Joseph Felix, in 1844. Despite St. Vrain's obvious fickleness, these unions forged with Mexican consorts, aside from obvious business advantages, may have been the most fateful and heart-wrenching events of his younger life on the border.

Although St. Vrain traveled between Missouri and Taos on numerous occasions, one of his main responsibilities was to oversee the Taos end of the trade at the company's store on the old town plaza. During this period he unquestionably became more than casually acculturated to the Mexican lifestyle and point of view. By 1831, St. Vrain became a naturalized Mexican citizen. In addition, he and Cornelio Vigil, both residents of Taos, received a substantial land grant in the valleys of the Cucharas, Apishapa, and Huerfano rivers in 1844. The grant was awarded for "services rendered to the citizens of Mexico" in promoting agriculture, stock raising, and colonization. The sizeable grant included what is today most of Colorado south of the Arkansas River. If it came to war, where would his loyalty lie?

With the successful coup executed in Santa Fe by Colonel Stephen Watts Kearny during the summer of 1846, all the lands comprising today's southern Colorado and northern New Mexico passed by military conquest into the hands of the United States. The war with Mexico was on in earnest. On September 22, 1846, Ceran St. Vrain's close friend and business partner, Charles Bent, was appointed the first civil governor of New Mexico Territory.

By the beginning of the new year, 1847, a group of Mexican and Indian patriots, fearful of wild rumors that the American invaders would ultimately eradicate Roman Catholic influence in New Mexico and abolish the parish churches, began to organize a secret resistance movement. About dawn on January 19, a band of men led by Pablo Montoya, "the self-proclaimed Santa Anna of the north," and Tomasito, a Taos Indian, crept silently through the quiet Taos streets toward the governor's house. Breaking down the heavy wooden door, the mob entered the parlor; although the sleepy Charles Bent tried to reason with them, they killed and scalped him. Bent's wife and children were left unharmed (possibly because of their Mexican bloodlines), but during that night five other Anglo-Americans were butchered in the streets of Taos while others were killed at nearby Turley's Mill (Arroyo Hondo) and the tiny hamlet of Mora.

When Colonel Sterling Price, the American military commander at Santa Fe, received word of the murders the next day, he condemned the Mexican insurgents as rebels and called for volunteers to hunt them down. On January 23, a force of 350 men marched on Taos. They reached the pueblo on February 3, bombarded it for two unproductive hours, then retired for the night. The next day the Americans stormed the church where the insurgents were barricaded. The defenders fled in panic. A group of volunteers posted on the opposite side of the church cut off the fleeing rebels. This later detachment was led by Ceran St. Vrain.

In fact, it was St. Vrain who had originally recruited the bulk of the American volunteers who accompanied Price's small detachment of regular troops on the march from Santa Fe. The revolt was over. New Mexico and southern Colorado lay securely in American hands. History does not record the anguish (if any) that St. Vrain might have experienced when he was requested to recruit volunteers for this retaliatory movement against the people he loved so dearly. But the die had been cast. Ceran St. Vrain had allied himself with the determined forces of Manifest Destiny.

During the fighting on February 4, St. Vrain's men were responsible for killing over fifty Mexican insurgents including Pablo Chavez, a revolutionary leader, who was wearing Governor Bent's shirt and coat. St. Vrain claimed to have personally shot the luckless Chavez. During one point in the battle, St.

Vrain engaged in hand-to-hand combat with an Indian insurgent. While seemingly losing the struggle, his friend and ally "Uncle Dick" Wootton approached the scene and quickly dispatched the Indian with a vicious blow from a tomahawk.

For the next quarter of a century until his death in 1870, Ceran St. Vrain remained passionately loyal to the advancement of American civilization in Colorado and New Mexico. The Mexican War and a subsequent cholera epidemic spread among the Cheyenne and Arapahoe had brought about the demise of Bent, St. Vrain and Company and forced the abandonment and destruction of the post on the Arkansas in 1849.

The advent of the Colorado Gold Rush in 1859, however, brought new hopes and dreams to St. Vrain and men like him. St Vrain became quite interested in the future of the "Pike's Peak" region and the prospects for Denver City. In 1860, William Byers, editor of the infant *Rocky Mountain News*, wrote: "Messrs. St. James and St. Vrain arrived with a large train of wagons, loaded with flour and a general assortment of goods, and opened a store in the first house from Cherry Creek on the south side of Larimer Street in the month of February, 1859. This was the first store opened in Denver."

Although the 1859 directory has no indication that Ceran St. Vrain was present in Denver during this time, William Larimer did note that cousin Edward St. Vrain was in business in the young town that year. Perhaps Ceran, getting up in years, was content to be an absentee financier for the business enterprise.

During the Civil War, the territorial government commissioned St. Vrain a colonel of the First New Mexico Volunteer Infantry recruited to repulse Confederate invaders intent on capturing the Colorado gold country. He resigned his commission during the first year of the war, however, claiming ill-health due to overweight, and turned the regiment over to Kit Carson.

The remaining years of his life belong exclusively to the history of New Mexico Territory. Ceran was responsible for establishing early flour mills and cattle ranches in the region, and successfully increasing the size of his original Mexican land grant in the process through careful litigation. He died of apoplexy on October 28, 1870, and was buried in the modest family plot, now obscured by time, in the hamlet of Mora, New Mexico.

Ceran St. Vrain has left his name on the map of Colorado. Towns, businesses, streams, glaciers, and even a nuclear power plant near the site of Fort St. Vrain all bear his name. Though others of his generation received more recognition for their daring exploits, the man whom the Indians called Blackbeard played a significant, if understated and perhaps tormented, role in preserving the rude desire of the young and restless American nation to bring the lands of southern Colorado under the banner of the stars and stripes.

George Griffith

Christmas Day, 1858, dawned bright and clear over the dusty plains adjacent to Cherry Creek. As faint tendrils of woodsmoke rose from the makeshift chimneys of several tents and cabins along the stream, a sorry-looking lot of anxious men began to stir under the bright sun of a pristine Rocky Mountain morning. A recent trade caravan from New Mexico led by the ubiquitous "Uncle Dick" Wootton had deposited a load of home-brewed whiskey, or Taos Lightning, to lift the spirits of the ragged miners so far from home during the holidays.

About six months earlier, a party of Georgia prospectors led by William G. Russell had washed a few hundred dollars worth of gold from a spot west of Cherry Creek. As news of gold in the western reaches of Kansas Territory spread eastward to Missouri, a number of fortune seekers set out across the plains to what they believed was the new Eldorado. They pitched their tents and constructed crude log cabins along the west bank of Cherry Creek and incorporated their town company into the little community of Auraria. Together with a rival camp across the stream known as Denver City, these early prospectors brought lasting American settlement and culture to the lands which eventually became Colorado. When this motley band of fortune seekers retired on that long ago Christmas night, they surely fell asleep dreaming of the wealth to be realized in the nearby mountains and foothills with the coming of spring.

Among the two to three hundred souls who comprised that first seed of American civilization in the Colorado gold country were two obscure brothers from Kentucky: George Griffith and David Griffith. Their subsequent fame, however, was not to be achieved along the banks of Cherry Creek, but in a canyon on the distant horizon through which flowed a tumbling mountain stream known as Clear Creek.

The Griffiths were members of a large party of immigrants that had assembled at Fort Kearny, Nebraska Territory, and plodded westward toward the Rocky Mountains earlier in the year. They arrived in Auraria on October 24, 1858. Although the brothers received one lot each in the Auraria Town Company that autumn by agreeing to build on the land, they arrived too late to stake a mining claim that would pay them the average ten dollars per day reputedly being realized by the first prospectors. With the advent of mild weather, the Griffiths would have to seek their fortunes elsewhere.

In May 1859, the two Kentuckians joined the stampede to Gregory Gulch where John Gregory had made a large strike. Again they were too late to stake a productive claim at the future sites of Central City and Black Hawk. By June they were prospecting further up Clear Creek. On June 15 the brothers camped on a spot where within a short time they would erect a small log cabin. Two days later George Griffith stumbled onto a good deposit of surface gold. Before the month was out, the news spread to the Cherry Creek settlements, and hundreds of prospectors rushed to the site. Soon, the miners discovered other deposits, and an instant city rose from the rustic valley.

During that first summer the Griffiths worked their small claim. Reputedly, they netted from fifty cents to a dollar's worth of gold dust per pan from washing dirt from the stream. By the end of the season they had realized a profit of approximately $500. The following spring found the brothers returning to work the pyrite ore which assayers had determined to contain gold. The miners formally organized the Griffith Mining District on June 25, 1860. George Griffith became the first recorder.

During that second season, the Griffith brothers brought additional family members into the burgeoning mining district. Their father, Jefferson Griffith, and their other two brothers, William and John, came with the family when it reentered the valley. So, possibly, did two women — Elizabeth and Elvira Griffith. Tradition has it that Elizabeth was the first white woman in the district. According to historian Liston Leyendecker, Elizabeth may have been a Griffith sister. Although her name appears in early accounts of the region, it is unclear exactly what her relationship was to the family. A history written in 1886 lists her as John Griffith's wife, but other accounts state that Elvira was John's spouse. Possibly Elizabeth and Elvira were the same person.

The summer of 1860 saw George and his family supervise the construction of the first road into the Clear Creek Valley. Its purpose was to enable the miners to haul heavy machinery up from Denver to process the gold-bearing ore extracted daily. Eventually, the road covered a distance of twenty miles from Eureka Gulch, west of Central City, to the Griffith District. The cost of construction through the rough terrain exceeded $1,500. To recover the costs of construction, the brothers charged a toll of one dollar per round trip. George Griffith and his brothers received bad publicity from their toll road, however. The *Rocky Mountain News* called for the various mining districts to raise tax moneys to purchase the road from the Griffiths and open it to the public free of charge.

During the fall of 1860, George Griffith brought in the first stamp mill to the region for the purpose of crushing ore. More prospectors came to the valley and erected cabins. The camp was christened "Georgetown" in honor of its leading pioneer — George Griffith. By the spring of 1861, the community and the mining district were formally surveyed and platted. Two stamp mills went into operation in the new town and ore paid between ten and fifteen cents per pound. By June at least seventy-five productive "leads" had been discovered in the region as more prospectors poured in every week. One observer reported that the area was the most productive yet discovered with the exception of the great Nevada District in Gilpin County.

Georgetown had come of age.

George Griffith and his brothers reached the peak of their productivity during the year 1861. After that time, reports of their activities began to dwindle. With the untimely death of their father (from unknown causes) and Elizabeth's increasing fear of the nearby Ute Indians, George Griffith and his family eventually sold both their mill and their mining properties to Stephen F. Nickolls, a Central City businessman, in January 1863. With that transaction, George Griffith and company exited from the annals of Colorado.

The brief saga of George Griffith and his family was fairly typical of the specultive nature of Colorado's mining frontier. And that is why so little is known about George's later life after he left the town which bears his name. The Griffiths found their attempts to crush ore increasingly difficult and generally unsuccessful. The deeper they dug for the precious ore, the harder it became to realize a profit with their primitive recovery methods. The necessary machinery to extract gold from complex ore was beyond the capabilities and the pocketbooks of most individual miners.

Although optimism characterized the first immigrants to new gold regions in the mountainous West, many of these would-be millionaires died penniless with only their broken dreams for epitaphs. Nevertheless, the sensationalist press of the mid-nineteenth century, eager to print news of opportunity in the wake of the panic of 1857, stimulated wild rumors regarding the gold region. When they finished their propagandizing, unsuspecting venturers acted upon the assumption that gold nuggets the size of eggs could be found lying around in the grass.

In the initial stages of any new boom, an independent prospector could realize a small profit from extracting surface or placer gold with little more than a pick, shovel, and pan. The development of the long tom and the sluice box aided him even more. Within a short time, however, given the influx of prospectors into a region such as Georgetown, the rich surface gold simply played out.

By far the greatest deposits of gold and silver lay beneath the surface of the earth in veins penetrating deep underground. To recover and process such ore required heavy machinery and outside capital from the East, and sometimes, from Europe. In addition, the smelting process which could extract gold from the rock increased recovery costs tremendously. The lack of effective smelters in Colorado during the early 1860s almost brought the gold rush to an abrupt end. Years later when smelting became a big business in itself, the costs were simply beyond the resources of the individual prospector who had perhaps invested his last penny on the long journey required just to reach the gold region.

Consequently, during the second phase of the mining frontier heavily capitalized corporations took over the business. Shares were sold outside the region to finance tunneling, crushing, and smelting. Those already wealthy individuals who could afford to purchase large shares in a prospective mine sometimes realized huge profits. The individual prospector would have to move on to the site of another strike where surface gold was available or be forced to work for low wages in one of the company mines until such time that he could afford to move to a new region. Some company towns, however, found ingenious ways to keep the hapless hard rock miner in debt for most of his life. This system made him dependent on company credit and kept him available as a source of cheap labor.

Much of the rock worked by individual prospectors like George Griffith contained silver. George and his family, in fact, let a fortune of the precious metal slide down the hill in the 1860s — ignorant of its value. In the end it was silver that made and destroyed personal fortunes in Colorado. By the 1870s, Georgetown was nicknamed the Silver Queen of the Rockies by its contemporaries. The discovery of great silver-bearing ore in Leadville, Silverton, Aspen, Creede, and dozens of other sites throughout the Centennial State solidified the economy of Colorado until 1893. From the point of view of many citizens, however, the greed for silver profits often put them at the ruthless mercy of an unregulated corporate economy. Colorado and the West was supposed to be a land of individual opportunity, but for many that dream of opportunity turned out to be nothing more than a myth.

"Poker Alice" Tubbs

On a bleak winter night in 1891, three heavily bundled figures stumbled through the four-foot snow drifts toward the warm glow of a window light. Even before they reached the iron gate that led to the small cabin just outside the town of Del Norte, a woman opened the door, and the three shivering hard-rock miners hurried in to warm their hands by the modest potbellied stove.

Prospectors had recently struck a new vein in the Old King Solomon Mine, and another boom was on during that cold winter. As an influx of miners flowed into the area, the ratio between boredom and moral transgression once again multiplied as it had throughout the nineteenth century in the rough-and-tumble mining camps of the West. The three men had made this trek through snow and bitter cold to bring some small joy to the miners of the King Solomon. They had never met this small, intractable Englishwoman hardened by years of living on the frontier and both loved and feared by countless miners throughout the West. They knew her only as "Poker Alice," and they knew she would come with them to the King Solomon.

The next day dawned crisp and clear as the motley party set out through the snow. When they arrived at the mine, a host of volunteers eagerly came forward and set about erecting a

"Poker Alice" Tubbs.
Western History Department,
Denver Public Library.

small cabin for the woman. Within a few days the structure was almost complete. Then they added a front room, and by the next week Poker Alice opened her game of chance and started the bright lights burning in the middle of the small, dirty camp to the great mirth of all the men present.

In the vast mining regions of the Colorado Rockies, as throughout the intermountain west of the nineteenth century, the American frontier became the scene of instant cities. Into these cosmopolitan mining camps poured every type of character imaginable. Rich or poor in their earlier lives, each individual shared one common bond, the belief that quick wealth was close at hand. Among the bizarre collection of people that migrated to the gold and silver regions were more than a few women. They covered the dusty miles with their menfolk, and more infrequently, alone, spurred on by the get-rich-quick philosophy that was the myth of the West.

Despite the inevitable disillusionment of many a would-be millionaire, evidence exists that the status of women improved somewhat in these rude camps. With the ratio of men to women sometimes exceeding 100 to 1 in the early years, and most of the men actively engaged in "making the big strike" in the mines, many of the commercial activities of the towns fell to women. Many urban pioneers of the male gender entered the gold and silver regions with the intention of profiting from the miners rather than in the mines themselves. Consequently, these businessmen relegated competing females to more domestic or minor economic enterprises such as laundering and cooking. It's also true, however, that a few women came to the mining camps alone with powerful capitalistic ambitions of their own. While many of the proceeds were compiled through the operation of gambling establishments and houses of prostitution, profits were reinvested into more socially acceptable operations once a town became stable. At the instigation of wealthy miners' wives, women entrepreneurs opened theatres, art centers, boardinghouses, and social service agencies, making them the true "civilizers" of the urban frontiers of the West.

The chronicle of women in the mining camps also illustrates changing opportunities in response to the environment despite society's attempts to simply reinstate traditional roles for these determined women. The early mining camps were little more than crude tent cities. Life was a constant chore. Despite the backbreaking work, however, the camps were always full of excitement. The rumor of a new strike farther up the river always sent men packing off to a better location, thus creating new business opportunities for the farsighted individual.

The one luxury the miner universally demanded in these instant cities was entertainment, particularly gambling, strong drink, and the pleasures of professional ladies of the evening. Somehow this gaming desire spawned by the mining rushes of the West revealed a basic gambling mentality inherent in the character of individuals of that day. In turn, that character demanded risky pastimes as a complement to the speculative nature pervading the socioeconomic structure of mining society.

According to historian Kent Steckmesser: "The restlessness and optimism that still seem to be American traits were found in extreme form among the floating population of the mining camps. The speculative nature of mining reveals a gambling mentality. Not only the prospectors themselves but those who 'grubstaked' the searchers or bought mining stocks were indulging in the great national pastime of the 1800s. This fever was revealed in the games of chance like poker, faro, or monte which were the chief recreations in the camps. One played in nature's great lottery all day out at the gulch, and then bet against the saloonkeeper at night. It was 'all hail' the winner and 'tough luck' for the losers in either place."

In numerous cases, the gaming saloonkeeper in question was a woman. One who came west with her family during the Colorado gold rush was a young, cultured Englishwoman by the name of Alice Ivers. She was destined to take her place in history via the gambling houses of western mining communities. By the 1880s, she would receive the deserved epithet, "the Queen of Gamblers." Eventually she became perhaps the most eccentric and colorful character ever to follow the houses of entertainment through the new Eldorado.

Born in Sudburn, England, on February 17, 1851, the daughter of a conservative schoolmaster, Alice Ivers moved to America with her family when she was still in her formative years. Raised in the sheltered conformity and social refinement of the cultured, class-conscious Old South, young Alice eventually graduated from an elite boarding school for gentlewomen. When she moved to Colorado with her family, she was still unworldly and innocent.

During the boom days of mining in Colorado's Lake City district, Alice Ivers' life changed drastically. In that homely frontier community, she married Frank Duffield, a mining engineer in the district. Moving to Leadville, where the couple resided for five years, Alice was introduced to the games of poker and monte in the great gambling halls and at the private parties of the town's aristocracy. Amidst flowing velvet curtains, lace tablecloths, and crystal chandeliers, the energetic young woman fell in love with the excitement expounded by the games of chance during Leadville's imperious days of lavish, ornate extravagance.

The untimely death of her husband in a mine explosion, however, left Alice with an urgent need to quell her grief and earn a living. She turned irrevocably to professional gambling. Migrating from one mining camp to another, Alice steadily built her reputation. Totally self-sufficient, she rapidly adapted the necessary skills to survive and become a true frontier individualist. After the great silver strike at Creede in 1891, Alice went there to provide entertainment. Reportedly, she felled trees in the nearby mountains, rolled them down the hillside, and built a cabin with her own hands. Georgetown, Central City, Del Norte, Alamosa — all of these towns knew her and loved her. She made her reputation when she broke the bank in Silver City, New Mexico, and brought home $6,000. By the 1890s, hard-rock miners and millionaires alike toasted her name. The rough-hewn, drafty log gambling halls became her palaces, and she was always the queen. Texas, Montana, Colorado, and New Mexico saw her determined presence as did the hard towns that were Tombstone, Arizona, and Dodge City, Kansas.

By mid-life the long years of frontier living and the trials of running gaming establishments had hardened Alice Duffield. The dangers of her profession required her to carry a pistol which she rarely displayed but knew how to use with skill. Perhaps as a more subtle display of authority and self-confidence, she began smoking large cigars, a habit that became her most vivid trademark. When asked why she acquired the habit, she would simply reply that "one could not stop a game to keep lighting cigarettes." She was known as a shrewd, honest businesswoman, intolerant of swindlers and able to meet men on their own grounds. Always fearless, never one to resist the need for providing sport to an isolated mining camp, the steely eyed, enigmatic Poker Alice came up the mountain that day to the King Solomon Mine, chewing vigorously on a black cigar.

Eventually, Poker Alice settled in Deadwood, South Dakota, during that town's boom years and there she married W.G. Tubbs, a gambler of local notoriety. The couple tried to settle down and homestead land some forty or fifty miles from the community of Sturgis. In the bleak winter of 1910, however, Tubbs died of pneumonia. During a raging blizzard, Alice hitched her team and drove to town to bury her husband's frozen corpse.

Finding the homestead too lonely, Alice returned to Deadwood, where reformers shunned her and eventually drove her out of town. She returned to Sturgis and began gambling seriously to support herself. Eventually she opened up her own place, ostensibly to monopolize the off-duty attentions of military personnel stationed at Fort Meade. For a time she did quite well providing the usual games, strong drink, and reputedly, the attentions of young women. Captain George Rawlins, an officer stationed at Fort Meade, vividly described Alice Tubbs: "Sometimes she wore an Army shirt and campaign hat, was completely equipped with belt, pistol and cigar, and was quite drunk but always able to navigate. . . . Though she was said to have three notches in her gun," he said, "I recall no incident of disturbance at her place. In fact she rather mothered some of the soldiers, especially recruits, limiting both their gambling losses and drinking."

In a sense, Poker Alice's establishment and countless similar saloons and gambling halls reflected a socialization process which came to be associated with the masculine free-spiritedness that stereotyped the West of frontier times. By the early years of the twentieth century, however, that idealistic image changed drastically, if only temporarily.

After several decades of scoffing at the radical prohibition advocated by such groups as the Women's Christian Temperance Union, the Anti-Saloon League, the Prohibition Party, and other reform groups, barkeeps finally closed their doors when the "grand experiment" of national prohibition became national law in 1920. Although establishments like Poker Alice's were soon to reopen illegally as speakeasies, a wave of reform sentiment had hit the nation. This attitude was nowhere more noticeable than in the West. Anxious to bury their wicked past, numerous former frontier cities began a campaign to not only remedy the perceived abuse of alcohol, but also to rid themselves of numerous forms of vice associated with territorial days.

Poker Alice's place became a prime target of reformers in Sturgis. Arrested for selling alcohol illegally, gambling, and running a "disorderly house," and charged with killing a soldier who allegedly attempted to force his way into her establishment, Alice lamented her fate as she awaited trial: "I thought he [the soldier] was the law and I didn't intend to hit him. Why, I wouldn't hurt a dog. What do they want to do, take my liquor and cigars away from me? I'm a good woman. . . ."

Alice had played her cards better than the reformers had suspected. Garnering protection and some measure of local political influence through her association with underworld interests of prohibition days, a series of petitions to the governor stayed an impending prison sentence on the grounds of her physical condition and advanced age.

The trial, however, broke Poker Alice both in finance and in spirit. Spending her remaining years in a ramshackle house in Sturgis, she was frequently seen tramping the hills, hunting and fishing, a relic of a bygone era. She told a reporter that her jaunts were merely for "recreation and peace." Actually, her pride prevented her from admitting that her hikes were in reality arduous searches for food. Frequently lonely and sick, Alice was not, however, without friends. Remembered by many older individuals as an honest businesswoman and an "astute good manager," she was frequently visited in her declining years. Citizens of Sturgis occasionally provided her with food, care, and money.

At age seventy-nine, Poker Alice laid her cards on the table for the last time. Told by a doctor that a dangerous operation was her only chance for life, she looked the physician in the eye and retorted: "Go ahead, I've always hated a piker." To a close friend she merely confided, "It's all in the draw."

But Alice lost this hand. On February 28, 1930, the Associated Press sent her obituary to newspapers throughout the nation: "Poker Alice Tubbs coppered her biggest bet today — and lost." She was buried in her beloved Black Hills. Today she remains a testament to the spirit of those frontier women who carved a life for themselves, sometimes alone, sometimes against enormous odds in a society that demanded adaptation, change, and the ability to "take a chance."

David Day

*F*rom America's very beginning, its western frontier was a magnet for the worst of society. True, as historian Frederick Jackson Turner once wrote, the West was a safety-valve for the nation's honest dispossessed — a place where hard-working commoners established not only their economic independence, but created national values as well. But the West also drew the dishonest dispossessed — thieves, outlaws, confidence men, land sharks, and others — and in the end it may have been as heavily populated by the worst of the national lot as by the best.

Colorado has known far more scoundrels than it has crusaders. Early Colorado, in microcosm, was a vivid reflection of early western patterns. It was home to hard-working miners and other men of honor, but it also teemed with men to whom work and honor were totally alien concepts. In a word, it was a rogue's paradise, a place where men took what they wanted from whom they wanted when they wanted. And those who condemned the process were voices in a howling wilderness.

David Day was one of the voices. A journalist by profession, a rabble-rouser by avocation, in the late nineteenth century he became protector, defender, guardian, and spokesman for a generation of southwest Coloradoans. His newspaper was small, but his voice was big, and he covered the San Juans with a steady thunder that lingers to this day.

David Day.
Colorado Historical Society.

There was little in David Day's birth and early life to suggest the path he would one day take. He was born in Ohio in 1847, but family problems forced him from his home while he was still a child. With no education on which to rely, he lived on his wits. At fifteen, he enlisted in the Union Army, and within three years — as incredible as it seems now — he was decorated with the Congressional Medal of Honor for consistent and conspicuous gallantry. Among early Coloradoans, only one other man shared this honor: William Jackson Palmer, founder of the Denver and Rio Grande Railway.

War's end left Day a man without a mission. He had no education and no promise, and a man who could neither add nor write had little future in the small rural villages of central

Ohio. Nor did Day have a calling; nothing beckoned him, nothing turned his head. At twenty, he was like many other veterans who drifted aimlessly away from the war, back into the American mainstream. Broke and unmotivated, he headed slowly from nowhere to nowhere again.

Nowhere in this case was Missouri. For no apparent reason, he settled there, buried his war memories, learned to write, tied an apron around himself, and became a small-town storekeeper. He married, had children, and lost his business to bankruptcy. At thirty, he was a failure. But he persisted. In 1879, he moved west with the silver tide. Abandoning everything he had ever had or had ever been, he moved across the plains to Colorado — to Ouray — where silver was king. There, Day became a giant. No one would have dreamed it. No one could have scripted it. But in the life of the San Juans, David Day became — and remains — a legend.

In Ouray, a tiny mining camp nestled among some of the richest mines and most spectacular mountains in the Rockies, Day founded his calling in journalism. With borrowed money he bought a newspaper — the *Solid Muldoon* — and turned it into one of the most powerful papers anywhere. Some people saw the *Muldoon* as an irresponsible, provincial, small-town muckraker, the personification of yellow journalism. But to others it was a beacon in a dark night. In an age where the passive press was the national norm, the *Muldoon* — cutting, picking, probing, never quiet, never satisfied with the status quo — was relentlessly active. In an age where even the strongest newspapers treated boosting as religion, the *Muldoon* treated it as a sidebar. In the end, the *Muldoon* was a peoples' paper, a friend, an advocate, a maverick as tough as its times. What made it so was clearly David Day. True, the old west was already in transition in the 1880s; the frontier was disappearing into a new, more civilized century, and much of its original nature was changing as a matter of sheer evolution. But in the San Juans, at least, evolution was assisted by the angry pen of David Day. It was this that made him one of the most significant citizens in Colorado's history.

Part of the man was show, and no doubt — like any journalistic demagogue — he sometimes played to the crowd. But at his core, Day was exactly what he seemed to be — a genuine iconoclast with a feeling for the commoner for whom he wrote. Perhaps it was his own early life that made him so — his own early brushes with failure, or his kinship with the dispossessed — but whatever it was, it infused him with a passion for "right" that bordered on obsession. All of it caused him a lifetime of anguish. He parried lawsuits from the day *Muldoon* was born to the day he died. More than once he published the paper from inside a jail cell, passing copy through bars to *Muldoon* staff members who had it in print the next day. But the paper also brought him rewards. In the final analysis, nothing deterred Day, certainly not jails and lawsuits. As the self-appointed guardian of the "people" of the San Juans, he let nothing stop him — not in 1879 and not during the next three decades.

Day often shot from the hip, but never at random. His targets were all clearly defined and carefully chosen. Not a day passed but that he did not attack the outlaw element of the San Juans — the thieves and killers and prostitutes who made crime there an institution. But more than that — and this is what set Day apart from other frontier newspapermen — he also dared to attack the region's powerful business establishment. The damage inflicted on people by claim jumpers and mine salters was clear, Day wrote time and again. The damage inflicted by greedy silver kings and railroad tycoons and their fawning allies in the legislature and press was more subtle. But, to Day, it was damage nonetheless, and its overall effects were far more devastating to society than the occasional theft of a cow or an act of prostitution. This belief underlay everything Day ever did or ever wrote. It was precisely what gave the *Muldoon* its special fire.

Ironically, the first and greatest of Day's targets were the silver barons among whom he lived.

In the 1870s and 1880s, Colorado was economically dominated by silver. From Georgetown to the San Juans, from Leadville to the Wet Mountain Valley, the white metal permeated every corner of the territory and underpinned every aspect of its financial life. In the span of a few short years, its extraction became the most important thing that ever happened to Colorado —

more important than gold, more important than cattle, more important than the agriculture beginning to root itself on the empire's ragged fringes. The late nineteenth century was a time when silver was king, and so were the silver barons and silver corporations who tended it.

David Day understood laissez faire economics with the best of his contemporaries, and he also understood — better than most — the Darwinistic nature of the frontier where the fittest survived, made their fortunes, translated economic wealth into political power, then ruled the rest. But Day also knew greed when he saw it. He knew the difference between investment and looting. Looking around himself at the silvery San Juans, he rejoiced in the life silver brought to his country. But at the same time, he also hated the avarice and opportunism that came with it. It was in that spirit that he attacked the silver kings and silver corporations who used the guise of developing the territory to mask their plundering.

Part of the problem, to Day, was the economic colonialism that pervaded the silver kingdom. As they did elsewhere in the West, outside corporations poured across the land, bled it of its mineral, then siphoned off its wealth and shipped it eastward. Their only interest in Colorado was what it could provide in dividends for eastern stockholders. When the land had served its purpose, the corporations simply moved on or moved out, leaving behind them a landscape littered with ghost towns and broken dreams. The value of these outsiders to Colorado itself was often nonexistent. If no one else knew it, David Day did.

Beginning in 1879, and continuing for years, Day published a daily "blacklist" identifying and indicting the corporations he hated most. "The Osprey Company of New York is an Abominable Fraud," read front-page headlines in December 1879. "The United States Gold and Silver Company of Chicago is a fraud." "The Ouray Mining and Discovery Company" of Boston "will bear close and constant watching." No company escaped his eye. And none was too big to fight. Though many of his contemporaries, even his friends, complained that he bit the hand that fed the San Juans, Day never wavered in his belief that he was right.

Typical of Day's attacks on the "system" was the bitter war he conducted against John R. Curry, a local mining entrepreneur with eastern ties. Curry, he believed, exploited the region with his mines, then sold depleted or worthless claims to others for far more than their value. The *Muldoon* indicted Curry as a "despicable, pitiful, filthy liar and whiskey bloat," a "libel on the name of dog" with the "conscience of a Judas Iscariot" and the "appetite and feeling of a hyena without its honor." Curry dared to suggest that Day was acting in self-interest and criticized the "filthy spewings of the Missouri Puke" (the *Muldoon*). But Day never let up. Again, when other area papers — boosters all — attacked him for imperiling the region's economy, Day still refused to quit. To the end he stood alone — against the Currys, against the boosters, against the looting corporations, even against many of his own people who did not realize what he was trying to do.

In the same vein, the *Muldoon* also attacked Colorado's big railroad men, most of whom Day considered as arrogant and anti-public as the silver kings. His greatest war was with the Denver and Rio Grande. Most Coloradoans either respected the great road or left it alone. It was, after all, Colorado's core road. Its spine, curving in a long arc from Denver to Durango, was in many ways the glue that held Colorado together. But Day collided with the Rio Grande over the question of a spur line into Ouray. Day believed the city deserved and needed one, but the railroad opposed the idea on economic grounds. In time, Day forced the Rio Grande to extend to Ouray. But once it was there, the question of high freight rates for short hauls pushed him into one of the bitterest fights of his career.

Charging inequitable rates — low rates for one city, high rates for another — was a practice as old as railroading itself. Railroad men had exploited American cities and played havoc with the economic fortunes of the American people from the day the first locomotive headed down the first track. But the practice was particularly bad in the West — vitally dependent on railroads to link it with eastern markets — where railroads charged what local traffic would bear. For all its own local ties, the Rio Grande was little better than outside railroads that came into the region. If a city could pay the "freight," it was charged for it, and more. If it complained, railroad men simply built another spur up another canyon and froze the city into oblivion.

As Day saw it, railroaders were vultures. And in that spirit, he conducted an almost incendiary campaign against the Rio Grande. In the short run, rates fell but little. But in the long run, the state of Colorado adopted rate ceiling legislation and in time every road in the state was brought, angrily and defiantly, into line. No one man was responsible for this, but certainly one more responsible than most was David Day.

In Colorado, as in most frontier states, the state legislature — at least until it was forced to bow to public pressure — invariably defended the actions of the silver and railroad magnates. Economic development was almost uniformly considered to be more important than the rights of the people. The prevailing view was that a state could feed itself on the actions of its producer-giants, but little of economic value ever came from protecting the rights of the workers.

Day, typically, disagreed, and he took constant issue with the legislature and its blind ratification of everything the captains of industry did. In one particularly memorable diatribe, he clearly summed up his beliefs:

Is that a salvation army?
No, my child, that is a band of horse thieves.
What are they doing that they look so excited?
They are suspicioned by the people and are debating a motion to
     investigate the charges.
What is an investigaion?
Investigation, my child, is the preparation of a self-amalgamated
     whitewash, introduced by the Colorado legislature in the latter
     part of the 19th century.
What is a legislature?
In Colorado it is a conglomeration of rural and metropolitan asses ele-
     vated by misguided suffrage to positions intended by the Consti-
     tution for brains, honor, and manhood.

As usual, Day's position was extreme. But it was also painfully close to the truth. Those who refused to admit it were destined to live with it.

Day also hated the press. He saw most state newspapers as shameless flacks for the state's political parties or as opportunistic mouthpieces for the big economic interests. Either way, Day wrote time and again, they were useless to the people. "God hates a coward," he wrote once, "yet there are several of them engineering so-called newspapers." And, he concluded, because the press was the only organization in Colorado that could force the interests to listen to the public voice, the cowardice cost society dearly.

Most of the evil, to Day, existed in Denver, where the legislature sat. It was there, he thought, that the various papers — all sycophants of the Republican party — made a particular mockery of their reason for being. The *Denver Times*, Day wrote, never "indulges in either pointed comment or criticism" and "avoids anything in the way of an original idea." When confronted with the dilemma of supporting the public interest over the interests' interest, it invariably chose the latter. Occasionally, said Day acidly, it "squirted taffy" at the powers that ran Colorado. But no more than that.

The *Muldoon* saved most of its venom for the *Denver Republican*. "It is a gallant, uproarious defender of the 'old party,' " Day wrote in 1882. "What it lacks in force it makes up in length. What it lacks in truth it makes up in pretense. What it lacks in frankness it makes up in hypocrisy. What is lacks in ability it makes up in stupidity. As a small, uninteresting, tedious fraud it has value. In no otherwise has it any value at all."

It may be, of course, that Day was wrong in the judgments he made of his brothers. But even if he was, the fact that he had the courage to challenge them *at all* was precisely what gave the concept of "the power of the press" meaning in Colorado. He seemed to understand, more than others of his time, that the correctness of his assessments was not the point. The point, in Ouray or anywhere else, was that the health of society relied almost exclusively on the ability of its institutions — like the press — to question. The day they did not, or could not — and the old Ohioan knew this as certainly as he knew the town he served — civilization would stagnate and die. The *Muldoon*, at least, would never have been a party to that.

In 1882, David Day moved his newspaper to Durango, but the change of address hardly changed the paper's style or tone. Though Day turned old and white-haired in Durango, and died there in 1914, his cause was as impassioned on the day he died as it was on the day he first put ink to paper.

In retrospect, some remember the old man for his grace and wit. Some remember him for his prose — often as beautiful as the setting in which he wrote. But most remember him simply for his courage.

When Day was a young man, living briefly in New York City, he made the acquaintance of one William Muldoon, a tough, scrappy Irish boxer who lost every fight he ever fought — but who never took a dive and who never quit. Day never forgot him. Years later, on the Colorado frontier, beginning a life of his own, Day began a newspaper and called it the *Solid Muldoon*. Its hallmark was integrity. Its focus was the lives of people. In the end, it achieved everything it set out to be. Of the old warhorse of the San Juans, William Muldoon would have been proud.

Chin Lin Sou

*H*alloween evening of 1880 was a macabre occasion for the citizens of Denver. Some of them celebrated by brutally beating and then lynching a helpless Chinese immigrant from a lamp post on the corner of Nineteenth and Lawrence streets. The event was only one incident which transpired during that wanton night of rioting in the city's Chinatown, situated along Wazee Street between Fifteenth and Seventeenth. To many whites, the neighborhood needed a cleansing anyway. The whole area allegedly festered with underground passageways leading to secret opium dens, dingy saloons, and foul-smelling cribs where Chinese whores plied their trade for white men's pocket change. "Hop Alley," it was dubbed. To many so-called respectable citizens of Denver, it was indeed Hell's fast acre.

No one knows for sure what started the violence. One account holds that it began as a saloon brawl between a white man and a Chinese resident. Another story has it that trouble began over a ten-cent difference of opinion regarding a laundry bill. In any event, many white rioters descended upon Chinatown between noon and midnight. They burned business establishments, looted homes, and even beat and murdered innocent people. Eventually, Mayor Richard Sopris, who hid several Chinese from danger, ordered David Cook and the Rocky Mountain Detectives

Chin Lin Sou.
Colorado Historical Society.

to quell the riots. Later, the city reimbursed the Chinese community for about $54,000 in property damages.

The Chinese Riot of 1880 was a sad event in Colorado history. Yet it was the culmination of racial bigotry that had intensified to the point of explosion since the early 1870s. The Chinese were more hated than any other immigrant group in Colorado's early years. Newspapers constantly editorialized against them. And much antagonism had built up over the death of an eighteen-year-old white boy who allegedly died from smoking too much opium. One week before the riot, on October 23, the *Rocky Mountain News* printed the following statement: "John Chinaman — The Pest of the Pacific Coast — The Heathen Who Have Ruined California and Are Now Slowly Invading Colorado — Workmen Starving and Women Following Prostitution Through Competition of the Wily Heathen." In essence, their different clothes, yellow skin, strange tongue, and stranger written language combined with a concept of life based on an incomprehensible code of living steeped in the ancient Confucian classics served to alienate them totally from the white community. Even the despised blacks and the hated Italians were Christians, it was asserted. The Chinese were viewed as heathens little better than Indians.

Although no proof exists, it seems likely that a proud six-foot-tall Cantonese immigrant by the name of Chin Lin Sou was present on that terrible night of violence. He was living in Denver at the time, and by 1880 he had become a highly respected figure among the overseas Chinese (as they called themselves), not only in Colorado, but throughout the West. Born in Canton in 1837, Chin Lin Sou was in his twenties when he stepped off the gang plank of the ship in San Francisco. Steeped in the ageless traditions of the Confucian civil service examinations, Chin was an educated man when he came to America. He also had a keen sense for business.

His queue, or pigtail, certainly appeared strange to Americans. But Chin would no sooner cut it off than he would die. In fact, that probably would have been the result had he parted with his braid. Ever since 1644 when waves of invaders from Manchuria swept China and established the C'hing, or Manchu, Dynasty the native Chinese were required to wear the queue as a symbol of subservience to the hated Manchu emperors. By the nineteenth century, many Chinese were allowed to work or study abroad but the queue always had to be worn lest the violator be discovered by one of the emperor's secret police who also walked the deserts and back roads of the American West. If Chin Lin Sou surveyed the destruction in Chinatown on that bleak autumn night in 1880, he surely must have vented his anger over American prejudice. After all, it was not the Chinese but the white, British imperialists, themselves considered to be barbarians among the Chinese, who introduced the noxious drug opium.

In 1842, the British had sailed their gunboats up the Yangzte River and opened China to trade with the western world. The event was known as the Opium War. It was nothing less than a coup by the technologically superior British navy. In the Treaty of Nanking, one of the so-called unequal treaties which ended the war, a balance of trade was established which clearly favored the British. Among the trade items dumped in China was the East India Company's annual refined crop of opium, a drug which had previously been used only for medicinal purposes, and the importation of which had been outlawed in China since 1800. The unequal treaties ruined China's delicate economy. As poverty spread, so did the opium habit. The refined drug was inexpensive and readily available. Internal dissension within the dynasty over the depression finally erupted with the bloody T'ai P'ing Rebellion in 1850. It started in Canton and spread throughout the nation. Its ultimate goal was the overthrow of the hated Manchu rulers. The rebellion lasted until 1864, and the devastation through almost twelve years of civil war led by many native-born Chinese to emigrate overseas. The emperor was glad to see the rebels go. Among them was Chin Lin Sou.

By 1864, the Central Pacific Railroad Company of Leland Stanford, Charles Crocker, Collis P. Huntington, and Mark Hopkins began recruiting overseas Chinese as workers on the rail network that would eventually link up with the Union Pacific Railroad to form America's first transcontinental line. As the word of such opportunity spread, even more Chinese migrated to the American West. Chin Lin Sou may have recruited many himself. "Crocker's pets," they were called, in deference to partner Charles Crocker, who bossed the Central Pacific's construction work. By 1867, there were 6,000 Chinese workers on the company's payrolls, including Chin Lin Sou, who was listed as a foreman. They proved to be indefatigable workers. As engineers blasted tunnels and rock shelves through the granite walls of the Sierra Nevada Mountains, the Chinese loaded the loose rock and wheeled it away in one-horse carts. Their energy was remarkable and they proved to be more reliable than the Union Pacific's Irish workers who, critics charged, drank and fornicated their way across the Nebraska prairie.

Meanwhile, Chinese laborers were industriously spiking down track in precise fashion eastward on a line toward Promontory, Utah. Finally on May 10, 1869, in a ceremony that bordered on comic relief, Chin Lin Sou watched Leland Stanford and Thomas Durant drive a golden spike commemorating the linkage of the two lines. The event stands today as one of the most significant in American history. It was now cost-effective to exploit the resources of the Far West. During the year after the link-up at Promontory, General Grenville Dodge of the Union Pacific spent the entire spring and summer reinforcing rails, smoothing grades, and in general, trying to bring the Union Pacific's trackage up to the standard exemplified by the Central Pacific's Chinese labor force. Chin Lin Sou was among those Chinese hired by the Union Pacific to help General Dodge. In 1870, Denver businessmen organized the Denver Pacific Railroad Company and constructed a localized, feeder line from the Union Pacific main line at Cheyenne into Denver itself. Chin Lin Sou was the foreman of the Chinese labor crew which brought that railroad to Denver.

Having decided to remain in Colorado, Chin almost immediately cast his lot with the Gregory Gulch mines. In 1871 he and a few friends moved to the gold rush town of Black Hawk and thus established one of the first Chinese settlements in Colorado Territory. Not many specifics are known regarding Chin's life in the area except that he was apparently very successful. That in itself is amazing. Throughout the mining camps of the West, the Chinese were persecuted as relentlessly as anywhere else. Local custom usually prescribed that Chinese could work only abandoned claims — they could not file original claims. This reality forced most Chinese in the mining camps into performing menial, but necessary, tasks like cooking and laundering. When they did labor in ostensibly worked-out mines, usually the entire Chinese community — men, women, and children would work the sluices and rockers jointly to extract very small amounts of placer gold — recoveries too small to be worth the while of white miners who had abandoned the claims. In a few cases this joint effort paid off in sufficient profit. It certainly did for Chin Lin Sou.

Despite a raging flash flood that wiped out his equipment, Chin struggled on, judiciously converting his gold into cash. One day he approached a Central City mine operator by the name of John T. Purcell and asked him to recommend a reliable bank. The First National Bank of Central City was suggested. What happened next is in John Purcell's own words. ''The eyes of the clerks bulged out when Lin Sue [sic] laid down sixty thousand dollars as his initial deposit and from that minute the

Chinese credit mobilier was set up as one of the fixities of the camp." By now Chin was in a position to finance passage for his wife to come to Colorado. Eventually, they had three children, two boys and a girl.

Sometime during the late 1870s, Chin and his family moved to Denver, where they witnessed the severe hatred that culminated in the infamous riot of 1880. Within the Chinese community, however, the industrious Chin Lin Sou was always looked upon as a leader. According to Purcell, who reflected the patronizing attitude of most whites at the time toward Chin's industrious qualities, he was described as having "intrepid traits" or being "more progressive than most of his sleepy eyed race."

Chin Lin Sou died in 1894 and was buried in Denver's Riverside Cemetery. For many years until his death in 1939, one of Chin's sons, William "Willie" Chin served as consensus mayor of Denver's Chinatown and was well respected for his views throughout the city. Indeed, the Chin family became, and still is, an important pioneer family in Colorado.

But in the records of the state and American West the contributions of the overseas Chinese are given scant attention. This oversight is perhaps due to their dwindling numbers in places like Colorado. According to historian Lyle Dorsett, Denver's Chinese population, which numbered nearly 1,000 people during the 1870s, dwindled to 306 by 1890 after the passage of the Chinese Exclusion Act, which ended recruitment of more laborers from China. Their numbers continued to decline during the twentieth century. In many respects the stereotype of the obsequious Chinese coolie of the nineteenth century is still persistent when the old stories of the American West are retold. Because they were not permitted to enter mainstream businesses or the professions, they can only be measured by their productivity as laborers. In numerous cases they were forced into grinding, menial labor jobs by the American community. Consequently, many whites have traditionally pictured Chinese laborers as slow and backward.

The careful placement of heavy iron rail along the sheer cliff faces of California's Donner Pass is today recognized as one of the greatest engineering and labor feats of the nineteenth century. If nothing else, men like Chin Lin Sou were responsible for providing the needed labor which finally brought the railroad to Colorado. Above all other factors at the time, the railroad was the one ingredient necessary to ensure that Denver did not become just another rotting ghost town.

Otto Mears

*T*hroughout the long, romantic saga of overland transportation in Colorado and the West, frontiersmen quickly realized the futility of constructing roads or hauling mail and freight without the support of government funds. The meteoric demise of Russell, Majors, and Waddell and the growing prosperity of the transcontinental railroads supported by enormous government loans and copious land grants demonstrated that fact quite clearly. Without a doubt, unaided private enterprise was impotent when it came to carving paths through the raw wilderness. Those individuals who thought otherwise usually ended their days wearing rags.

Fortunately, no one ever explained this basic truth to a diminutive scraggly-bearded, Russian Jewish immigrant by the name of Otto Mears. Chiefly through his own efforts, this unlikely drifter to Colorado almost singlehandedly linked southwestern Colorado to the outside world. First through a series of hardscrabble toll roads and then through the even more demanding construction of narrow gauge rail across the heart of the high mountains, Mears succeeded in opening Colorado's Western Slope to profitable mining for the first time. In doing so, he ensured the prosperity of such communities as Silverton, Ouray, and Telluride.

Otto Mears.
Western History Department,
Denver Public Library.

Otto Mears was born in the Courland Province of Russia on
May 3, 1840. His mother was a native Russian, but his father
was a British subject. By the time that Otto was three years old,
he was an orphan. Before he reached the age of ten he had
been shuttled among a host of uncles in both the old world and
the new. After residing for a time in New York City, he was
finally shipped off to live with one of his more ambitious uncles
in raw San Francisco of gold rush days. Crossing the Isthmus
of Panama by horseback and then sailing up the Pacific coast,
a journey of several months from New York, the lad's luck finally
ran out. No one in the city by the bay had ever heard of his
uncle. Finding himself destitute and alone he grubbed for room
and board by selling newspapers along San Francisco's tawdry
Barbary Coast. According to his own confession he never entered a classroom after the age of ten.

Surviving in the streets, however, gave young Otto a more
practical education. As a teenager he shifted from gold camp
to gold camp throughout California. When the Civil War broke

out, twenty-year-old Otto Mears enlisted in the First Regiment of California Volunteers and helped repulse a rebel invasion into New Mexico at the Battle of Val Verde. After his discharge from the Union Army in 1864, Mears wandered into Santa Fe and briefly clerked in a store. By the next year he found himself in Colorado Territory, where he would finally find happiness and fortune.

In 1865, Mears took out a homestead in the sage-speckled San Luis Valley. His intention was to grow wheat to supply a crude gristmill he had constructed with his own hands near the little Hispanic village of Conejos. Together with some rudimentary lumber operations, Otto Mears expected to supply nearby Fort Garland with both flour and timber. By the time his harvest was complete, however, Fort Garland was no longer a viable market. Undaunted, the young man loaded some wagons with his produce and headed toward the gold camps of California Gulch, where fifteen years later boisterous Leadville would thrive in the lavish squalor of fortunes made too quickly. The lack of a reliable road over Poncha Pass almost stopped the young entrepreneur in his tracks, however. To get his wagons through he had to hack his way across the mountains with an axe. On the descent down the pass, Mears' wagon overturned, spilling the produce into a precipitous gorge. Perhaps by sheer fate, the part owner of the huge Baca Grant in the San Luis Valley, William Gilpin, ex-Territorial Governor of Colorado, happened to ride by at this very time. According to legend, Gilpin suggested to Mears that when he finished his journey, he should go to Denver, pay five dollars, and charter his recent trailblazing as a toll road. Mears took Gilpin up on the idea — a move which brought him unprecedented fame.

In 1867, Otto Mears, age twenty-seven, began constructing southwestern Colorado's first major toll road. Beginning at the new town of Saguache (also pioneered by Mears when he built a store next to his homestead), the road ran over Poncha Pass to connect with the road from Denver to California Gulch. Mears erected a toll gate at the pass to collect fees. He later boasted that he recovered the total construction cost of $14,000 in three months' time due to the booming strikes at Leadville — a claim which sounds preposterous.

While doing business in the town of Granite one day, Otto Mears met and courted a local girl named Mary Kampfschulte. They were married on November 17, 1870, in Saguache. Throughout their long life together, Mary seldom hesitated to accompany her husband on his dangerous journeys through the high San Juan Mountains.

Two years before Otto's marriage, the Ute Indians had agreed in the so-called Kit Carson Treaty to relinquish their lands in the San Luis Valley in exchange for a reservation west of the Continental Divide near Cochetopa Pass. By 1872, however, the discovery of silver-rich ores on the new Ute reserve prompted miners to file over 100 illegal claims in the region. The government responded in characteristic fashion by deciding to move the Indians once again. Chief Ouray of the Utes, who was outraged by the violations of the Kit Carson Treaty, was not disposed to uproot his people when the whites had been at fault. It was suggested that Otto Mears, who had met Ouray a few years earlier, talk to the chief and persuade him to move.

After conferring in private with Ouray, Mears made a proposal to Felix R. Brunot, the principal negotiator for the U.S. government. The Utes were to be paid an annual annuity of $25,000 and Ouray would be paid $1,000 a year as long as he was chief. In exchange the Indians would agree to take a new reservation in the Uncompahgre Valley. Although indignant at first, Brunot finally agreed to the payoff. The Utes signed a new treaty on September 13, 1873, at the Los Pinos Agency, and Chief Ouray, accompanied by Otto Mears, was treated with a trip to Washington, D.C. at government expense to meet the president. For all his expertise at compromise and persuasion, it is interesting to note that Otto Mears chartered a new toll road into the relinquished Indian lands even before Congress ratified the treaty on April 29, 1874.

In 1875, Mears helped organize the Lake City Land Company for the purpose of boosting settlement on the former Ute lands. He commissioned yet another road into the region. By connecting the already existing route from Del Norte to Antelope Park and thus to the newly platted town of Lake City, Mears created one of the primary routes into the San Juans. Within two years the town had over 900 buildings and a population of 2,000 inhabitants.

In order to secure his financial situation, Mears received a small contract from the government in 1876. The agreement stipulated that Mears would carry mail to the isolated town of Ouray. The job was risky and so was the contract. It imposed a steep fine should Mears fail to meet his once-a-week schedule. Mears built relay stations twenty miles apart and used dog sleds and skis to carry the mail over the high trail. During the harsh winter Otto Mears' dog sleds were Ouray's only link to the outside world. The sleds carried freight as well as mail; sometimes the loads were so tremendous that the top-heavy sleds crashed to the bottom of steep, snow-filled ravines, crushing the fashionable hats and dresses that the good ladies of Ouray ordered from Paris or New York.

When the spring thaw turned the trail into a quagmire of mud and slush, it became obvious that neither sled nor mule would be able to reach the isolated mining community. If the deadline was not met, Otto Mears would be bankrupt. His hired drivers refused to move. In order to prevent such a disaster, the undersized dynamo from Russia strapped on a heavy backpack containing the mail and set off on foot over the "impassable" trail. With a knee-deep quagmire of mud and snow covering the route, the icy water sucking at his leather boots, Otto Mears took almost a week to traverse the seventy-five miles between Lake City and Ouray. He succeeded. He got the mail delivered before the deadline. Once again Mears beat the odds of the wilderness which had destroyed other men by the score.

By 1878, Otto Mears' determined efforts at road building began to pay off in earnest. That year the great silver strikes at Leadville created a market which brought produce by the ton out of the San Luis Valley and over the original Poncha Pass toll road. The rush to Gunnison during the same year inspired Mears to construct another road over 10,846-foot Marshall Pass. The road paid handsome dividends, as did his road to Ouray, which saw Mears collecting frequent tolls from the Army, which used the road grudgingly but regularly. Eventually, Mears sold his Marshall Pass route to the Denver and Rio Grande Railway, which used much of the road to lay rail into Gunnison ahead of the rival Denver, South Park & Pacific Railroad.

This series of events by 1880 made the once-penniless orphan from the Baltic a wealthy and influential man for the first time. From there his fortunes skyrocketed. Before long, he built wagon roads into virtually every town in the San Juans, some of them traversing mountain passes so steep that Mears' works were recognized as tremendous engineering feats. The most famous (and fearsome) of all was the precipitous Circle or Rainbow route ascending out of Ouray on a shelf of solid rock 1,000 feet above the valley floor. The road skirted the grandeur of Red Mountain and finally snaked its way into Silverton.

The numerous toll roads completed from 1867 to 1885 became Otto Mears' ticket to success. By the 1880s, the tenacious little path builder had already foreseen that the future of transportation in southwestern Colorado would be vested in steam locomotives. William Jackson Palmer had already proved the feasibility of utilizing narrow gauge track (three feet between the rails) to link the larger mining centers of the Western Slope to Denver and points east. In 1887, Otto Mears began selling stock in his newly organized Silverton Railroad Company. Among the corporation's numerous investors were southern Colorado businessman Fred Walsen, the Guggenheim family which was making a fortune from the Leadville mines, and imperious David Moffat, one of Denver's greatest financiers. Mears' objective was to link Silverton to the newly organized mining camp of Ironton in order to haul ore from the Silver Bell and Vanderbilt mines in the Yankee Girl Mining District on Red Mountain.

Mears received permission from the federal government to employ Ute Indians to prepare the right-of-way. For a while the work proceeded at the proverbial snail's pace because the Indians kept chasing the numerous marmots or "whistle pigs," as they were locally known, which were considered to be a great delicacy on the dinner table. The work continued, however, and by hand labor alone the company finally completed the line between Ironton and Silverton by 1889. During one single year of operation the Silverton Railroad carried over 30,000 tons of ore from the Yankee Girl mines to nearby smelters.

Eventually, southwestern Colorado miners extracted $38 million in ore during the golden days of the Red Mountain region. In an effort to popularize his railroad among eastern dignitaries, Mears commissioned several Denver and Santa Fe jewelers to design V.I.P. railroad passes cast from solid silver. The so-called "Mears Passes" soon became trendy collectors' items with the "social flys" of New York and Philadelphia.

In 1895, Otto Mears incorporated the Silverton Northern Railroad Company. The plans called for tracks to be laid from Silverton to Animas Forks and finally to Lake City over the bed of the old toll road. The line had reached Animas Forks by 1904, but Mears never completed the line to Lake City, probably due to his absence from Colorado during that period. He had gone east to take over the presidency of the Washington and Chesapeake Railway.

The most ambitious railroad effort Otto Mears ever embarked upon, however, was the 172-mile Rio Grande Southern begun in 1890 and completed in 1892. The line connected with the Denver and Rio Grande at Ridgway and then proceeded over another of the old toll roads to the boom town of Telluride. Historians agree that the completion of the Rio Grande Southern was one of the grandest feats in the long history of western railroad building. One of its enormous trestles near the town of Ophir was reputedly so high that engineers allowed uneasy passengers to leave the train and walk rather than ride over the frightening chasm below. According to legend the conductors on the Rio Grande Southern announced just prior to the terminus: "Last station stop, TO-HELL-U-RIDE!"

Although the Southern operated until 1951, it was never particularly profitable and usually in debt. Its fate became a harbinger of the future for Otto Mears. In 1892 he proposed yet another railroad. The Ouray-Ironton Electric Railway would, if built, have to negotiate a 7.7 percent uphill grade thus making the use of steam engines impossible. The plans for the new line never got off the ground. By mid-1893 the great silver crash and resultant nationwide financial panic ruined railroad building throughout the West.

By summer of that year the great Union Pacific, Northern

Pacific, and Santa Fe railroad systems went into receivership. So did Otto Mears' Rio Grande Southern. Many years later a local verse summed up the situation quite irreverently:

> "Otto was my loving daddy
> He had great hopes and plans for me,
> And I did a thriving business
> Until the crash of ninety-three."

In fact, the loss of the Rio Grande Southern was such a severe blow to Otto that he temporarily left Colorado in 1897 to take over the presidency of the financially distraught Washington and Chesapeake Beach Railway. He returned to his beloved San Juan Mountains in 1907, however, and purchased a home in Silverton. From there he tended his investments and some local mining interests until his wife's failing health forced the couple to relocate to Pasadena, California, in 1917. Three years later his wife Mary died. It was at La Crescenta, California, on a bright June day in 1931 that Otto Mears peacefully passed away in his bed. According to his last wishes, friends held a memorial service over his ashes in Silverton, Colorado. Then they dispersed his ashes and those of his wife Mary over the site of the old toll gate on the Rainbow Road south of Ouray, today's "Million Dollar Highway."

There is no doubt that the life of Otto Mears reflected a slight flaw in the harsh reality of life on the frontier. It is true that he succeeded where other men had failed. In actuality, very few entrepreneurs of the Old West succeeded in developing viable transportation systems without substantial government support. For the most part Otto Mears built his empire chiefly on insight and a keen sense for timeliness and opportunity. Through the appropriate sale of stocks and the honest use of the interlocking directorate device of control, a system which scandalized much larger railroad companies, the "Pathfinder of the San Juan" was able to build an empire mainly through individual effort. Rarely did the prosaic quest for western independence reap such high dividends. It is doubtful that the riches of Colorado's Western Slope could have been tapped quite so quickly or efficiently without the foresight, optimism, and tenacity of a former newspaper boy named Otto Mears.

Nicholas C. Creede

Nicholas Creede was dead! There was no doubt about it. A servant had discovered him lying unconscious in the rose garden of his Los Angeles home, and although medical treatment had been quickly administered, he died within two hours. The cause, said the attending physician, was morphine poisoning. The date was July 12, 1897. The next morning the front page of the *Denver Republican* reported: "LOS ANGELES, CAL, Jul 12 -- Nicholas C. Creede, the millionaire mine owner, after whom the town of Creede, Colo., was named, committed suicide with morphine this evening at his home in this city because his wife, from whom he had separated, insisted upon renewing their marital relations."

Financier L.E. Campbell, a onetime associate of Creede, looked up from the telegraph he was reading in his plush Denver suite. He had made a decision. Within a very few minutes he sat in the office of the *Denver Republican* making a statement to the press. "He never killed himself," Campbell told the reporter. "And I said so when I read the dispatch from Los Angeles this morning. Creede was too brave a man to die that way. I do not doubt the statement about him having died of morphine poisoning," Campbell exclaimed. "In fact I knew of two or three occassions when he came very near dying from the same cause."

Nicholas C. Creede.
*Western History Department,
Denver Public Library.*

"The fact is not very widely known," Campbell went on, "but Mr. Creede had for several years been hopelessly addicted to the morphine habit. He acquired it in 1892, when he was living in Creede. . . . For some time then (Mr.) Creede had been drinking heavily, always whisky, and finally he got into such a condition that it was deemed necessary to call in a physician. . . . His (physician's) method of curing the whisky habit was to furnish the patient with a substitute stimulant — and he chose opium."

"The opium prescribed for him then started Mr. Creede in the morphine habit, and he continued to use morphine afterwards. Whenever he was worried or anything went wrong with him, the regular dose did not have the desired effect, so he used to take a second and a heavier dose. . . . I believe that when his wife was about to come back to him, out there in Los Angeles, he decided to cast her off for good. In order to brace himself up for the interview with Mrs. Creede he resorted to morphine, and in his disturbed condition he probably had to take a second dose, as usual. He was an old man, going onto 60 years, and was unable to rally from the effects of the drug. It is my opinion, that this was how his death occurred. Take my word for it," Campbell concluded, "N. C. Creede will never fill a suicide's grave."

What had gone wrong with Nicholas Creede? Immediately, his so-called "friends" like L.E. Campbell blamed drugs and an unhappy marriage. Creede himself had allegedly sought a divorce on the grounds of his wife's supposed addiction to morphine.

On the surface Nicholas Creede was a Horatio Alger hero. He was a quiet prospector described by his acquaintances as "reserved in manner, not convivially inclined, square shouldered and well made." They portrayed him as being "thoroughly honest," but possessed of only "average intelligence." Nicholas Creede started with nothing, a man estranged by his Iowa home and family. Between 1870 and 1892 he could be found prospecting the majestic peaks of the Colorado Rockies, in the later years accompanied only by his little dog Whiskers, searching for the one big strike that would fulfill the promise of the West. And finally he discovered it. Almost overnight he became famous — giving his very name to the rugged land. By 1893, Creede was living in luxury. His dog Whiskers wore a leather collar studded with nuggets of pure gold. He married for the first time in his life. The story of Creede's exploits and his determined individualism was the stuff and substance of the West that lured people by the thousands to the frontier.

And then four years later he was dead — a victim of morphine poisoning. Even before his burial his apparent heirs began a long struggle that would eventually span the first decade of the twentieth century, to claim his estate valued anywhere from $50,000 to $100,000 — an estate that should have been ten times richer. In the end, the life of N.C. Creede mirrored the reality, rather than the promise, of individual effort exerted on the frontiers of Colorado's mining camps.

N.C. Creede had been born on a farm near Fort Wayne, Indiana, sometime in 1843. When the lad was only four years old, the family moved to Iowa Territory where he lived until he was 18. At that time his name was William H. Harvey. According to early testimonies he fell in love with a local girl who was also being courted by his brother. Supposedly, the young lady finally chose the brother and young William Harvey renounced his home and family and set out into the world under the alias — Nicholas C. Creede. He went to Omaha where until 1863 he sold lumber felled along the Platte River.

During the Civil War, Omaha was a rude outpost on the Great Plains. It served as a jumping off point for frontiersmen making their way up the Platte toward the shining Rocky Mountains. With the withdrawal of federal troops during the war, Captain Frank North formed the illustrious Pawnee Scouts to protect the trail from the marauding Sioux. N.C. Creede joined the unit and quickly became a first lieutenant. By 1865, the scouts helped guard the advance of the Union Pacific Railroad across the plains from Omaha toward its rendezvous with the Central Pacific at Promontory Point in Utah. Across the Nebraska prairielands, the bold Sioux still raided. The Pawnee Scouts were kept busy protecting track crews and engineering parties. It was during this time that Creede first met his future business partner, Major L.E. Campbell, at Fort Kearney, Nebraska.

By the time the transcontinental railroad reached Cheyenne, Wyoming, Nicholas Creede turned his thoughts to prospecting. A recent trip to the Black Hills provided him with the knowledge he needed. By 1870, he found himself wintering in Pueblo, Colorado, ready to make the big strike when the warm zephyrs of spring blew down from the north. During the next few years he prospected around Del Norte and in Custer County and as far south as Elizabeth, New Mexico. He also ventured into Leadville and Chaffee County. Fortune eluded him all the way.

Eventually, he wandered into the rugged San Juan Mountains and then into the Sangre de Cristos. Near the little town of Bonanza, Creede discovered the "Twin Mines" which he developed and later sold for $10,000. This was his first taste of success, and with renewed enthusiasm he ventured off to Arizona, Utah, Nevada, and California. The trip was largely unsuccessful.

In 1886, the almost penniless Creede formed a four-year partnership with Salida financiers George L. Smith and Charles H. Abbott. With the grubstake provided by his partners, Creede left once again for the hidden valleys of the majestic San Juans. Just as the term of the partnership was about to expire, Nicholas Creede made the big strike. According to legend, while Creede was aimlessly prospecting above Wagon Wheel Gap, he picked up a chunk of ore from a nearby outcropping. Examining the ore closely, he became very excited. In astonishment he finally grabbed his dog and shouted, "Holy Moses, Whiskers, we've struck it rich!"

Creede and his partners needed capital to exploit their Holy Moses Mine. Major L.E. Campbell, Creede's old friend from his Nebraska days, was then serving as quartermaster of Fort Logan, but Campbell had side interests in mining. It was to Campbell that Nicholas Creede turned for needed funds. Campbell and his associates, Sylvester T. Smith and David H. Moffat, Jr., the powerful financier of Denver's First National Bank, lent Creede $65,000 in return for the controlling share in the mine. It was from this point forward that N.C. Creede's problems multiplied.

During the time that L.E. Campbell was managing the Holy Moses Mine, he engaged Creede to prospect the lands adjacent to the property. Creede received forty dollars a month and was to receive a one-third interest in whatever he might discover. On August 8, 1891, a telegram arrived at the office of David Moffat. It read: "I have found a million dollar mine. N.C. Creede." The new mine was named the Amethyst and the discovery stake bore the names, "L.E. Campbell, D.H. Moffat, and N.C. Creede." Development work began at once by the Amethyst Mining Company organized by Moffat and his associates.

The Amethyst vein turned out to be one of the richest silver strikes on record. Within a few weeks the story of Creede's discovery spread abroad. Soon, "a thousand burdened burros filled the narrow, winding, wriggling trail." One of Colorado's last great rushes was on. Very shortly, the new camp in the San Juans had thousands of inhabitants. After much discussion the rival camp of Jimtown (or Gintown as it was sometimes called)

was fused with the new camp on the far side of a high cliff and
the entire community was named Creede. L.E. Campbell named
the town as well as constructing its first permanent building.

Without doubt Creede became one of the bawdiest mining
camps in the West. Gambling halls, saloons, and bordellos pro-
liferated in the lawless town. The likes of Poker Alice Tubbs,
con man Soapy Smith, and Jessie James' boyish assassin Bob
Ford ran the community openly and insolently. Vice so characterized the town that its newspaper editor Cy Warman was
inspired to write his now-famous poem, "Creede," ending with
the lines:

> "It's day all day in the day-time,
> And there is no night in Creede."

With ore from veins fifteen feet wide producing 85 to 120
ounces of silver per ton, the Amethyst Mine was an immediate
success. And Nicholas Creede found himself in seeming
opulence.

In 1892, with his fortune apparently assured, Nicholas Creede
took a wife. Louise Patterson (at the time Mrs. Frank Kyle) ran
a boardinghouse in the nearby town of Del Norte, though in
the past, to supplement her income, she had starred on the
stage of Jud Calkins' dance hall in Del Norte. Before she married
Kyle, Lou Patterson had befriended Nicholas Creede, then a
poor, unknown prospector. When Creede returned from his
frequent trips into the mountains, he usually lodged in Lou
Patterson's boardinghouse. Purportedly, they became intimate,
Lou even accompanying Creede on a prospecting journey to
the nearby La Garita Mountains.

After the money began to roll in from the Amethyst Mine,
Creede hired carpenters to build a log cottage at the head of
West Willow Creek. Soon afterwards, Lou Patterson obtained a
divorce from her husband and scurried off to Las Vegas, New
Mexico, with Nicholas Creede. The couple was married by a
justice of the peace in the Hot Springs Hotel.

By 1893, Nicholas Creede should have been a very happy
man. After all, the firm of Moffat and Campbell was supervising

the Amethyst Mine and sending Creede a check for his third of the profits every month. According to L.E. Campbell's own account to the newspapers, Creede's receipts totalled over $340,000 "during the two years he had been associated with the Amethyst Mine."

But Nicholas Creede was not a happy man. In the spring of 1893 journalist Cy Warman paid him a visit. Warman remembered that Creede had been reading *Huckleberry Finn* when he entered the room. In the corner of the room a big music box tinkled away. Whiskers was wearing jewelry. "How is the Amethyst?" Warman asked. Creede spoke not a word but instead handed his visitor a slip of paper. On the paper was written the figure $30,000. According to Warman, "they [the figures] had been marked down by that big, busy man in Denver, Creede's banker and benefactor, and represented Creede's share of the net earnings of the Amethyst for the short month of February."

"A thousand dollars a day," cried Warman. "You ought to be happy."

"Yes," said Creede, "I ought to be." Then he looked out where the March winds were sweeping the mesa. Warman noticed that "there was silence for some moments, during which I wondered why this man could be so sad. He could not know that, even then, a Judas was at the old miner's board — a Judas whose kiss, it is claimed, has since caused one of the awful, unwritten tragedies of the West."

Within a few weeks Nicholas Creede, convinced that his mines were filling up with water, sold his shares in the Amethyst and Holy Moses for a paltry $15,000 and moved to Los Angeles with his wife. While living in California, Creede adopted a baby girl named Dorothy, the daughter of a destitute actress. By 1897 he had grown disenchanted with his wife. He paid her $20,000 to leave Los Angeles whereupon he began divorce proceedings. Shortly thereafter Creede was found lying prostrate in his rose garden dying of a morphine overdose. His wife, who had allegedly visited him with the intention of reconciling their differences, was actually discovered living in Iuka, Mississippi. She had no comment.

Almost immediately a nasty court battle ensued over the estate valued only somewhere between $50,000 and $100,000. Brothers, half brothers, and a jilted wife all filed claims in court. Creede had named his adopted daughter, Dorothy, his sole heir.

The main focus of the contest, however, was not the modest sum Creede had left behind. It was the Amethyst Mine! By 1897, the property, which Creede had sold for $15,000, had produced nearly $6 million in ore. It was one of the largest producing mines of the time. And Creede had sold it to Moffaat and Campbell for a song!

In May 1899, attorneys for Creede's estate filed suit in district court against the firm of David Moffat, L.E. Campbell, and their partners Walter Cheesman and Sylvester T. Smith. The charge was fraud!

Allegedly, Creede's partners misrepresented the potential future of the Amethyst Mine when they approached him about selling his share. According to L.E. Campbell's report to the *Denver Republican:* "In [summer] 1893, water then hampering the operations at the Amethyst Mine, Creede sold out his third interest in the property." Soon after the sale, pumps were linked from the Holy Moses Mine to the Amethyst to drain the latter, and Moffat and Campbell found themselves sitting atop some of the richest ore in the world. Dorothy Creede's attorney charged that the partners lied to Creede, telling him that the paying days of the mine were over, when in fact it was paying more than ever. The charge against Campbell in particular was that "he in whom Creede had reposed great confidence and sincere friendship," (since the days of the Pawnee Scouts) had "courted the friendship" and had "imposed upon his weakness, gained his confidence, and passed himself off as a sincere friend that he might lead Creede into a trap." The attorney charged that Campbell "had so frightened the old miner, whose nerves were shattered by drink and morphine, had so fraudulently and intentionally misrepresented the facts to the incredulous old man" that he had but little choice to sell his share.

The attorneys for Moffat and Campbell claimed that Dorothy Creede's attorney, John T. Jones, only "discovered fraud" after Creede's case came into the courts. The case took an interminable thirteen years to settle. After numerous appeals the matter was finally resolved on July 3, 1910, when Judge Phillips of Superior Court ruled in favor of Moffat and Campbell, stating that "Creede had disposed of his holdings of his own free will." He ordered the case dismissed. In a separate action Mrs. Louise Creede lost all claim to the estate while little Dorothy Creede, now living with her real mother, who had previously given her up for adoption, retained all of Creede's remaining assets.

The *Rocky Mountain News* called it "one of the most sensational mining scandals" in western history. Whether N.C. Creede was actually defrauded or not will probably never be known for certain. Legally, he sold the property of his own free will. At the very most, Nicholas Creede himself was guilty — guilty of being a poor capitalist.

Throughout the saga of Colorado and the West the same theme occurred repeatedly. From the early days of the free trapper during the Rocky Mountain fur trade to the time of the family homesteader staking out his 160-acre sand waste reserve, through the rude mining camps which saw all the N.C. Creedes of the world make their big strike, the result was often the same. Once independent frontiersmen discovered potential prosperity, the great capitalists were soon on the scene reaping the bulk of the profits. It might be the powerful Hudson's Bay Fur Company forcing the independent trapper into its employ for low wages. It might be one of the behemoth railroad corporations overcharging the once optimistic homesteader and recovering his prime land when he finally gave up his claim — or a feudal cattle syndicate ruthlessly using the blacklist to control its empire. In the case of N.C. Creede it was the Amethyst Mining Company capitalized by David Moffat, L.E. Campbell, Sylvester Smith, and Walter Cheesman. By fair means or foul they all found ways of leaning on the independent frontiersman until he gave up. In a land where many people at least believed, despite the hardships, that individual effort would be rewarded — it was, in truth, the corporate dynasty which ultimately won the West.

Alferd Packer

*E*ven today, the black forested wilderness along the
Lake Fork of the Gunnison River is a treacherous land. The
monstrous cold fronts that howl in like foreboding spectres
seem to pulverize the majestic San Juans with uncontrolled fury.
During these times the storms unleash such enormous amounts
of snow that modern motorists, caught in the throes of nature
at her worst, wonder how their ancestors could have survived
in such a hostile environment and still remain, shall we say,
"civilized."

George F. Ruxton, an early British visitor to this Rocky Mountain empire, observed with a keen sense for detail how nature
could shape the character and temperament of American frontiersmen pitted against the merciless rage of the wilderness
environment. He wrote that "their habits and character assume
a most singular cast of simplicity mingled with ferocity, appearing to take their colouring from the scenes and objects which
surround them. Knowing no wants save those of nature, their
sole care is to procure sufficient food to support life, and the
necessary clothing to protect them from the rigorous climate."

During the deadly winter of 1873-1874, a group of twenty-one
prospectors had the chance to test the limits of human endur-
ance in the face of this very Rocky Mountain wilderness. Leaving
their camp at Bingham Canyon near present-day Provo, Utah,

Alferd Packer.
Western History Department,
Denver Public Library.

the men were optimistic that they could reach the gold diggings along the Blue River at the rough-and-tumble mining camp of Breckenridge, Colorado. The guide for this group was a thirty-one-year-old panhandler with flowing jet-black hair and small, deep-set eyes. His name was Alferd Packer. The other prospectors had grubstaked Packer because of his self-proclaimed knowledge of the "Colorado" which he said "he knew like the back of my hand." Consequently, Packer was appointed the leader of the group.

When the ragged band of frontiersmen set out on their venture, the golden days of Indian summer blessed them in their journey and they made good progress. Eventually, however, the ever predictable forces of nature came rushing into the mountains in the form of an early snowstorm. The blizzard slowed their pace to ten miles per day and their food supply dwindled. Sustaining life on their horse's feed, the men finally descended into the more temperate Uncompahgre Valley of Colorado on

January 21, 1874. It was in this very small valley that a band of Ute Indians under Chief Ouray was camping for the winter. After convincing Ouray that the party was merely a group of prospectors on their way to Breckenridge and that they had no intention of violating the treaty between the United States and the Utes, Ouray extended his hospitality until the weather cleared and the men could resume their odyssey. Some of the party, including Packer, accepted the offer. The remainder of the twenty-one, eager to reach the gold country and stake their claims, pushed on in the face of uncertain weather.

Among the party that left the Ute camp in early February 1874 were O.D. "Lot" Loutsenhizer, George Driver and his brothers, Isaac and Thomas Walker, and Mike Burke. Their destination was the Los Pinos (Ute) Indian Agency located in the Cochetopa Hills southeast of where Gunnison, Colorado, is located today. Once again nature intervened. The party became hopelessly lost in a raging blizzard. Wandering in circles for days without food, it came to the brink of starvation.

Separated from the others, Loutsenhizer and Burke ran into a stray government cow, itself emaciated by starvation. The two men killed the animal with their bare hands and sucked its warm blood to stay alive. Three days later and by pure chance, Loutsenhizer and Burke stumbled into a lonely cow camp operated by government cattlemen James Kelley and his partner Sidney Jocknick. The two cattlemen immediately loaded a sled with provisions and set out to find the remainder of the party, still lost in the mountains. After locating the half-dead prospectors, Kelley and Jocknick recoiled in horror at what they saw. Standing in the front of a pitiful campsite was one of the men ravenous with hunger and half wild with madness. According to Jocknick, the man's "eyes fairly glistened with childish delight. . . ." With matted hair and beard, his clothes ragged and torn out at the knees, this pathetic survivor was raving and uttering jibberish undistinguishable to Kelley and Jocknick.

What was more amazing was the gruesome thing he clutched to his chest like a mad man. Coming closer through the eerie silence that inevitably accompanies new-fallen snow, Kelley and Jocknick could distinguish with revulsion the half-eaten remains of a coyote's head. The party had located the emaciated animal a few days before and had tracked him until the animal gave out. The Loutsenhizer party was saved from the unforgiving clutches of the wilderness. The prospectors remained at the cow camp for three weeks until they recovered from their ordeal; then they set out through the snowdrifts to the Los Pinos Reservation.

Meanwhile, back at Ouray's camp on the Uncompahgre, the gold fever took hold once more, and on February 9, a second party departed through the snow in another attempt to reach Blue River. Six men comprised the rough group: Sixty-year-old Israel Swan, a sixteen-year-old lad by the name of George Noon, Shannon Wilson Bell, James Humphrey, and a German butcher named Frank Miller. Leading the party was six-foot-tall Alferd Packer.

Chief Ouray warned the men to stay close to the banks of the Gunnison River to avoid getting lost. Because they expected to reach the government cow camp easily, the men carried only six day's worth of rations. Preston Nutter and James Montgomery, two of the original twenty-one who had decided to remain behind, watched the party of six depart through the deep drifts and into the teeth of yet another snowstorm on February 10, 1874. It was the last time any of the party, except for Alferd Packer, was ever seen alive.

The events that occurred during the next sixty-six days will forever be shrouded in controversy and mystery. Nevertheless, early on the morning of April 16, 1874, a disheveled and exhausted Alferd Packer stumbled into the mess house at the Los Pinos Indian Agency. He was the sole survivor of the party of six men that had left Chief Ouray's camp in February.

Packer told authorities that when he became snowblind, the others had left him behind in quest for food and shelter. When they failed to return, said Packer, he somehow managed to survive by eating wild rose buds and struggling a mile or so each day until he found his way out of the treacherous mountains. At first people at the Los Pinos Agency believed Packer's story. Yet his possession of Miller's Bowie knife and Swan's Winchester did not seem to fit his account of what happened.

Claiming to be destitute, Packer sold the Winchester for ten dollars and left the reservation for Saguache, still hoping to reach the gold diggings at Breckenridge.

While in Saguache, Packer began spending money freely. While under the influence of alcohol in Dolan's saloon, he repeatedly began telling new versions of his ordeal in the mountains. Many people grew suspicious. Controversy was such at the Los Pinos Reservation that Indian Agent Charles Adams went to Saguache and escorted Packer back to the agency for questioning.

Under pressure from Adams' interrogation, Packer broke down and in his high-pitched, whiny voice gave the first of his confessions to a bizarre set of events. Packer related to Adams how food had given out and the aged Israel Swan succumbed to the elements and died after about ten days out. The party partook of his flesh as food to stay alive. Several days later, Humphreys and then Miller died, and the remaining three men stayed alive only by eating their flesh raw or cooked on a stick over an open fire. When the supply of meat ran out, Packer recalled, the three men became nearly insane with hunger. Accordingly, Bell shot the sixteen-year-old George Noon and then turned on Packer. After Bell shot at Packer and missed, Packer supposedly turned on Bell and killed him with his hatchet. Packer admitted eating the flesh of Bell and Noon until he escaped from the mountains. Packer swore and signed his confession on May 8, 1874.

Eventually, a search party was organized and Packer reluctantly agreed to lead it in search of the five missing corpses. Upon reaching the Lake Fork of the Gunnison near Lake Cristobal, Packer grew restive and claimed he was unfamiliar with the country in the immediate vicinity. The search party returned to the Los Pinos Agency empty-handed. By the following August, however, grisly evidence was discovered in the wilderness surrounding Lake Cristobal.

According to one of several conflicting accounts, an artist by the name of J.A. Randolph found the decaying bodies of the victims while sketching material for *Harper's Weekly*. When discovered, all five bodies bore the marks of hatchet wounds and all of their boots were missing. Due to the decomposition of the bodies, however, little else was ascertained. Nevertheless, the deep gashes in the bodies revealed marked inconsistencies in Packer's confession.

When the gruesome find was reported, Alferd Packer was placed in heavy irons in the flimsy Saguache jail to await a hasty trial. The court never convened, however. On the very night that he was jailed — and under mysterious circumstances, perhaps bribery — Alferd Packer escaped his captors. Search parties scoured the hills in vain. Surviving members of the original twenty-one swore vengeance. But at the moment, it was not to be. For the next nine years Alferd Packer remained a fugitive from justice, a $5,000 reward on his head.

On a bleak winter night in March 1883, with the snow and ever-pervasive wind blowing around a pine log hotel in the tiny frontier town of La Perle in Wyoming Territory, a scruffy peddler by the name of Frenchy Cabazon tossed fitfully on his hard bed in a useless attempt to sleep. On the other side of the wall, through the drafty pine logs, he kept hearing a whining, high-pitched voice. He had heard the voice years before deep in the San Juan Mountains. The next day he sought out the voice. It belonged to a man who called himself George Swartze, but Frenchy recognized the black-haired figure immediately as Alferd Packer. Frenchy had been a member of the original twenty-one and had long ago sworn revenge against the man that the unforgiving press referred to as the "man-eater."

Frenchy sought out the local sheriff, and on March 11, 1883, Alferd Packer was once again arrested. General Charles Adams came from the Los Pinos Agency to Cheyenne, where Packer was taken to await extradition to Colorado. Adams escorted the prisoner to Denver, where Packer gave yet another confession. Vividly, Packer related how, when food ran out, he was appointed to climb a nearby hill to search for "signs of civilization." Upon returning from the hill, Packer said he discovered Bell roasting a piece of flesh over the campfire. The bodies of the other four men were arranged in a row, their heads split open with hatchet wounds. Upon being caught in the act of cannibalism, Packer said, Bell attacked him with a hatchet. In self-defense, Packer shot Bell in the side and then finished him off with the hatchet.

According to Packer's own testimony, he remained in the camp for sixty days unable to get out through the enormous snow-drifts. He subsisted off the flesh of his former partners. When the snow finally began to crust over, he said, he packed the remaining flesh, took the men's money, and made his long journey to the Los Pinos Agency.

Alferd Packer was taken to the newly developed mining town of Lake City in Hinsdale County near the site of the alleged crime. There on May 9, 1883, he went on trial for murder. Un-doubtedly, the jury heard rhetoric about other cases of can-nibalism on the western frontier. How, for example, the luckless Daniel Blue, who tried to cross the plains to Denver City in 1859, became lost in a spring blizzard, and when his brother Charles perished, ate his flesh to stay alive. Perhaps they even heard the more remarkable story of the unfortunate Donner Party, which became stranded in the Sierras on the way to California in 1846. The party stayed alive until spring only by eating the remains of the deceased. Hearing testimony from surviving members of the twenty-one, the prosecution's case rested not on the act of cannibalism but rather on the motive of robbery for money or food or both. Packer took the stand in his own behalf relating how the ill-tempered Bell was the most belligerent of the group and greatly feared starving to death. The jury heard expert witness to the effect that Bell had been shot in the back rather than the side as Packer had professed. This damning fact led the jurors away from the claim of self-de-fense and after only three hours of deliberation, they found Packer guilty of the charge of murdering Israel Swan. Judge Melville Gerry sentenced Packer to hang on May 19.

A ridiculous legend was born at the sentencing of Alferd Packer. According to fancy, Larry Dolan, a Saguache bartender testifying at the trial, (according to one version) quoted Judge Gerry as saying, "There was only seven Dimmycrats [sic] in Hinsdale County and you, you voracious man-eatin' son-of-a-bitch, you et five of 'em! [sic] I sentence you to hang and may God have mercy on your Republican soul!" In actuality, the articulate Gerry very eloquently sentenced Packer to the gallows.

The story of Alferd Packer might have ended here, but it did not. The hanging never took place. Seizing upon an omission in the laws of the new State of Colorado, Packer's defense attorneys moved for a retrial. Their plea was accepted, and the change of venue moved the proceedings to Gunnison before District Judge William Harrison. Essentially, the old territorial murder statute of 1870 had been repealed without a savings clause when Colorado attained statehood. The missing clause would have provided for the right to try individuals for murders committed prior to the repeal of the old law in 1881. Consequently, the Colorado Supreme Court reversed the death sentence in 1885 and Packer won a new trial in Gunnison the following year. This time Packer was tried on five counts of manslaughter, found guilty again, and sentenced to forty years in the Colorado State Penitentiary in Canon City.

A model prisoner, Packer took an interest in horticulture and became an expert florist. After twelve years, parole was recommended and Packer was released from prison on January 10, 1901. He was fifty-nine years old. The terms of Packer's release required him to remain in Colorado for the remainder of his life. He settled in Littleton, where he worked copper claims in nearby Deer Creek Canyon and befriended many children in the community. He died on April 23, 1907, maintaining his innocence to the last. He was buried in the Littleton cemetery overlooking the South Platte River.

During the late nineteenth and early twentieth centuries, a great body of folklore grew up around the Packer case. The yellow journalism of the period perpetuated myth over fact when it would sell newspapers. Perhaps no report was as outrageous as the one printed by the *Gunnison Tribune* on June 24, 1893. The paper exclaimed that: "Another party ultimately found the camp with the remains of his [Packer's] five friends butchered like beeves, with their flesh hanging on the limbs of trees to jerk in the sun."

Consequently, we may never be able to sort out all the facts from the fiction surrounding the colorful "Cannibal of Slumgullion Pass." Perhaps Packer was truly innocent of premeditated murder. His testimony about shooting Bell in the side rather than in the back may have been an honest mistake. After all, night had fallen, both men were snowblind, and perhaps Bell was turning around when Packer shot him. We may never know.

What is more important about the ordeal of Alferd Packer and his unfortunate companions is the relationship they had with the unforgiving wilderness and how they reacted to it. Throughout the nineteenth century, thousands of men and women ventured west. Facing them was the relentless frontier, which at times was void of many life-sustaining elements. Adaptation and change in response to that environment were necessary if individuals or families were to survive very long. Those pioneers who methodically planned and learned how to use nature to their advantage helped build a great nation in the wilderness. But those opportunists who saw the chance for quick wealth and went to the frontier without respecting its potential for violence faced a danger far greater than Indians or highwaymen. When these individuals were forced to change, it was too late.

Change, therefore, came in extreme and radical ways to meet the forces the wilderness had unleashed upon them. Who is to say that any of the other members of the unfortunate party of six would not have reacted like Alferd Packer if pushed only a little bit further. According to Packer's own testimony, they did.

Violent death from numerous sources was rampant on the frontier — it was accepted as a part of life — but among all of these causes, the worst villain of the Old West was by far nature herself. She came swift and furiously, be it on the windswept open plains, the scorching deserts of the Great Basin, or amidst the killing blizzards of the mighty Colorado Rockies.

Frances Jacobs

Riding the riverboat to Westport, Frances Jacobs must have wondered about the new world that lay before her. On the Missouri, in the winter of 1863, her home and family were already distant memories. At the end of the river lay Westport, then the frontier. Riding the paddlewheeler west, Jacobs must have wondered — and worried — about it all.

In retrospect, she need not have. Twenty-nine years later, when she died, Frances Jacobs was one of the most significant women Colorado had ever known. To be sure, there was irony in the fact. She had no great color, no flair. Among men of silver and steel, she was a bolt of slate-gray cloth; in a world of dominion and power, she was always at its edge, not its center. In a sense, Frances Jacobs came and went so quietly in life that few knew she had ever been there. But she had. And without people knowing it, she had touched them all.

Frances Weisbart was a child of the frontier, born in Harrodsburg, Kentucky, in 1843, and raised in Cincinnati, Ohio. Her upbringing was traditional midwestern and traditional Jewish: Well-educated and lavished with affection, she was trained for life as a loving wife and providing mother. She taught school briefly in Cincinnati, and it was there that she met Abraham Jacobs, a handsome young Jewish merchant moving up

Frances Jacobs.
*Western History Department,
Denver Public Library.*

and moving west. Their time there was short; she was sixteen, with family ties too strong to release her, and he was twenty-five, with too little time to court. In 1858, moving westward with the tide, Jacobs settled first in Omaha, then, in 1859, in Denver. The next year, on the cutting edge of the gold frontier, he moved to Central City. Only then, established behind the cluttered counter of his mining outfitters' store, did his thoughts finally return to Ohio and the Jewish school teacher he had left behind.

On a February afternoon in 1863, beneath a white canopy in a Cincinnati synagogue, Abraham Jacobs married Frances Weisbart. The ceremony was a simple one, rich in Jewish tradition, and when it was over, the small, dark-haired woman with laughter in her voice boarded a steamboat for the West. Out of St. Louis, standing at the steamer's rail, watching dark water disappear beneath its bow like so many fragments of her life, Jacobs must have experienced the great fear of anyone who moved into the wilderness. On one side of her stood her husband and her future. On the other sat a small box holding a white tablecloth, a small quilt, and her grandmother's brass candlesticks wrapped in a shawl. They were her past, or her last links to it. Looking upriver, her face to the wind, weighing it all, she must have wondered again about the choices she had made.

The frontier was a brutal place for women like Frances Jacobs. Many like her had gone before her — young, eastern, cultivated, physically frail, and mentally unprepared for frontier life. The new world they found themselves in had devoured them. If the frontier broke men, it broke far more women. But Jacobs survived the river trip. She also survived a harrowing wagon trek across the prairie from Westport, where Indians shadowed her every move, and where for days on end, searching for water, she and her companions found only acrid water holes and miles of dust. Above all, however, she survived Central City, and in so doing she established a pattern for the rest of her life.

In the early 1860s, Central City was several square miles of lean-tos and tarpaper shacks scattered up and down a narrow draw, a wild, smoky, ticky-tack village of some of the hungriest men in the West. Abraham Jacobs moved easily through its streets. As a wily, frontier-wise businessman with apprenticeships from Louisville to Omaha to the kingdom of Gilpin, he knew the Central City psyche well. Operating his store at a profit, and a southbound stage line as well, and investing his earnings in properties from Denver to Georgetown to the new mining country farther west, he played his cards and he won his hands. While he did, his wife adapted to frontier life. Satisfied and comfortable in a small home on a low-rising hill, surrounded by children to love — two survived the early days in Central City, one did not — she spent her days, as she had been trained to, nurturing them. She had no outward aspirations, no dreams that anyone could see. For all intents and purposes, she shut out the raucous world around her. Even on late spring days, when she walked the town's muddy streets, her mother's shawl around her shoulders, she glided along the boardwalks seemingly oblivious to everything around her. In her husband's store she spoke to those around her, but nowhere else did she. Perhaps it was her way of coping, as if detachment from heat and cold and noise and rancor was simply the only way to survive. Looking at the thin woman with dark eyes and pearl-colored skin, no one could have known.

Like most mining camps, Central City ruined more men than it made, but as the years went by, fortune smiled broadly on Abraham Jacobs. Realizing enough profit from his Central City store to launch a new one in Denver, he slowly became one of the most prominent merchants in Colorado. Frances emerged with him. As his career expanded, so did her life, and in time she shook much of her youthful shyness — as the wives of powerful men had to do — and drifted into the elite circles of the gold town's young society. At the same time, though, almost paradoxically, she also began to demonstrate a growing sympathy for those who did not prosper with her. In any event, no one who met her forgot her. The Cincinnati Weisbarts had taught their daugher well, and her sophistication, intelligence, and concern for others made her almost starkly visible in the streets of Central City.

For a decade life was good there. For Frances, the long trip west was forgotten — its memories brought back only in the lighted candlesticks at family dinners — and her first fears dismissed. But in 1874 fire destroyed Central City and the Jacobs' store with it. It brought her quickly back to reality. Standing on a smoky hill, watching flame fill the sky, she could not have known it, but her life was soon to change forever.

In a sense, Abraham Jacobs never recovered from the great fire. With his store gone, and $50,000 with it, he moved his family to Denver. There his OK Clothing Store became, in effect, his last stand. Once in the city, he sold his wares and dabbled in politics and charity work. But he seemed to have lost his spirit in Central, and it never returned to him again. In 1885, his Denver store failed, and so did he. The once-great merchant, the enterprising stage owner, the mayor of Central City and politician of Denver literally disappeared from sight. At the turn of the century he was a dump guard for the city, and when he died at age seventy-nine — his wife and most of his family gone — he was nothing at all.

As her husband receded into the background, Frances Jacobs advanced to the front. In reality, her unusual emergence as a force in Denver life was probably not so much a conscious act of moving forward as it was a simple matter of drift. At all times, even to the end of her life, Jacobs was an exceedingly shy woman, distant and introverted, and dedicated primarily to fulfilling the roles of wife and mother. But, slowly, her children grew up (Evelyn became a teacher and Ben moved toward law) and her husband's empire disintegrated. And none of the three, in her eyes, needed her as they had before. For the first time in her life she had a void to fill. It had not been her nature to seek out causes or fill her days with activities for the sake of it. What happened next was less the action of a woman with a goal in mind than it was the drift of a woman who had lost the need to be needed. But whatever it was, in time it brought her great personal gratification, and it brought everlasting benefit to the city in which she lived.

In the mid-1870s, shortly after the family's arrival in Denver, Frances Jacobs became the driving force in the city's nascent charity movement.

In the late nineteenth century, as Denver moved from childhood to adolescence, the city possessed virtually no mechanism to help those who could not help themselves. It had no relief agencies to sustain its rapidly growing underclass, nor did the territory or state around it. Its citizens, like those everywhere else in America, embraced the laissez faire Social Darwinism of the time: Socially, they said, the fittest survived, or if they did not, they were not meant to. It was not the function of government to prop up the weak, said the people of the Queen City, for the weak only undermined the strong — and whole civilizations fell from that weakness.

Philosophy aside, though, parts of late nineteenth-century Denver were immersed in the kind of poverty that was slowly sapping the life of the city. Whole sections of it were inhabited by destitute immigrants, few of them with the means to help themselves. And beyond them were children with no parents, consumptives with no clinics, the aged with no shelter. In a city dedicated to business enterprise and little more, no time seemed to exist for those with means to concern themselves with the masses with none. So the masses lived in limbo.

Frances Jacobs, at a turning point in her life, seemed to be searching for personal fulfillment at precisely the moment the underclass became a public problem. Impulsively, perhaps, she responded to it. At first she joined, then led, the Hebrew Benevolent Ladies Aid Society, a small but important network of Jewish women — most of them, like Jacobs, maternalistic and well-to-do, with civic influence far beyond their numbers. Almost alone among them, however, it was Jacobs who early understood that Denver's problems were neither "Jewish" nor "Gentile," but universal, and that in any case they were far too vast for any one organization to solve. Too dedicated to her own peoples' cause to abandon it, she nonetheless began working in other areas of Denver's charity life as well. And as she did, whether she planned it or not, she became the core of what began to emerge as a unified and widespread city charity movement.

Jacobs championed everyone from consumptives to homeless newsboys to alcoholics to the aged. She quickly became the heart and soul of the new Ladies Relief Society, which focused on dispersing food and clothing to the needy and establishing everything from clinics and day nurseries to free kindergartens and homes for destitute women and children and the elderly. A small woman with a strong and vibrant voice, and a kind of manic energy that amazed everyone around her, she literally spent her days begging for the voiceless. Slowly, she catalyzed the many fragmented charities around her into one, then infused them with her own passion. In the mornings she made speeches to anyone who would listen to her. In the afternoons she collected funds. In the evenings, long after the sun had set on most of Denver, she carried the fruits of her days' labors from shelter to shack to brothel to saloon until she was too tired to stand anymore. And in doing it all, she was still virtually alone.

As the years went by, Jacobs became a legend in charity circles. One week would find her in Baltimore and San Francisco, speaking at conferences where she became a nationally known and respected figure, and always, when she spoke, her topics were alcohol and abuse and the need to educate children and shelter the old and the homeless. Another week — most weeks — would find her walking the dark back streets of Denver. In the summers she endured the sun and dust of the near west side and the smelter towns and the immigrant enclaves on the South Platte. In the winters, she prowled the icy reaches of the railroad yards. Wherever she went, she carried what she could. Sometimes soup, sometimes brushes, clean rags, and tea. Sometimes cookies for children. In cold houses she built fires, and in filthy ones she washed curtains and dishes and swept out ashes from packed dirt floors. She nursed the sick, counseled alcoholics, read stories to children, and clothed them, and sometimes she took them to school. Her days were full of the best of people, and the worst. It was said that Frances Jacobs "looked more poor and wretched people in the face than any person in Denver." What allowed her to survive it, said her friend J.S. Appel, was her humor. It was "the safety valve that kept her heart from bursting at all the sorrows she witnessed."

Slowly, Jacobs expanded her work. By the mid-1880s, she was secretary of the Board of Control of the House of the Good Shepherd, promoter of the Newsboys' Home, member of the National Council on Charities and Corrections, and still highly active in both the Ladies Relief Society and the old Hebrew Benevolent Ladies Aid Society. She was also the primary force behind Denver's new free kindergarten movement that finally resulted in the city's first such institution in 1891. And at a time and place where womens' rights were still one of the most divisive issues of the day, she fought doggedly for the rights of women workers in a marketplace that treated them like chattel. In a word, there was no humanitarian issue in two decades that she did not support, no cause she did not fight for. And, still, every night she left her home on the edge of Capitol Hill and walked into other worlds that most Denverites did not even know existed.

In 1887, it was Frances Jacobs, with ministers Martin Hart and Myron Reed, who finally brought Denver's twenty-two charities together in one organization and gave them a collective power that they had never had before. In a sense, the so-called Charity Organization — later the Community Chest and forerunner of the United Way — was the culmination of Jacobs' life.

Even so, she still turned to one last crusade.

Like a handful of other Denverites, most notably Walter von Richthofen, who had dreams for a great spa on the prairie to the east, Jacobs had long hoped to establish a free hospital for consumptives — those who suffered from tuberculosis. Berating eastern agencies for "sending sick people to Colorado, then forgetting them," she began to lobby local Jews for help. Her reasoning was that the women who had helped launch the charity movement in the first place would now make an effort to help the thousands of consumptives who poured into Colorado each year. The response was immediate. A Jewish Hospital Association was formed to raise money for a consumptive hospital to be built on Colfax Avenue on the prairie east of Denver. As the plans crystallized, Jacobs, as usual, was at their center.

On an early August day in 1892, Frances Jacobs finally pushed herself beyond her limits. In the stifling heat of a downtown tenement room, she collapsed with pneumonia and was taken to her small home on Clarkson Street to be tended by her family. Her doctors gave her a clear choice: She could rest and live, or she could work and possibly die. She made her choice. For the next three months, as summer heat turned to winter cold, she worked. As late as November 1, gaunt and pale and nearly too weak to walk, she delivered medicine to a sick woman on Larimer Street. Two days later Jacobs was dead. At 8:30 on the morning of November 3, after emergency surgery for blood poisoning, she died at Marquette Sanitarium a few blocks from her home. Appropriately, it was one of the many agencies she had helped.

In the days that followed, Denver said a long and sorrowful goodbye to the "Queen of Charities." Not long after her death, standing on a lily-decked pulpit in the First Congregational Church, and behind a soft chorus of "Lead, Kindly Light," the state's former governor, John L. Routt, eulogized Jacobs as an uncommon woman who "thought of nothing but to do good to others." "More than anyone I know," said E.J. Jeffrey, president of the Denver and Rio Grand Railway, she "appreciated a helping hand going with a tender heart." It was Jeffrey who proposed that the new Jewish Consumptive Hospital, currently under construction, bear her name. And every listener agreed.

On November 4, a day that began with dark clouds covering the sky and ended with sun streaming through stained glass windows onto Jacobs' casket, crowds spilled into the street at her service at Temple Emanuel. In a voice filled with emotion, Martin Hart remembered her days spent in the homes of the poor, of her whole recent life spent in the lifestreams of the poor. "And this weak woman," he said, "did it for no earthly recompense, seeking no reward save the gratitude of the needy and the 'well done' of the great God above us." Wrote the *Rocky Mountain News* the next day, "She was beloved by people in every walk of life. In her death the poor have lost an earnest and sympathetic friend. She knew no creed or denomination when a cry of distress was heard." And because of it all, she was unique.

In time, of course, Frances Jacobs was forgotten by most. As Mayor Platt Rogers said at her funeral, "The human mind is so constituted that we look for our heroes to those who have been connected with some great epoch." Jacobs was no soldier, no statesman, and certainly she was connected with no great epoch. She was an ordinary woman who rode a riverboat to the West, who loved her family, and who cared for the poor. So, slowly, she drifted from public memory. True, the great sanitarium briefly bore her name — the Frances Jacobs Hospital — but in time it closed because of financial problems, and when it reopened in 1899, it did so not as the Frances Jacobs Hospital, but as the National Jewish Hospital for Consumptives. The first child born there was given her name, but after that, her name remained on nothing at all.

But if the public forgot Jacobs, her friends did not. In 1899, largely due to the influence of Otto Mears, one of Colorado's most influential Jews, Jacobs was honored by the installation of a stained glass window of her likeness in the Colorado State Capitol. In an original group of sixteen pioneers, she was the only woman. Today her home is gone, torn down for a funeral home parking lot, and one of the greatest hospitals in America no longer bears her name. But her face, at least, still shines in stained glass.

In retrospect, Frances Jacobs, said Rabbi William S. Friedman, was "one of the great women of Jewry. Her duplicate does not exist today." Friedman came closest to capturing her essence when he said that "in every day she saw but only an opportunity for good. Weak herself, she buoyed up a despairing soul, she raised the weary, she passed through life happy herself and made others happy with her. And in the end she helped make every son of man equal in the sight of God." Platt Rogers said that he was "proud that her life was spent" in Denver, but most of all, he was happy that she had galvanized people to carry on after her. "They sow the seed," he said, "that will spring up long after the sower is dead."

Riding the paddlewheeler to Westport one evening, Abraham Jacobs turned to his wife. "You'll find many wonderful things to do in Colorado," he said. He was right. She did. But most of all, in a selfish and often brutal time she gave everlasting testimony to the beauty of the human spirit.

Tom Horn

A loud shot rang out through the crisp pre-dawn air. It resounded through the Iron Mountain foothills with such clarity that its sharp report reminded the young boy of a thick wooden board being sharply snapped to pieces.

It was the last thing he ever heard.

A moment later, he lay silent in the dust amidst the sagebrush of his father's sheep camp, a rock neatly placed under his head like a morbid pillow. Only the erratic clanging of a few bells around the necks of the alarmed ewes muffled the methodic hoofbeats of a lone horse and rider as they made their way rapidly east across the barren Laramie plain toward the pink light of a July dawn.

In Cheyenne and Greeley the whispers began within a few weeks.

Horn!

Tom Horn dry-gulched fourteen-year-old Willie Nickell.

In cold blood!

Never had a chance!

Two years later Tom Horn lay stoically on a lumpy bare mattress in the Laramie County Jail puffing on a cigar. Outside, a "horseless carriage" rattled up the pock-marked street, raising clouds of dust as it backfired sharply. As soon as it passed, Horn resumed listening to the tests of the trap door on the

Tom Horn.
*Western History Department,
Denver Public Library.*

scaffold outside his barred window. The abrupt drop of the wooden trap reminded him of the muted slap a Mexican saddle makes when slung on the back of a nervous bronco. A moment later his thoughts trailed off to another more romantic time when his actions would have been respected. What had happened to his life and the world he had once known? Less than two decades before, in Arizona, he had been a local legend.

Born to a Missouri farmer on November 21, 1860, Tom had left home around age sixteen and soon found himself amidst the troubled strife of the turbulent San Carlos Indian Reservation in Arizona Territory. An accomplished hunter, he was offered a job as an army scout. Because of his quick ability to learn, he soon mastered both Spanish and the Athapascan tongue spoken by the Chiricahua Apache wards on the reservation. Consequently, he was promoted to the position of interpreter under the tutelage of the famous chief of Apache scouts, Al Sieber.

Throughout the early 1880s, Tom developed the keen eye and iron nerve necessary to track the elusive Apaches as they periodically left the reservation and scattered to their vast mountain hideouts on both sides of the Mexican border. Attached to the command of General George Crook, Horn once penetrated the mountain stronghold of the wily Geronimo, and there amidst the pungent smell of junipers and the needlelike Spanish bayonet of the Sierra Madre, he won the chief's respect and cajoled the defiant Apaches to return to the reservation, if only temporarily.

During 1885, Talking Boy, as the Indians called him, distinguished himself for valor by helping save the Third Cavalry from disaster across the international border during an ambush by Apaches and Mexican troops which saw the slaying of the expedition's commander, Captain Emmett Crawford. By this time, the Indians specifically requested council through Horn and no one else. He dealt firmly, but fairly, with the Chiricahuas, and he was rewarded with a promotion to chief of scouts. In 1886, Lieutenant Charles B. Gatewood of General Nelson A. Miles' "flying column" finally subdued the Chiricahuas. Soon after the surrender, they, along with the Apache Indian scouts who had ironically helped secure their surrender, were loaded in boxcars and sent into exile into Florida. The Indian wars had come to an end in Arizona, and Tom Horn, chief of scouts, found himself unemployed.

After his tour of duty with the military, Horn worked sporadically as a drover in the Arizona and New Mexico territories. He was generally regarded as an expert with a rope at round-up time. Eventually, he came to Colorado and accepted employment as a Pinkerton detective; there he learned the trade that finally made his hired gun renowned throughout the West. He hunted down train robbers in the parched lands surrounding Meeker and Rifle, but he admitted later that the work was "too tame" for him. "While Pinkerton's is one of the greatest institutions of the kind in existence," he wrote, "I never did like the work so I left them in 1894."

That year, he drifted into the vast range lands along the Colorado-Wyoming border. After working briefly for the baronial

Swan Land and Cattle Company, he joined the Wyoming Stock Growers Association as a livestock detective, a move that marked the beginning of his downfall.

The Wyoming Stock Growers Association was composed of politically influential cattle kings who were sometimes financed by British capital. Through a territorial law dating back to 1884, the association controlled all livestock affairs in Wyoming. It used this authority to terrorize and sometimes liquidate competitors who included rustlers, homesteaders, and small ranchers.

Usually, the association acted without distinction among the three. It seized cattle from anyone remotely suspected of rustling and paid no respect for due process of law. Any cowboy suspected of rustling was blacklisted from employment in the region. The association was especially intolerant of small ranchers who attempted to introduce sheep to the ranges. By cropping the precious gamma grasses low to the ground, sheep created an overgrazing problem that was anathema to the large cattle interests. Consequently, many a "snoozer" would find his sheep clubbed to death during the night, or, on occasion, driven over a nearby cliff.

The landholdings and influence of the association extended into Colorado. It employed private livestock detectives like Horn to bring to justice suspected rustlers who hid out in Coon Hole, Brown's Park, or the Hole-in-the-Wall across the Wyoming line. In essence, this "range land mafia" governed its domain with an iron fist that commonly defied both federal and state law. Instead, it embraced a ruthless code of "justice" meted out by secret mercenaries.

While in the employ of the association, Tom Horn was suspected of stealthfully penetrating several gangs of rustlers and eliminating selected men identified by the association. In each case, the victims were shot with the new .30-.30 rifle then making its appearance in the country, and the corpses were almost always discovered with a rock neatly tucked under the head. In many cases, Tom Horn would visit the camps or ranches of supposed rustlers, and over a steaming cup of coffee, around a fire in the crisp evening air, he would spin yarns. He would tell of his experiences as a manhunter, both real and imagined, of his deeds during the Indian wars and on the open ranges. The gruesome tales were his trademark and quite often provided an effective deterrent to cattle rustling for weeks throughout the districts where he made his visits.

When the Spanish-American War broke out in 1898, Tom enlisted and served as a packer with General William R. Shafter's army in Cuba. Although much speculation surrounds his desire to enlist, most evidence points to the association's decision to dismiss him. It is generally believed that J.M. Carey, chairman of the secret detective committee, fired Horn on the grounds that he was more interested in killing men than in securing evidence for use in court. Guilty or innocent, the killings ceased when Tom Horn entered the service, and the association was relieved that the embarrassing matter was finally over.

After the war, Horn returned to the Wyoming-Colorado borderlands and was promptly hired on a private basis by some of the association's big cattlemen, allegedly to assassinate enemies. For this grisly work, he received five hundred dollars per victim. The names of Ora Haley and John C. Coble have most notably been identified as Tom Horn's employers after 1898, although it is likely that there were others as well.

In any case, the range murders resumed after Horn returned. Small ranchers and rustlers alike trembled wherever Tom Horn rode the deadline. Undoubtedly, he killed four men, two in Wyoming and two in Brown's Park, Colorado, in 1900. Probably more men fell to his deadly aim, but only hearsay evidence could be collected and the quiet, mild-mannered Tom Horn was not arrested.

Then on the morning of July 18, 1901, young Willie Nickell was murdered near his father's Iron Mountain ranch. Kels P. Nickell, Willie's father, had made the mistake of introducing sheep to the Iron Mountain Range. In addition, he was known to have slashed John Coble with a Bowie knife during a quarrel back in 1890. His son Willie was large for his age, and wearing his father's coat and hat and riding his father's horse, the boy was undoubtedly mistaken for the elder Nickell, the bitter enemy of John C. Coble, Horn's reputed employer.

The citizens of Cheyenne and Denver were outraged. They demanded swift justice. By 1900, the "wicked" frontier reputations of cities throughout the West had come under attack by reformers. From prohibitionist to populist, western citizens were determined to rid themselves of the vestiges of their controversial past and vigilante-type justice. Six months later the sure-sighted ex-scout, Tom Horn, was arrested for the murder of Willie Nickell.

To get evidence, a deputy U.S. marshall by the name of Joseph LeFors, while cleverly discussing his own past experiences as a manhunter, baited a slightly intoxicated Horn into making a casual and barroom-like comment about the Nickell murder. Meanwhile, Charles Ohnhause, a stenographer, and Leslie Snow, a deputy sheriff in Cheyenne, hid in an adjoining room and listened through a crack in the door. When Snow later swore under oath that Tom Horn had admitted to the killing, the cowboy was put behind bars on the strength of this "unsigned confession," a chicanery that most assuredly would not stand up in modern courts of law.

The ensuing trial in the Laramie County courthouse was lengthy and jaded by the prosecution's inability to establish a clear motive. Horn's rancher friends assembled the most able legal minds in Wyoming to defend him. John W. Lacey, Timothy F. Burke, R.N. Matson, T. Blake Kennedy, and Nellis E. Corthell argued long and brilliantly, but they could not save him.

The prosecution's case relied strongly upon the so-called LeFors-Ohnhause "confession." Allegedly, Tom had looked sternly at LeFors when casually questioned about the Nickell killing and boasted, "That was the best shot I ever made, and the dirtiest trick I ever did." Horn adamantly denied making the statement. He claimed that Ohnhause had been paid to change his notes by adding the damning statement when he translated them from shorthand. Many key witnesses were not heard from in a satisfactory manner. These witnesses included John C. Coble and Tom's lady friend, Gwendolene Kimmell, a local school teacher who was denouced by the prosecution for introducing "theory as evidence."

Horn's own testimony was strong. He recalled names and events with clarity. Although he was in the Iron Mountain district on the day of the murder, he vividly related his solo journey to the Bosler Ranch during the time of the killing. Cowboy friends, however, who were called to the witness stand to attest to Tom's whereabouts at the time of the murder were easily cajoled and intimidated by the prosecution into giving twisted testimony. In the end their accounts were more condemning than they were helpful.

The jury, too, composed mostly of small ranchers and middle income citizens was by occupation, if for no other reason, hostile to the big cattle interests that represented the defendant. Populist sentiment of the era was predisposed to contravene anything that smacked at big money, including imperial cattle barons.

The press also jeopardized Tom's case. Tainted with the yellow journalism characteristic of the circulation wars of the age, Cheyenne and Denver newspapers attained new subscription highs by ostensibly molding public opinion against the hapless cowboy and the cattle kings. By fastidious and sensational reporting, the journalists garnered facts about Tom's life that held no bearing on the trial but were nonetheless damaging to his character. Politically, a new trial was impossible. In the end the prosecution was able to turn the guilty verdict and gleefully hear the judge pronounce the death sentence amid throngs of reporters and curious onlookers. The date of execution was eventually set for November 20, 1903.

During the entire trial there had been much excitement in southeastern Wyoming and in Colorado. Many people believed that if Tom Horn was guilty, his employers could not afford to let him hang lest he reveal their identities during his last moments. Citizens of Arizona who knew him well could not believe the verdict. Al Sieber, former chief of Apache scouts and Horn's tutor later wrote: ". . . knowing him, as I do, and taking all into consideration, I cannot, and will not, ever believe that Tom Horn was the man the [news] papers tried to make the world believe he was." Sieber was adamant. "These words and sentiments cannot be put too strong," he said, "for I can never believe that the jolly, jovial, honorable and whole-souled Tom Horn I knew was a low-down miserable murderer."

Then on August 10, 1903, the citizens of Denver awoke to the following headline in the *Rocky Mountain News:*

"TOM HORN AND JOHN MCCLEOD THE TERRORS OF THE RANGE MAKE A BREAK FOR LIBERTY AND AFTER AN EXCITING MANHUNT BY ARMED CITIZENS ARE RETURNED TO THEIR CELLS."

Tom and his prison mate John McCleod had assaulted Deputy Sheriff Richard Proctor on the morning of August 9 when Proctor attempted to pass a cup of water to the men in the cell. After a brief struggle, Horn grabbed Proctor's keys and ran out the side door of the jail. Seeing no horse to make his escape, Tom ran into the pallid Cheyenne streets with Proctor's new Browning revolver. Proctor had cunningly engaged the safety latch of the gun, rendering the weapon essentially useless to Horn, who was unfamiliar with the model. Deputy Sheriff Lee Snow saw what was happening and, according to the *Rocky Mountain News*, sounded the alarm with the "ringing of bells and the firing of guns. From every direction men came hurrying with guns. Women rushed into the streets at the sound of the firing and stood screaming, adding to the confusion."

Across the street was a children's merry-go-round operated by a man named O.A. Aldrich. When the mammoth Aldrich saw Horn flee up the alley, he pursued the convicted felon with sixshooter blazing. At the corner of Capitol Avenue and Twentieth Street he fired at Horn, grazing his head. Clubbing the dazed cowboy with the butt of his revolver, Aldrich finally subdued his victim and Tom surrendered as more angry men approached the scene of the excitement.

Only after Deputy Sheriff Snow rode up and administered a vicious blow to the temple of the luckless Horn was he hastily shuffled back to a steel cell in the Laramie County jail along with the recaptured McCleod. During the melee, Kels P. Nickell harangued the mob in the streets and attempted to incite its passion to the point of lynching Horn on the spot.

Seeing his fate before him, Tom had done the only thing he

felt he could; being the free spirit of the vanquished, open range that he was, he sought freedom in a fashion that at one time would have been admired had his attempt been made from a camp of warlike Apaches.

The deed sealed his fate, however.

In the consciences of Cheyenne and Denver's "progressive" citizens who had pondered the accusations of jury-fixing at the trial, Tom Horn clearly illustrated his guilt with finality in the squalid back alleys of Cheyenne. Any hope for a gubernatorial pardon was now almost out of the question.

Tom's occasional sweetheart, Gwendolene Kimmell, however, journeyed to Cheyenne to plead Tom's case with Governor Fenimore Chatterton. Although the press intensely reported the "frequent interviews the governor held with the school-ma'am," in actuality she only saw him once. Living on the Miller Ranch in the Iron Mountain district, Miss Kimmell claimed to have heard a confession to the murder from eighteen-year-old Victor Miller, whose family hated the Nickells. Admittedly, the school teacher, who had an admiration for the young Miller, had tried to protect him through her silence at the trial. The governor was seemingly uninterested in this sensational development. "I held but one interview, worthy of the name, with the governor," she wrote, "and in this his questions were very evidently prompted more by a curiosity concerning my personal, private affairs than by an anxiety to inform himself upon the true situation."

In actuality, the public sentiment stirred by the sensational press was against Horn in the end, as it was during the trial and the governor knew it. Testing the waters of public opinion through numerous telephone calls from the statehouse and more than the usual number of appearances at county fairs during the autumn of 1903 convinced Chatterton that any commutation of sentence would be politically unwise. Although threatened with the withdrawal of financial and political support by some of the big cattlemen, Fenimore Chatterton was keenly attuned to the changing times and the evolving attitudes of the majority of Wyoming's electorate in their opposition to the baronial cattle empires. At 3:30 p.m. on November 14, Judge Lacey received a written decision as he sat smoking a fat Cuban cigar in his chambers.

The governor would not interfere with the death sentence.

When November 20, the day Tom Horn would die, finally arrived, the citizens of Cheyenne and Denver held their breath to see if Horn would finally admit his guilt in the Nickell murder and implicate some of the big cattlemen. Saloons did a record business amidst a carnival atmosphere and a lot of money changed hands on bets that Horn would talk. Many patrons even wagered that at the appointed hour, the condemned man "wouldn't swing" at all.

Hundreds of people crowded the streets before the appointed 11:00 a.m. hour. Masses of onlookers jammed their way toward the Laramie County courthouse. Cordons of police patrolled the town to keep order. Guards were placed on top of the county building in case of violence. Although a high board fence had been erected to keep out the general public, friends and witnesses filed into the arena an hour before the scheduled execution. Most of them shivered if not because of the grisly scene which they would soon behold, then because of the northerly Wyoming wind which blew over remaining patches of snow from a recent storm.

Eventually, the condemned prisoner, handcuffed and emaciated from two years of confinement but still walking with the slight swagger that characterized the vanishing breed of range riders to which he belonged, mounted the creaking wood scaffold with Deputy Sheriff Proctor. The coolest man in the crowd was Tom Horn. As Tom stood surveying the witnesses with extraordinary calm, Proctor announced that Charlie and Frank Irwin, two of Tom's closest friends who would not desert him in his last hour, would sing an old "cowboy-railroad ballad." Stopping on several occasions, the brothers had to swallow hard to regain their composure. Finally, they finished their rueful song.

"Thank you," Tom said, and the two old friends were up on the platform within seconds.

"Tom," Charlie asked, "did you make a confession to the murder of Willie Nickell?"

"No."

"Well Tom, a man's got to die only once and it has to be, so be game."

"You bet I will."

Joseph Cahill, the Laramie County clerk, was on the scaffold with Proctor. Tom looked at Cahill and said, "Well, Joe, I hear you are married and doing well; that you are county clerk. Is that so?"

"Yes, Tom. It's true," answered Cahill.

"Well, by God, I'm damn glad to hear it."

Tom Horn's arms were then bound and he twisted his body to actually assist in the operation. When Cahill unsteadily went to bind his feet, Horn looked at him straight in the eye and retorted, "What's the matter Joe? Ain't losing your nerve, are you?"

Eventually, Proctor placed the noose and the black hood over Tom's head, and he was placed over the trap door. Instantly, it clicked. Water began to run from a tank beneath the scaffold. When enough ran out, the trap door would automatically release. In this fashion, no human hands would spring the trap on the condemned man. Clenching his fists tightly, Tom waited and listened to the water for thirty-five seconds, forty, forty-five, fif — Tom Horn dropped six feet through the trap door without a sound except for a muffled "chug" of the rope as it drew taut. A faint cracking noise signified to the crowd that his neck had been broken. The body bounded up a few inches, swung around, and was still.

"He sure died game," Charlie Irwin was heard to say and the witnesses began passing out from the yard and into Nineteenth Street. Outside, a quiet Kels Nickell waited.

When a reporter emerged from the yard, Nickell sauntered up to him and asked, "Is he dead?"

"Yes, getting cold now."

Still unconvinced, Nickell waited until he saw a body wrapped in a black rubber sheet being placed in a wagon. Even then he followed the wagon as it creaked up the busy street toward the undertaker's office. After viewing the contorted, blue countenance of the corpse, Nickell raised his head and muttered, simply, "at last."

When affluent residents of Park Hill opened their *Rocky Mountain News* the next day, they were greeted with banner headlines:

"TOM HORN EXPIATED HIS GUILT WITH SEALED LIPS:
GOES TO HIS DEATH WITH A JEST OVER ACTIONS OF
NERVOUS OFFICER
Stoutly Protesting His Innocence to Last, Cattle Detective
Suspected of Many Other Crimes Faces Hereafter Without
Quiver and Swings into Eternity With Songs of Friends Ringing
in His Ears — Awful Tension Relieved in Wyoming"

The same day, Tom Horn's forty-third birthday, his body was shipped to his brother Charles in Boulder, Colorado. John C. Coble had purchased the best casket that money could buy. The casket was made of fine oak and lined with copper and white satin trim, and Charles Horn personally inspected its contents at the funeral parlor. There had been rumors that profiteers wished to steal the corpse for public exhibition.

Finally, the arrangements were made and on the following day 2,500 people waited at the Horn family plot in Boulder's Columbia Cemetery. Hundreds more lined University Boulevard, doffing their hats as the somber hearse made its way down the seven blocks to the cemetery.

The funeral of Tom Horn symbolically marked the passing of the wild, open-range days of the Colorado-Wyoming frontier. Times were changing, and Tom Horn and others like him were never quite attuned to those changes. It is doubtful that Tom Horn even liked the world as he knew it after 1900. Akin to the rugged frontiersmen of his youth, Tom Horn had simply outlived his era.

Perhaps Gwendolene Kimmell expressed it best when she told a reporter a year later that "His enemies can call him a desperado but his life was spent keeping the desperate in check. His experiences were broad and deep, and he rendered much gallant service to his country. Riding hard, drinking hard, fighting hard — so passed his days, until he was crushed between the grindstone of two civilizations." The great era of frontier individualism and the hearty men it bred was gone, forever.

Back on his ranch near Bosler, Wyoming, a fatigued John C. Coble took off his elegant gray-wool overcoat and high-peaked Stetson hat. He carefully placed both on an expensive oak hanger in the corner of the stately living hall. Coble virtually fell into the rich leather chair appropriately trimmed with shiny brass studs. He stared at the embers glowing fainter now in the ponderous open-hearthed stone fireplace. Lighting his pipe, he began fumbling with the wrapper on the package he had just received.

Inside was a lengthy manuscript written by Tom Horn describing his experiences as a "Government Scout and Interpreter" during the Apache wars in Arizona. On top of the manuscript was a letter, Tom Horn's last correspondence to his former employer. Coble began reading intently. The letter detailed how Tom, on the morning of the Nickell tragedy, had ridden onto the Miller Ranch and was, for a second time, offered money by the Millers, from a third-party source, to "kill off the Nickell outfit." He had refused the offer and ridden on throughout the day to the Bosler Ranch.

He read how LeFors had supposedly framed Tom with the infamous "confession" and then, Coble's heart jumped as he came to the last paragraph of the letter.

"Your name was not mentioned in the Marshal's office. This is the truth, as I am going to die in ten minutes. Thanking you for your kindness and continued goodness to me, I am,
Sincerely yours,
Tom Horn

John Coble slumped down in the leather chair, a smile came over his face, and he breathed a great sigh of relief.

"Always mindful of obstructions, do your duty, never fail,
Keep your hand upon the throttle, and your eye upon the rail.
You will often find obstructions; look for storms of wind and rain;
On a fill, or curve, or trestle, they will almost ditch your train."

— Ballad sung at the hanging of Tom Horn
Cheyenne, Wyoming
November 20, 1903

Ann Bassett

*O*n hot summer afternoons, the sun turns the country around Brown's Hole into a shimmering-hot no-man's land. For as far as the eye can see, the desert of northwestern Colorado — Brown's Park and beyond — stretches to the horizon. All that breaks the monotony of the flat symmetry are lumpy clusters of cedar and sage and small knots of cattle. It is a hard country. Savage in summer, worse in winter, only the strongest — even now — can survive it.

It was here, on some of the toughest land in Colorado, that Ann Bassett became a legend.

In her own time, no one really knew who Ann Bassett was, and now, nearly a century later, most still do not. To some of her contemporaries she was a simple cattle thief, a common parasite no better than the rustler men she ran with on the cattle kingdom of northwest Colorado. But to others she was a heroine, a gallant champion of the little ranchers against the larger cattle barons. No one, probably, will ever know the full truth about her. But one thing is certain: Her actions and attitudes — good or bad, it matters little — clearly typify the spirit of turn-of-the-century Colorado.

Like Molly Brown, there was an air of "unsinkability" around Ann Bassett from the day she was born. She was the first white

Ann Bassett.
Western History Department,
Denver Public Library.

child born in northwest Colorado (in 1878), the third child of
Brown's Park pioneers Herbert and Elizabeth Bassett. Through
a quirk of fate — her mother had no milk — she was nursed
by a Ute woman from a nearby camp. In many ways she absorbed more than Ute milk; she also absorbed a fiery independence — typical of the wild, free-running Utes of the Colorado
Plateau — that early on set her apart from most other people
of her time. There was never a moment in her life when she
was not her own woman. Impetuous, defiant, arrogant to an
extreme, she earned the title of queen of Brown's Park because
of her imperious ways. If the title meant little, though, her ways
did not. In the great valley along the Green River, they served
her well from the beginning. They also left a mark on the land
that still endures today.

   Like most pioneer children, Ann Bassett grew up in one place
and never left it. As a child, she had the run of one of the most
important ranches in the territory, a spread that sprawled across
the mouth of Brown's Park and dominated entrance to and exit
from it. From the first snow to the last branding, her father's

ranchhouse was filled with visitors — some known and some not, some good and some on the run — and from them she gained an early understanding of the world beyond Brown's Park that few other young people there ever had. She learned to ride and rope with the best, and even the toughest cowboys learned to accept her on her own merits. But when she was sent away to school, first to Salt Lake, then to Boston, she also — like Molly Brown — learned culture. In the end she became a genuine curiosity — a frontier hybrid of both toughness and beauty, part poet, but part hellion too, who smelled at once of damp leather and eastern perfume, and who at all times remained an enigma to those around her.

When she returned to the family ranch after the death of her parents, her fame had already spread. She was known as an iron-willed woman who could bust a bronco with the best of men. But she was also known as a graceful, auburn-haired beauty who could quote Shakespeare. From Baggs to Craig to Vernal it was agreed: Ann Bassett was the "queen" of Brown's Park.

As a young woman, Bassett had many dreams, but the main one was to maintain her family's ranch. In a way, she was torn between two worlds. Raised on bootleg copies of the *Police Gazette* and midnight rides with liquored-up cowboys, but weaned on Chaucer and Renoir, she had roots that ranged from the hard ground of Brown's Park to the genteel, cultural soil of Boston. But the home roots grew deeper, and at the turn of the century she settled down in Brown's Park for good.

Predictably, trouble found her almost immediately.

Like other small ranchers of her time and place — and northwest Colorado was filled with small hardscrabble operators scratching out livings along the cedar-covered draws — Bassett hated the cattle kings who dominated most of the land. For twenty miles on each side of the Green and ranging into both Utah and southwestern Wyoming, a score of powerful cattle barons preempted the land, ran their herds on it, and held all other operators at bay with roving bands of hired guns. What existed — and there was no "law" to stop it — was a condition of social and economic terrorism. Those who opposed it were destroyed — blackballed, driven from the range and local markets, and sometimes killed. It was this condition that Ann Bassett was raised with, and it was this status quo, as a woman returned to save her family ranch, that she refused to honor.

It took her only a brief time to develop tactics to deal with it. More than once she and her riders drove herds of "trespassing" cattle off cliff walls to die in the area's deep canyons. More than once they triggered moonlight stampedes. And more than once — in defiance of one of the West's most sacred codes — they covered brands of strays found on or near Bassett property. Bassett loved her land and feared no one who encroached on it, and part of what she did stemmed simply from that fact. But there was also a kind of obsession in her actions, a certain irrationalism that seemed to transcend the issue of land and cattle. Some suggested that her war on the cattle barons was motivated by some kind of inner demons that no one else ever saw. Perhaps the real issue was power, but no one ever knew for sure. No one argued that Ann Bassett was a driven woman. The question that everyone asked — and never answered — was why.

As she staked out her place on the Brown's Park range, Bassett came into conflict with every large cattleman there. But no one did she hate more, or fight harder, than Ora Haley, the brooding, iron-willed master of the Two-Bar Ranch. Their fight, long and ugly even by the legendary standards of the great West, was one of the fiercest in the annals of the American cattle industry.

In a word, when Bassett attacked Haley and his herds, Haley fought back. Operating on the assumption that Bassett was nothing more than a rustler — an assumption large cattlemen commonly made about their enemies in order to justify what they did to them — Haley unleashed his own night riders. Legend has it that his top gun was Tom Horn. To the end of her life, Bassett blamed the death of her fiancee, Matthew Rash, killed in a Brown's Park ambush by an unseen assassin, on Horn. And feeling his presence in her own shadow more than once, rarely did she herself sleep far from a rifle.

Bassett never forgot the pain of Rash's death. Haley became an obsession. Almost certainly she fought back by rustling his cattle. And almost certainly she harbored others — including the Hole-in-the-Wall gang that foraged out of southern Wyoming year after year — who did the same. In an effort to break Haley, she even married his foreman, Hi Bernard, and took him away from the Two-Bar. With Bernard gone, the giant spread faltered. Haley's fortunes declined. Marrying a man two decades older than herself, and marrying out of vindictiveness instead of love at that, Bassett played a high-risk game. In the end, she both won and lost. She brought Haley to the brink of ruin, but her sad and hollow marriage also ended in divorce. At thirty-four, she had already lost two men, and the effects of the loss on her personal life lingered for years.

In the fall of 1911, confronted by the remains of a young steer freshly exhumed from her property and bearing a mutilated brand, Ann Bassett was finally put on trial for rustling. Across the courtroom from her sat Ora Haley. From the very start, though, the issue was not rustling. In fact, the steer had been slaughtered and buried on Bassett land by Ann Bassett's enemies. And most people around Brown's Park knew it. The real issue was whether or not small ranchers had either the right or the strength to challenge the cattle kings on the land they claimed as theirs. The issue, too, was Ann Bassett herself — a woman in a man's land, playing men's games by men's rules, and winning.

After a long and dramatic trial, the decision sent shock waves rolling across the park: In August 1913, Bassett was acquitted. For days, small ranchers and their hands celebrated in the streets of Craig and in small fields of bunch grass along the Green. The Queen had won, and they had won with her.

Life, for Ann Bassett, at least, was never so exciting again. In 1923, she married again, to Frank Willis, a cattleman. They moved to Leeds, Utah, where she spent the rest of her life with him. Only in the summers did she return to Brown's Park. She died at Leeds in 1956, just short of her seventy-eighth birthday. She was buried in Brown's Park, "the only thing," she once said, "I ever selfishly loved."

In retrospect, Ann Bassett was as significant a symbol of her time — the turn-of-the-century West — as Colorado ever produced. A small rancher in a sea of predators, a woman in a world of men, she faced some of the most immovable obstacles the frontier offered. And she moved them all.

Ironically, the last person who would have understood all this was Bassett herself. She saw herself as a woman, not as a symbol. And she never saw Brown's Park as a battleground between forces of social and economic change. To her it was simply a habitat to be loved and nurtured.

To this day, no one really knows who Ann Bassett was. They know she was a woman of grace and beauty who quoted Shakespeare and rode like the wind. And who may have been a rustler. But beyond that, they know little. To a surprising degree hers was a life lived in shadows, where three men she loved came and went, and where death finally came at seventy-seven. But, as befits local legends, she was never forgotten. On hot summer afternoons, when the sun turns the country around Brown's Park shimmering-hot, and the ghosts of Tom Horn, Ora Haley, and the Hole-in-the-Wall gang parade across the hard land, one can still almost see Ann Bassett, on horseback, framed against the sky, scanning the horizon for strays.

Jefferson Randolph (Soapy) Smith

*T*he West, it was once said, was settled by successive waves of bums! Those individuals, who for one reason or another could not compete with their rivals back east, who had lost family or property during the Civil War, or who sought to escape the law, saw the frontier as a chance for refuge and new opportunity. Add to these misfits a host of opportunists who believed, or wanted to believe, that the gold and silver diggings of the Sierra Nevadas and Rocky Mountains or the embryonic frontier communities of the plains would offer fantastic chances to get rick quick and you have a cross-section of a sizeable proportion of frontier society.

As mining camps, cattle towns, and cities sprang up throughout Colorado and the West, seemingly overnight, a host of urban pioneers poured into the budding settlements to seek a fortune. Some succeeded. Most did not. In many cases these people expected to make their fortune in mining, farming, or ranching, but after assessing their chances, many saw new opportunities in the economic structure of the new towns.

For every urban pioneer who operated within the expected moral standards, there were others who compiled fortunes outside the social sanctions acceptable to more solid citizens or the laws back east. Throughout the West these opportunists plied

Jefferson Randolph
(Soapy) Smith.
*Western History Department,
Denver Public Library.*

the questionable "trades." The young, emerging frontier city of Denver during the last two decades of the nineteenth century was no exception. Undoubtedly, one of the most colorful and convincing confidence men ever to land on Larimer Street was a mannered, jovial rascal with steel-gray eyes. His name was Jefferson Randolph Smith. Colorado and the West were never quite the same after his untimely departure from this world in 1898.

The dapper Smith was born in Georgia in 1860. According to sketchy accounts of his early life, his family moved to Texas sometime during the late 1860s, because its fortunes had been devastated during the Civil War. As a teenager, Smith signed on with a Texas cattle outfit and made the long drive up the dusty Chisholm Trail to Abilene. It was in that wide open cattle town that the young cowboy first became fascinated with the confidence games that became his trademark. Losing his wages in a shell game, Smith borrowed twenty dollars from a fellow drover who asked, "You don't mean you're going to try again?" "No," retorted Smith. "I'm going to join the show and learn that game." Soon after, the optimistic Jefferson Randolph Smith left the open range cattle business to be tutored by one of the Old West's true masters of deceit, Clubfoot Hall.

In 1878, Smith turned up on the streets of booming Leadville to begin plying his new-found trade. Like other western mining towns, Leadville was a con man's heaven, and the young Smith had no trouble taking advantage of a populace already oriented to a gambling mentality. Allying himself with local politicians, the silken-tongued Smith first learned the meaning of power, corrupt as it was, and enjoyed his first taste of success under the tutelage of expert gamesters.

By the early 1880s, Smith was ready to go into business for himself. Confident in his newly acquired abilities, he moved to bustling Denver to set up his soap box on Seventeenth Street between Larimer and Market streets near Union Station. Cornering new arrivals to Denver from Union Station, Smith would begin his pitch by wrapping $1, $5, $10, $20, and $100 bills around bars of soap. He then placed a blue paper wrapper around each bar and shuffled the mess into a large basket. "For $5 you get a bar of soap and maybe $100," he barked. Of course one of his cronies in the audience would come forward, pay his money, and receive a bar of soap with a crisp $100 bill neatly wrapped around the soap under the blue wrapper. By this time the multitude was upon him sticking $5 bills in his face. Few of them received any cash. Smith had put small creases in the blue paper containing money and made sure they were not passed out except to his cronies. After netting at least $250, Smith would fold up his operation until the next day. This scam soon won Smith the nickname "Soapy," a title that would follow him for the rest of his life.

Soapy Smith succeeded in Denver due to his shrewd political sense. Taking advantage of the social incohesiveness that existed in the city during the last two decades of the nineteenth century, he allied himself to the thriving underworld and its bosses. Lou Blonger was the king of that underworld. Blonger made sure that hustlers stayed away from Denver's permanent citizens, but allowed his henchmen to prey openly on newcomers. Soapy obeyed the rules. By doing so, his money and power grew. He

must have justified his scam in his own mind by warning patrons: "Watch carefully" and then "Take a chance." "Use this
soap to wash away your sins! Cleanliness is next to Godliness,
but the feel of a crisp greenback in the pocket is paradise."

While in Denver, Soapy married and fathered three children.
Not really a family man, however, he attended mainly to his
"business enterprises," which grew by leaps and bounds before
1892. Like an octopus he moved in on more and more of the
rackets in the leadership-starved city. He ruled a mob of cut-
throats who made him quite influential in Denver's underworld.
When public opinion began to turn against him, he was fore-
sighted enough to leave town for a while. He moved to the
new, bustling, and wide-open mining town of Creede. There
he became an absolute dictator.

Even with his reputation preceding him, Soapy was welcomed
in Creede. The new silver strikes meant that money was available
in a boom town that was swelling in population by 300 souls a
day. After a few days of casing the town, Smith and about
twenty of his henchmen simply announced that they would
run the place. The only potential stumbling block to Soapy's
aspirations was the owner of the Exchange Club, a bustling
drinking and gambling establishment. The owner's name was
Bob Ford, known throughout the West as the baby-faced assassin
of the outlaw Jessie James. When a meeting between Smith and
the ill-tempered Ford was arranged, Ford realized he was in the
company of a far superior con artist than he was. The two men
agreed to cooperate. Within a few weeks, however, Bob Ford
was shot to death in his own club by Ed O'Kelly.

Now unrivaled, Soapy Smith established his famous Orleans
Club on Creede Avenue. There he openly ran the town. Potential
competitors were run off — or worse. Establishing a link with
the almost nonexistent government, Soapy Smith created a
machine within the city limits of Creede. Newcomers were welcomed and even helped by the Smith machine so long as they
complemented his operations. All new "businessmen" in town
were advised to see Soapy Smith first. "What Smith says in this
town goes" was the closest thing to law that Creede possessed.

During his Creede days, Soapy Smith carried out one of his

most famous and outrageous scams — the excavation of "Colonel Stone." Ordering a cement and plaster figure of a man from Denver (according to one version), Soapy had the figure taken to a nearby mine in a crate labeled "heavy machinery." The plaster man was buried in the mud near a stream where a short time later it was "discovered" by one J.J. Dore. Although contradictory evidence suggests that Smith may not have dreamed up the idea but merely purchased the figure shortly after the "discovery," Soapy eventually wound up with "Colonel Stone." It was said the "Colonel" had met his end at the hands of Indians when he was a member of the John C. Frémont expedition in 1842. Later he became petrified in the mud. Soapy had the "Colonel" taken to the Orleans Club, where eager visitors paid twenty-five cents each to view the "amazing discovery." Soapy milked the petrified man story for all it was worth and then sold the statue to a circus promoter. It was last reported in the state of Washington in 1897.

Eventually, the people of Creede became discontented with the Smith regime. By late 1892, even his gang was losing interest in the bunco artist's operation. After the death of his close friend and partner, Joseph Simmons, Soapy himself lost interest in Creede. He sold the Orleans Club and left town, forever.

Returning to Denver as a wealthy man, Soapy Smith opened up the Tivoli Club at the corner of Seventeenth and Larimer streets. The magnificent Victorian edifice contained plush velvet-valour carpets, flowing drapes, and expensive mahogany furniture to complement the lavish paintings of nudes throughout the establishment. There Soapy and his companions would deal poker and monte, the latter game becoming an obsession with Soapy Smith. He made and lost fortunes seemingly overnight.

In 1894, Smith endeared himself to Denver's political bosses when he, along with other city officials, barricaded himself inside city hall in defiance of populist reform governor Davis Waite's order calling for the resignations of two Denver fire and police commissioners. During this "City Hall War," Waite's administration attempted to force needed reform among Denver's bureaucratic structure by eliminating the commissioners. Men like Soapy Smith would have none of it. When Waite called out the National Guard, which promptly besieged City Hall, Smith reputedly shouted at the soldiers, "If your men take one step against City Hall, you and Waite will be dead!"

Waite called off the troops at 9 p.m. on March 15, 1894. Eventually, the questionable commissioners were removed by a court order. The first rumblings of reform sentiment that would eventually end Soapy Smith's "reign" in Colorado had begun.

Nevertheless, Soapy gained the respect of city hall officials because of the incident, and he prospered for three more years. Over the door of the Tivoli Club he shrewdly placed a sign. Inscribed in Latin were the words "caveat emptor" (let the buyer beware). On at least one occasion the sign saved Smith's establishment when he was hauled into court on charges of fraud. "We should not be classified as gamblers," he told the judge. "I am running an educational institution. The Tivoli Club is a cure for gambling . . . the gambler learns a valuable lesson. He cannot win." Soapy Smith was acquitted of all charges.

By 1897, Colorado was suffering severely from economic depression following the collapse of silver prices in June 1893. Consequently, the mining industry went into sharp decline and with it went the lucrative nature of businesses like the Tivoli Club. In addition, the reform movement was finally squeezing power from the bosses who ruled old frontier Denver. One such reform measure ordered Soapy Smith to pay back half of his gambling profits for graft to the police. He left Denver and Colorado for the last time shortly thereafter.

The story of Soapy Smith might have ended here, but it does not. The bearded "gentleman Jeff" had one more hand to play. In the summer of 1897, he sailed to Skagway, Alaska Territory, to exploit the last frontier of the North American continent, the boisterous Klondike Gold Rush.

As he had done in Creede, Smith moved in on the wide-open town and gained power almost overnight through his alliance with the underworld. By the next year he wrote a friend: "I am now in complete control." From his saloon, "Jeffs Place," he ruled Skagway according to his own will. After a shooting in his saloon in which bartender John Fay was later acquitted through Smith's maneuvering, Soapy was proclaimed the "King of the Klondike." The ability of his gang to kill with impunity made his position unchallengeable. He even ordered a parade on July 4, 1898, in his honor. He was the "Sultan of Skagway." He was supreme — that is, until four days later when he was killed by a would-be rival in a gun battle on Skagway Wharf. He was buried in Gold Rush Cemetery. A simple wood marker marked his grave.

Thus ended the colorful reign of the personable, smooth-talking Soapy Smith. Many would call him a huckster at best, a ruthless ringleader of organized crime, at worst. Like many others of his kind, a great deal of legend has grown up around Soapy Smith. Most of it has at least some basis in truth. What can be said in retrospect is that men like Soapy Smith and his fellow con men were like the secret committees of vigilance, inevitable in mushrooming frontier communities devoid of fully evolved agencies of law and order. In some respects, men and women like Soapy Smith concentrated their shady activities in localized establishments and thus tempered the crude frontiersman's need to expel his energies upon others of his kind, rather than upon the common populace in the open streets and residential areas. When law and order caught up with frontier towns, the taxes and revenues accumulated through saloons, gambling halls, and houses of prostitution were significant to the economic evolution of the community. In many cases these businesses netted even more profits than adjacent mining or ranching activities which were the primary economic endeavors of the region.

What is little noticed about Soapy Smith was his obvious sense of philanthropy. Whether to ease a possible guilty conscience or to cover a scam, Soapy Smith's generosity contributed to the evolution and growth of Denver. He gave away fortunes to the needy in an age when private charity was the only means to that end, even among so-called "respectable citizens." He helped clergymen whose parishes were in desperate need of money and even patronized the Peoples Tabernacle of the Reverend Thomas Uzzell. On Christmas Day he would set up his soap stand as usual and pass out hundreds of dressed turkeys to the poor with the greeting, "Merry Christmas and Good

Luck." The beneficiaries of the Christmas dinners would reply, "God bless you, Soapy."

There have been many who "took from the rich and gave to the poor," and their basic crimes could not and should not be condoned. What can be said, however, is that individuals like Jefferson Randolph Smith played a significant role in the development and lore of Colorado's frontier cities.

Casimiro Barela

*D*uring the troubled summer of 1864, citizens of Denver City were too angry to take much note of the lethargic state of affairs in southern Colorado Territory. The Civil War had caused problems out west, and bold Arapahoe and Cheyenne warriors had all but cut off supplies to the infant city. Troops were training at Camp Chambers, near Boulder City. A campaign against the Indians during the fall was imminent. If it failed, the swelling tide of American civilization in Colorado might be halted for many years to come. Certainly, no one in 1864 cared about the poor New Mexican padres outfitting caravans in Taos and Mora for their annual journeys over Raton Pass to the squalid collection of adobe hovels called Trinidad.

Ever since the founding of San Luis in the great southern valley during 1851, modest numbers of Hispanic immigrants had filtered into the sage-covered lands bordering the Sangre de Cristo Mountains. When Colorado became a separate territory in 1861, their poor communities were carved out of New Mexico Territory. The inhabitants became isolated politically, economically, and socially. Most Americans in Denver and in the gold camps could have cared less about them. The Indians were the immediate problem. As long as the Mexicans remained confined to the southern portion of the territory, they posed no

Casimiro Barela.
Western History Department,
Denver Public Library.

threat to the glorious pageant of Manifest Destiny being played out up north. The politicians in Washington had made them an instant minority group within the boundaries of the new territory, and the Anglo-Saxon population wholeheartedly approved.

Consequently, no one knew, and no one cared, about a seventeen-year-old lad by the name of Casimiro Barela, who made the hard trip over Raton Pass that summer in the company of the padres. The youth immediately fell in love with the new land. Being the son of a poor farmer and freighter, he returned to New Mexico in time for the harvest. Within three years, however he returned with his family to the valley of San Francisco Creek, twenty miles from Trinidad, to start a farm. Soon the citizens of Denver would know the name — Casimiro Barela. Beginning in 1876, this immigrant from New Mexico would begin a tenure in the Colorado State Senate which would last until 1916 — one of the longest of any state senator in the history of the United States.

Casimiro Barela was born on March 4, 1847, in the town of Embudo, in what became New Mexico Territory. Educated by the clergy in the local mission churches, Casimiro showed extraordinary academic aptitude and leadership ability at an early age. When he migrated to Colorado at age twenty, he came prepared with a plan to start a small freighting business. After staking out quarter sections under the Homestead Act, the Barela clan planted grain and raised cattle. In the fall, the Barelas took their produce in wagons to be sold at Fort Union and other isolated way stations along the old Santa Fe Trail. A little village grew up on the family's land, and they named it, appropriately, Barela, Colorado.

In March 1867, Casimiro briefly returned to New Mexico to marry Josefita Ortiz in the chapel at El Sapello. He brought his new bride to Colorado and settled down to a life which would bring him many financial and political rewards.

Within five years, Casimiro's genius for business made him a very successful man. With early profits, he started a sheep ranch. He invested in the budding open range business. He imported over 1,200 head of Texas Longhorns into Barela to stock his growing ranch. From there his investments and corresponding wealth multiplied, extending to railroads, real estate, and banking. During the 1870s, Barela built "El Porvenir," a veritable castle at the base of a small mountain. The luxurious stone mansion was resplendent with drawbridges, gardens, and reflecting pools. Turreted spires allowed Casimiro to look down upon his sheep and cattle empire below the village named for his family.

In 1871, Casimiro Barela went to Denver as a territorial representative from newly organized Las Animas County. His commanding use of the English language spoken with an eloquent Spanish accent immediately impressed his fellow legislators. In 1875, he was chosen to be one of the forty-nine delegates to the convention that drafted the Colorado state constitution. At Barela's urging, the laws of the new state were printed in English, Spanish, and German. In arguing his case, Barela exclaimed, "You may say that ignorance of the law does not excuse the breaking of it. I say it is the only excuse." With statehood in

1876, Barela was elected senator from Las Animas County and thus began a career which extended into the second decade of the twentieth century.

Casimiro's wife, Josefita, died in 1883. Within a year he married Damiana Rivera, a wealthy woman from New Mexico. The senator built yet another town, naming it Rivera in honor of his new bride. His own assets combined with those acquired through this second marriage elevated Barela to a position of wealth unequaled among the Hispanic peoples of southern Colorado. By the mid-1880s, he was one of the three wealthiest stockmen in the state. His horses were recognized as among the finest in the nation. From his famous sire, Senator, came many of the noblest quarter horses and polo ponies to ever please the tastes of eastern sophisticates. In business and private life, Casimiro Barela was very successful.

More notable than his financial accomplishments, however, is his record of achievement in helping the Hispanic people of Colorado while concurrently displaying the pragmatic political sense to keep himself in a position of power during an age of severe racial prejudice. By the dawn of the twentieth century, Casimiro Barela had set the state well on the path toward listening to the concerns of people in southern Colorado. But the task was not an easy one.

Throughout his long career, Barela used his eloquence as a speaker to advance his many causes. Not without a sharp temper, he had the ability to outshout the best of them on the floor of the Senate. He always seemed to get his point of view across in boisterous fashion. Within a very short time, many people believed that Casimiro Barela would become a major force in the Colorado Senate. And they were right.

In order to garner political support and inform Hispanic people about his activity in the Senate, Casimiro Barela established two printing businesses. *Las Dos Republicas* was centered in Denver where Hispanics were starting to congregate toward the end of the nineteenth century. The other press, *El Progresso*, was located in Trinidad to serve his constituents in Las Animas County. Leaflets and news releases, printed in Spanish, frequently rolled off the giant iron presses and were distributed, free of charge, throughout the Denver barrios and in southern Colorado. To aid Hispanic immigrants in their transition to American culture, Barela served as the Denver consul for the republics of Mexico and Costa Rica. He always made time to listen to the concerns of his people.

Toward the turn of the century, the discovery of coal deposits in southern Colorado shattered the cultural isolation of Hispanics around Trinidad. As more and more Americans poured into the region, Barela found himself constantly doing battle with the more numerous Anglos in an attempt to protect his people's land holdings — some of which dated back to land grants allocated by the Republic of Mexico before American annexation in 1848. On one occasion two Hispanic cattle herders by the name of Vasquez and Abieta walked into Casimiro Barela's office with a sad story. A few years before they had purchased 640 acres of state land near Trinidad for grazing purposes. Now one Dr. John Grass (a political rival of Barela's) claimed that the transaction was fraudulent. Barela became furious. Immediately, he summoned Dr. Grass and his lawyer, W.A. Garner, to the capitol.

Meeting in the governor's chambers, Barela accused the two men of being agents for the powerful Colorado Fuel and Iron Company, whose land was adjacent to the Vasquez-Abieta ground. Coal had recently been discovered in the 640-acre tract, and the two men had refused to sell out to Colorado Fuel and Iron. Grass and Garner became enraged. They challenged Barela to state his accusations in writing. Coolly, the senator from Las Animas County pulled out a sheet of paper from his cumbersome leather briefcase and wrote out his accusations. Governor James B. Orman intervened. The whole matter was referred to the state land board for investigation. Within a week the board's appraisers resolved the matter by reporting that no fraud had existed in the sale of the land in question to Vasquez and Abieta.

Not only did Barela champion the cause of individual Hispanics, he fought for better relations between the United States and Mexico as well. At the end of the nineteenth century, Barela delivered one of his most moving, typically Victorian speeches on the floor of the Senate when he successfully argued that the state return several battle flags captured during the Mexican War. "Let us return to the Mexican administration all the trophies of war," Barela said. "They will touch the hearts of that people and stimulate them to closer ties with ours. They will be kept not only as momentoes of their independence, but as relics that will make dear even to Mexicans the bones of American heroes that yet lie bleaching at Chapultepec, and like the new cement between our North and South, Mexico and Uncle Sam will strew flowers alike over the graves of victor and vanquished."

Casimiro Barela did not go unchallenged by his numerous enemies. During a speech delivered to the people of Hoehne, Colorado, on Halloween evening of 1896, that point was made all too clear. No one seemed to notice a window being raised on the second story of an adjacent wood frame building as Senator Barela rose to speak. Within a few moments, five shots rang out across the plaza. People screamed. The senator fell to the ground, blood flowing down his cheek. Fortunately, Barela was only grazed. But the crowd wanted action. A posse was organized to round up two men who had been seen fleeing down a dusty alley. "We'll hang them on the spot," was the violent reaction from the incensed crowd. Barela motioned them to be quiet. "Violence," he said, "is not the answer. Let the law take its course."

By 1900, opposition to Barela and the concerns of the Hispanic population in southern Colorado increased. Anglo opponents forced close elections in Las Animas County after that time. After one especially hard-fought campaign, Barela won reelection to the Senate by a very slim margin. His opponent insisted that the election had been unfair. He claimed election fraud. Showing no anger, Casimiro Barela offered his defeated opponent $100 to help pay for the protest. After a recount, Barela was once again returned to the Senate.

Despite his staunch stands and unrelenting desire to help his people, Senator Barela maintained the cool political sense necessary to flow with changing times. After the administration of Populist Governor Davis Waite was blamed for the depression of 1893, both Populist and Democrat alike were out of favor with most Colorado voters. After 1901, reform sentiment, which culminated with the regulatory changes spearheaded by Republican President Theodore Roosevelt, was taking the nation by storm. With the dawn of a new century, Casimiro Barela thus switched his allegiance from the Democratic Party to the Republican Party. Consequently, he was able to win reelection in 1902, sweeping in on the coattails of Governor James Peabody. To strike a balance between the interests of his Hispanic constituents and the interests of the state as a whole, Barela very shrewdly supported popular stands in Colorado. He was an ardent supporter of the silver standard, populism in the 1890s, and the progressive movement of the early 1900s.

By the turn of the century, Barela depended more and more on Anglo votes to remain in office. Finally, in 1916, it all came to an end. Barela was defeated for the Senate by Wesley De Busk. For the first time in forty years he was not returned to the state capitol. He retired to Rivera, where he spent the remainder of his life in seclusion. On December 18, 1920, the "perpetual senator" peacefully passed away. He was buried in the old cemetery at Trinidad.

Today, the prairie winds blow wild across the weathered remains of the old town of Barela, Colorado. The community is no longer on maps, but the ambitions of its founder, Casimiro Barela, are still very much alive. Barela was successful during his generation because of his unusual sense of pragmatism. He was, after all, "el patron." Ever since the early settlement of southern Colorado, the Mexican plaza system of community development had its political patrons. These local politicians received political support in return for the obligation of providing employment and political favors for their constituents in the villages. After 1876, Casimiro Barela transferred this age-old concept to the state level. By that time, however, the arrival in Trinidad of the Denver and Rio Grande Railway and the eventual discovery of coal in southern Colorado brought ever-increasing numbers of Anglos into Las Animas and adjacent counties. The resulting cultural conflict doomed the plaza system and impoverished many Hispanics. Casimiro Barela witnessed this collapse. He remained in power only so long as he was able to bridge the gap between the interests of the two ethnic groups in his constituency and in the state at large. When he left office, much of his cause fell silent for a time.

The problems of illiteracy, poverty, and exclusion from the job market were, and still are, persistent among Hispanics in Colorado. By the middle years of the twentieth century, they sprang up in the larger towns and cities, including Denver. Not much was done about it before the late 1960s. During that de- cade, however, and through the 1970s, the Hispanic civil rights movement began advocating a form of separatism based on the concept of ethnic pride and awareness. The La Raza Unida political party started by Rudolfo "Corky" Gonzales attempted to instill ethnic pride by preserving the social and economic integrity of the Hispanic cultural communities. By the 1980s, however, much of the old militancy of the 1960s and 1970s had cooled.

Today's Hispanics are working more and more within the system. Public officials like Polly Baca, a senator from the Denver area, became major forces within the state. Then on June 21, 1983, Federico Peña, a thirty-seven-year-old lawyer and son of a south Texas cotton broker, was elected mayor of Denver. Over- night he became a national figure. Peña became the only minor- ity mayor in America in a large city not dominated by minorities. Peña's organization was successful in aligning Hispanics, blacks, and predominantly young, professional, Anglo voters behind the common causes of environmentalism, limited growth, and civic pride. In a campaign reminiscent of the Kennedy years, the Peña election was a major political upset — the biggest in Denver's history. By appealing to the tastes of the young, white, urbane, professional voters who saw themselves as trend set- ters, Federico Peña was able to bridge the gap between ethnic groups once again — if only slightly. Time will tell whether or not his modern sense of pragmatism will bridge the gap even more and proceed to the extent that one woman voter in 1983 believed when she said, "He's not just for the Hispanic people — he'll do the best he can for all the people." Senator Casimiro Barela would heartily approve of that position.

Walter von Richthofen

*I*f history were written in colors instead of words, the story of Walter von Richthofen would be dazzling. For here was a man — a big, red-bearded, barrel-chested, giant of a man — who made a unique mark on one of the most volatile eras in Colorado's history. Here was a man who very nearly outshone his times.

For those who ask who he was, he was a dreamer. In a land of men who dreamed big as a matter of course, in a time where dreams were the essence of frontier life, Richthofen dreamed far more intensely than most. None of his dreams came true, of course. None were ever destined to. In retrospect, in fact, his great visions seem impossible enough to be ludicrous.

But this is not the point of his life. The point is that, win or lose, he reached for the stars. Whether he was a success or failure matters not. What matters is that Richthofen taught a generation of contemporaries — and those who followed him as well — that there were no limits to the ability to dream. And given the fact that Colorado was given birth by dreamers, that it exists today only because of the willingness of men and women a century ago to think and act beyond the normal bounds of what was then "possible," it was a valuable lesson indeed. In a way, Richthofen was a lodestar for a generation. And to those who remember him, he might be still.

Walter von Richthofen
and wife Louisa.
Colorado Historical Society.

Richthofen's early life reads like a long chapter from an exotic novel. He was born in 1850 in Breslau, Silesia, the son of Prussian aristocracy. It was his misfortune to be born into a warmaking state at a warmaking time. Enlisting in the Prussian army at sixteen — as sons of Prussian lords were expected to do — he fought in the Austro-German War, then took part in Prussia's invasion of France not long after. Riding slowly back and forth along the long, gray Prussian line, the tall young lieutenant saw more death by the age of seventeen than most men see in a lifetime. And he decided — maybe on some remote French battlefield, maybe even before — that he could go no further. Whatever his dreams were, they did not include war.

Returning to Prussia, the young baron went to college, then married. But he never settled down. Dishonored for laying down his arms, burdened by a marriage he never really wanted, he finally fled to America.

Richthofen, intense and self-assured, was ready for the new world he found. Briefly he stopped in Chicago, then moved on; like most people at midcentury, he traveled always westward. Working toward the Rockies as a railroad section hand — more for the excitement than the money — Richthofen finally found Denver. In 1870, the year he first walked its dusty streets and boarded in a room at the Corkscrew Club, the Queen City was a boisterous, brawling yearling, as wild and untamed as the land beyond it. But it was also a city of opportunity. For an enterprising adventurer like Richthofen it must have been Eden.

Over the next two decades, little happened in Denver that Richthofen was not a part of. Richthofen money helped launch the city's Chamber of Commerce and support the short-lived, but ambitious, Circle Railway. In an age of gaudy young amusement parks, it was Richthofen money that built the gaudiest of them all — the Sans Souci Concert Gardens on the prairie street Denverites called Broadway. Massive and pretentious — a huge, walled castle from a bad Teutonic dream — the great beer hall briefly played to the largest sporting crowds in Denver's history. In time it died, a spectacular failure; but before it did, its success marked Richthofen, once and for all, as a man to be reckoned with. Clearly, nothing was beyond him. Nothing was too big or too grand or too absurd. Already, though he could not have known it, he could have been writing his epitaph.

In building the Sans Souci, Richthofen found that entrepreneurship seemed to be his calling. The timing was right. Despite the fact that he had lost heavily on the Sans Souci (and more heavily still on Jewell Park, a recreational venture that actually eroded more of his fortune than the beer garden), Richthofen realized that the times still begged for men with capital who could invest in the prairie empire. The baron still had capital. And he still had an overwhelming desire to create. Shrugging off the Sans Souci, which some *still* called one of the most attractive resorts in America, he turned his attention elsewhere.

What finally caught his eye was the desert that swept eastward out of Denver toward Kansas. The land there was as blank as paper, and life was ruled by wind and prairie dogs. Even in the booming 1880s, when downtown Denver was exploding with business blocks and commercial growth, no one save an occasional optimistic homesteader considered the ability of the eastern plains to sustain human existence on a very large scale. It was precisely here, though, that Richthofen finally cast his lot.

In the early 1880s the baron bought the 320-acre homestead of dry goods king John Jay Joslin — a vast, sweeping expanse of buffalo grass, small cottonwood groves, and prairie dog colonies east of Denver in a region loosely called Montclair. There he formulated the greatest plan of his career. Jewell Park, the Sans Souci, the Circle Railway — even then snaking along the Platte — were forgotten. Montclair was to be the culmination of his enterprising life.

What Richthofen envisioned was one of the first planned residential communities in the West, a pastoral enclave on the desert that would rival any settlement in the world. It would cater to two groups: Upper middle class urbanites weary of city life, and health seekers, primarily consumptives. It was not enough for Richthofen simply to create a suburb; the suburb had to be populated — "seeded," perhaps — by the right people. It was clearly a place with a purpose, and the purpose — typical of the Prussian mentality — was social planning.

Richthofen's first thrust was the development of what he called a "high class" residential section carved out of the dust. His hope was that on the maze of lots that crisscrossed Montclair — some developed by him, some developed by others and bought by him — a "club of congenial families" would take hold, put in lawns and trees, establish solid middle-class institutions, and wall out the rest of a city that was growing too fast and too wildly for them to cope with. What Montclair was to be was a sanctuary for rural-minded people with rural values caught in modern times; it was to be a place where they could *see* the city and travel *to* the city, but where they could still live apart *from* the city in security and peace. Separated from the stench of a growing metropolis, isolated from its social problems, miles away from its noise and filth and corruption, they could sit under grape arbors on summer evenings and watch the sun set over the mountains completely untouched by it all.

This was Richthofen's dream.

In retrospect, Montclair was founded on arrogance. Only large lots were sold, to discourage the poor, and a "board of trustees" had to approve all house plans.

Richthofen's covenants rigidly restricted anyone using "vulgar, indecent, and abusive language." Outlawed above all was the sale of liquor. By 1900, forty-five handpicked citizens had planted trees along Montclair's rambling dirt streets. Homes, however slowly, were sprouting from the dirt. Where Montclair would go, no one could properly say. But an idea at least had been born.

Richthofen also envisioned a haven for consumptives. No one ever knew why the man — an aristocrat and elitist — embraced masses of tuberculars, many of them precisely the kind of people he wanted kept out of Montclair, in a day and time when national policy, essentially, was to ignore them. Maybe there was something in his past that bonded him to them — a family death, perhaps, or a personal brush with the disease — but if so, it never came to light. Perhaps in this sense Richthofen was exactly what he seemed to be: A man who cared about the sick and was committed to the use of his own resources to make them well. In any event, it was a side of Richthofen that set him apart from most other members of Colorado's business establishment.

Richthofen's plan for consumptives bordered on fantasy. In the middle of Montclair, ringed by the mansions of the pastoral elite, Richthofen modestly envisioned the "largest and most noted health resort on the face of the globe." Patterned after the great spas at Potsdam and Carlsbad, he planned a 300-room hotel with a bathhouse, its hot mineral water piped from Idaho Springs, sixty miles away. Some smiled at the plan, but not Richthofen. It never occurred to him that he could fail.

His plans set, Richthofen finally began the last work of his life.

First he put his personal life in order. In the mid-1880s, he divorced his first wife, who had lived with him briefly in Denver and borne him two children there, and married a gentle, caring Englishwoman, Louise Ferguson. The couple had first met in 1884 at a dinner in the old Corkscrew Club following an afternoon of horseracing at Jewell Park. "He was tall, handsome and energetic, an impetuous lover," she recalled later, but too "unsettled." Not until "his career had taken a more definite form" did she consent to become his wife. The relationship — which began on a gray Jewell day when a young Englishwoman first saw a scarlet-coated horseman from her carriage window — was to last the baron's lifetime.

For the new baroness, who refused to live simply, Richthofen built a palace on the Montclair prairie. Sitting on the plain, like a mirage on a hot summer day, the great hulking castle was one of the most stunning structures in Colorado. In a sense, the building was a reflection of the man himself — big, stately, striking, strong, and sturdy enough to seem indestructible. Its huge, hand-chiseled limestone blocks, its towers and turrets, its dark fortress battlements, and especially the brooding sandstone bust of Frederick Barbarossa carved on the mansion's corner, all eloquently mirrored Richthofen's Teutonic nature. But at the same time the gloomy grayness of the castle also seemed at odds with Richthofen's flair.

In any event, it deeply displeased a baroness more accustomed to the misty English countryside than the chalky bleakness of the Colorado prairie. When she balked at moving in, Richthofen scattered large groupings of geraniums and roses around the castle's grounds, transported wagonloads of trees and shrubs from Bear and Turkey Creek canyons west of Denver, and set loose flocks of canaries who filled the Montclair sky with color. In time the estate became a thing of beauty. Antelope and deer ran free from one end of it to the other. Bridle trails and bicycle paths laced its dusty lots. Flowers grew everywhere, surrounded by new greenery and pine trees filled with songbirds. The baroness moved in. Briefly, at least, her life and her husband's were full and good.

In the late 1880s, Richthofen turned his full attention to the development of Montclair. Circulars were printed and mailed all across America. Those who replied, who journeyed to Denver to see Montclair, were met at the train station by shining tally-ho coaches and handsome young coachmen, then driven down tree-lined "boulevards" to the new city. There, invariably, they were met and greeted by a tall, crimson-coated man on a white bay, wolfhounds at his heel, manor mistress by his side, riding in the wind. Some bought lots. Some did not. But all must have been impressed by the baron. And few forgot him.

Richthofen also proceeded with his spa project. Across from his castle, connected by a 300-foot passageway so that the baron could reach it even in bad weather, he built a large, blocky "milkhouse" (the Molkerie) which was to be the nucleus of everything else. There consumptives rented small rooms with screened-in porches, breathed Montclair's pure air (lightly scented with pine from the castle's small forest), and drank fresh milk from the finest herd of Jersey cows on the plains. How many lives the "Swiss Milk Cure" saved in Montclair was never known. But for Richthofen, if even a single life was saved, it was a beginning.

In the last days of the 1880s and the first days of the 1890s, Richthofen's life was good. He had his health, a beautiful and loving wife, and the kind of security most pioneer Coloradoans could only dream about. Around him lay a slowly growing neighborhood of his own planning, populated by hard-working men and women of his own choosing. Beyond him lay the spa project. And to the south, in the booming "Golden Bowl" of Cripple Creek, he held stocks of immense value in one of the richest mining districts on earth. He had succeeded in virtually everything he had done. Accordingly, he lived the rich life of the baron he was. By day he and his baroness rode the prairie, wolfhounds in their wake. By night they dined by candlelight at Tortoni's and enjoyed the opera at the Tabor. They were never a part of Denver society, which shunned divorcees with a passion, but they never needed to be. Montclair was their world. They needed no more.

But in 1893 the world ended. When economic depression settled across America, and silver crashed in Colorado, Richthofen's empire crashed with it. In Denver real estate values plummeted, and overnight Montclair froze in the dust. With what he had left, Richthofen floated renewed plans for his "Colorado Carlsbad," then watched them die because no one could buy his stock. As paralysis slowly spread across the mountains, then the plains, it engulfed Richthofen like a rising tide. Standing on the prairie, watching everything he had ever planned slip away, he finally saw his life change forever.

The lavish living stopped. Summer trips to Europe and winterings in southern California ended. Hemmed in by poorly selling gold stocks, loan defaults on his Montclair lots, and mounting tax liabilities, Richthofen even tried — and failed — to sell the castle. Nothing worked. The Midas touch was gone. "We've lost everything," he finally said.

For five years Richthofen lived in a dark world of ruined plans and broken dreams. Abandoning the castle, haunting Denver real estate offices, desperately looking for land deals that would revive him, briefly even selling books on the road, he finally became lost, disoriented, and as broken as his own dreams. In effect, Richthofen disappeared entirely from the Denver scene. The last time anyone saw him was on a brilliant spring morning in 1898 when lines of young Colorado soldiers marched through Union Station to board trains for the Spanish-American War. As the men stepped up to the cars, each was presented with a garland of blossoms by a haggard-looking man beside a wagon full of flowers, attended by a handful of servants. The man was Richthofen. The flowers were geraniums from the castle.

On May 8, 1898, only days after he stood in the shadows of the station, Richthofen died. In a brief newspaper article it was noted that Walter von Richthofen was dead at forty-eight, killed by appendicitis. Doctors, it said, had worked on him in vain, but he died, his wife by his side, in a dingy room at the Imperial Hotel. When he died, it might have added, he was miles and years away from the castle in Montclair.

Those who knew Richthofen, though, said it was not appendicitis that killed him. They said that a person who had fought in two European wars before he was even a man could never die of something as ordinary as appendicitis. What killed him, said his grieving wife, was failure. "Under the burden of his worries," she said, "his health failed." Mental depression enhanced physical. The spirit died. And the body died with it.

In the month of May 1898, with cactus patches and sagebrush stands reclaiming Montclair, the baron was buried in the family vault in Breslau. On his deathbed he had asked his wife that nothing at his funeral be "inappropriate for a private citizen." It was not. And if he was widely mourned either there or in Denver, the record does not show it.

Richthofen left a legacy so sweeping in scope that his own generation probably had not the perspective to understand how significant he had been. In retrospect, though, what he left behind — even if unfinished, even if unfulfilled — was awesome. Jewell Park, the Sans Souci, the Circle Railway — whose last spikes were drawn from their ties during the last days of Richthofen's life — were all his. The Molkerie, where consumptives found a home. A larger spa system unrealized by the baron himself, but later brought to life — on Richthofen ground, with some of Richthofen's plans — in the form of the Agnes Phipps Sanitarium. A planned neighborhood that gave to the Denver of the 1880s a glimpse of the city's future.

But there was still more than this.

What Richthofen really gave Colorado was a lesson: That great societies are built on great dreams; that even if unfulfilled, great dreams are the genesis of civilization. In his time, probably no Coloradoan dreamed greater than he. In Richthofen, Colorado found a man to match its mountains.

Lewis Price

*T*he world that Lewis Price lived in was a world drawn in white. Its institutions were white, and its values, too. White race, white language, white faith, white thought — it was a world immersed in whiteness, a civilization absorbed by whiteness, a people obsessed with whiteness. It was a world where white ruled, and black — if it could — survived. Like darkness against a clear sky, black was stagnation in the midst of productivity, ignorance in the midst of knowledge, degeneracy in the midst of morality. Black was intrusion in the whole process of white civilization.

The time was postwar, the 1870s. The world was Colorado. And right in its midst — angry, proud, and black as night — was Lewis Price.

Price was born a slave in Clay County, Missouri, in 1849. He never knew his father, and barely knew his mother. Like other slaves, chattel that they were, he took the name of his master, Sterling Price. But he hated the man, a Confederate general, and he hated his name. And like most chattel slaves, he hated his life.

As a boy seeking identity, Price found nothing. To the world around him he was just another slave — a slight and slender black man with wide-set eyes, a light mustache, and short stubble set back on his head. At fourteen, though, he knew enough

Lewis Price.
Western History Department,
Denver Public Library.

to know that he was tired of chains. In Ray County, Missouri, he ran from a new master and left slavery behind forever. He surfaced briefly near St. Louis, serving with the 62nd Missouri Colored Infantry in the last days of the Civil War. But when the war was over, he found his way to Kansas. He stopped in Atchison and looked west. In 1865, at sixteen, he was free.

For the next six years Price drove a borrowed wagon across the plains and back — to Colorado mining camps, then home again — freighting goods in and out and making a living good enough to survive. Despite the fact that he operated in Indian country, alone, he was never harmed. Perhaps he was lucky. Or perhaps, as he himself believed, the presence of a lone black man in such an alien land was unusual enough, or mysterious enough, to keep the Arapahoe at bay. In any event, he saved the money he earned — which was never much — and in 1867 he made his way to Cheyenne. For three years he operated a laundry there — one of the few frontier enterprises realistically open to blacks — then lost all of his profits in real estate. In

1870, with nothing to his name but the horse he rode, Lewis Price went to Denver. There he hoped to reestablish his life.

The Denver that Price found was a city drawn in white. In 1870, perhaps only eighty blacks lived there, a minority so small as to be almost unrecognizable, but still large enough to be feared and disliked by the white majority around it. For that reason, black life in Denver was not happy. Blacks had no place in the city or its affairs. They had no recognition or status. They had no future. They were little more than part of the city's physical landscape — like the prairie and the cottonwoods that surrounded the town, and the plank sidewalks on Blake Street — part of Denver's furniture instead of part of its life. Denver blacks were not hated, and they were not actively persecuted. They were simply ignored, as if they did not exist, treated with a kind of institutionalized condescension that ate away their pride, destroyed their spirit, and kept them a perpetual underclass in a white land.

Racism confronted blacks at every turn. They quickly learned, for example, that they could not live where they chose; they lived where whites allowed them to live — in the seedy boardinghouses and rundown shacks of the lower downtown and along the Platte River bottoms in tarpaper shanties that sprouted like wildflowers. There they boarded — they did not own — segregated by a city that did not like them, and cynically fleeced by landlords who took advantage of them.

Blacks early understood that the way out of despair was education and jobs, but they were effectively denied both. Black children were routinely excluded from Denver schools, relegated to a traveling "colored school" that met when it could in the back rooms of black churches, administered by black teachers who knew little more than their students. "We do not propose to eat, drink, or sleep with Negroes," said William N. Byers, editor of the *Rocky Mountain News*, "and neither do we think it right that our children should receive education in Negro classes." Sadly, he spoke for a generation.

Good jobs were as scarce as a good education. In the very early life of Denver, when enough work existed for all, blacks took their share. Briefly, they were seen — and treated — as contributors, not competitors. But by 1870, when society had become more developed, whites had taken the best jobs, condemned blacks to the worst, and created an insidious job caste system that was to last for generations. In 1870, 97 percent of Denver's blacks were manual laborers — day laborers, porters, cooks, teamsters, waiters, coachmen, and servants. E.H. Hackley, editor of the black *Statesman*, vehemently argued that "the colored man is not confined to any single channel of trade. He is an all-around man and a success." But Hackley wrote a lie. A handful of his "all-around" men owned barbershops — the highest level a black man could reach in early Denver — but the rest owned nothing at all. And they were not successes. Ironically, just as black slaves had been characterized as the "mud sill" that had supported white civilization in the South, so might Colorado's black freedmen have been characterized in economic terms as the mud sill that supported Denver.

Nor did discrimination and despair end with the loss of educational and employment opportunity. Invariably, they carried over into social affairs as well. Blacks could not eat in white restaurants or sleep in white hotels. They could not join white clubs or gamble at white faro tables. Even in white saloons — the frontier's commonest denominator — they could not drink with white men, or if they did, they did so at their own risk. Instead, mired in a city where economic and educational elites translated their domination into social terms, they were allowed to socialize only with each other. So black men gambled at black faro tables, drank in black saloons, played billiards in black billiard halls, and wondered all the while what had happened to them in the land of promise.

Finally, they faced white law.

As late as 1865, blacks living in Colorado technically existed in a condition of slavery. Until then, at least, they knew exactly what their rights were and were not. During the postwar, though, their status changed: The Thirteenth, Fourteenth, and Fifteenth amendments to the Constitution freed them from slavery, gave them the right to vote, and accorded them the full rights of all citizens. Then, armed with the rights brought by change, they sought to improve their lives.

They quickly found out, however, that their rights existed on paper, not in fact, and that any black people asserting their constitutional "rights" on the Colorado frontier (as anywhere else in America) were doomed to bitter disappointment. The reality of their lives in Colorado was the fact that distant words on distant parchment were only as effective as the white majority interpreting them allowed them to be. The reality of their lives was that on the Colorado frontier, where the white majority had consistently denied blacks any semblance of civil rights, had not allowed them to vote, to serve on juries, to testify at trials, or to own property, nothing could be changed quickly by edicts from Washington. The result was that people who had once known what their rights were and were not, no longer did; they lived in a kind of legal limbo where paper said they were free, but white landlords, saloonkeepers, and politicians said they were not. Ideally, Reconstruction-era changes in civil rights law should have protected blacks from abuses in the other areas of their lives. It should have liberated them in fact as well as in theory. But it did not. At best, it was neutral toward them; at worst, operating against them instead of for them, it made their existence even more miserable than it already was.

In the end, Colorado blacks suffered indignities that white men could not have possibly imagined. They found no educational system that would adequately educate them. Fundamentally rural and lacking even basic urban job skills, they found no economic system that would equally employ them. Just up from slavery, they found no legal system that would protect them. To survive, like the Jews, they turned passively inward to themselves and to their families. But they knew from the start that the only thing that would really improve their lot would be action. So it was that they constantly looked for the appearance among them of men who would, by example, force change on the white society they lived in.

In the fall of 1870 Lewis Price arrived in Denver. Renting a small room at the Tremont House, he began work for merchant John Armour. Saving almost all the twenty-five dollars a month that he made, Price slowly amassed — for a black — a fortune. In 1873, with what he had, he acquired a small farm near Nortonville, Kansas, then bought his first Denver lot, in central downtown, for $150. From the beginning, Price was more style than substance; just as he had lost all his investments in Cheyenne, so did he lose them in Kansas and Colorado (his farm was sold ten years after purchase at a $500 loss and his Denver property failed altogether). But he never quit. With a growing circle of blacks around him watching his every move — expecting him, like them, to fail — he never quit. And, slowly, by example, the stranger from Cheyenne began to lift his people.

In 1876, still with virtually nothing to his name, and still living in the bleak back rooms of the Tremont House, Price tried again. With borrowed money, he bought a small Denver laundry. Then, living frugally, barely eating, buying only what he had to, and working the laundry with no help, he finally began to prosper. Within a year, two at the most, he was on the road to success. And as he walked it, he slowly became a symbol to those who did not.

For Price, financial success led to personal awakening. As he came to understand his growing position in the black community — the heady prominence of the black entrepreneur — he slowly began to take a more active part in its leadership. Until then — until 1880 — he had not. Until then, an itinerant Kansas bullwhacker with no successes to his name and nothing of value to offer his people, he had existed largely parallel to his own community, more interested in personal survival than racial causes. But the acquisition of money — no matter how little, no matter how slowly gained — changed him. In the late 1870s, joining with a handful of other local black leaders, Price became a force in the closest thing to a civil rights movement Denver had ever had.

The men Price joined had been in Denver for ten years before his arrival. Immersed in the city's racism for a decade, they had much to teach him. John Gunnell, Thomas Parnell, and Henry Wagoner — another son of a slave — sat the young man in their barbershops on cold winter mornings. Then, like old Indian chiefs preparing young braves for life in a world they did not know, they regaled him with stories of their Denver trials. What

Price did not learn from them he learned from others. From some he learned the power of patience. From others he learned the power of perseverence. But from all of them he learned the power of power.

Two mentors, in particular, influenced him. William Hardin, son of a free quadroon and a white father, had arrived in Denver in 1863 at the age of thirty-two and single-handedly forced the inclusion of civil rights provisions in Colorado's constitution. From him Price learned the value of confrontation. Hardin, a one-time barber and pool room manager, may have been the most hated black in the West; before he was driven from Denver for marrying a white woman, he taught Price lessons in courage that he never forgot. From Barney Ford, Colorado's "Black Baron" — the only successful black businessman in the territory — Price learned the value of business success. Success, Ford preached, was the only language white men knew, and business success was the only thing that offered black men entry into their world. Ford, like Price, was the son of a white plantation master and his slave woman mistress. Sold in his youth, a veteran of the north Georgia gold fields and Mississippi River paddlewheelers by the time he was fifteen, he built a Denver barbershop, then a restaurant, into a small fortune. By 1864 he was as wealthy as all but the richest of Denver's white elite, and by 1872 his glittering InterOcean Hotel was a western landmark. Where Hardin confronted, Ford impressed. Either way, though, they both held their own among enemies. And from them both — the fiery politico who used anger like a bludgeon, and the riverboat gambler with talk as smooth as the fine suits he wore — Price learned about life. Adopting Ford's quiet cunning and Hardin's passionate temper, Price in time became a fusion of both.

In 1880, a year of awakening for Lewis Price, he pooled all the money he had — as he had in Cheyenne — and again rolled the dice. This time the game was not real estate. This time, with $6,000 he had saved from his laundry, he founded and began publishing the *Denver Star*, the first black newspaper west of the Missouri River. Through it — much like Byers proselytized whites through the *Rocky Mountain News* — Price attempted to organize the city's blacks and give them a sense of identity they had never had.

Price was no journalist. He could barely even write his own name. But through the pens of a small handful of black writers he hired, he eloquently argued for the rights of a people who did not even know what rights were. Ironically, he had no quarrel with the past. While slavery had been wrong, he said, it had been constitutionally protected in the South, and illegally abridged; for that reason, arguing the argument that white southerners had hurled at abolitionists for a generation, Price maintained that the South should have been compensated for its losses. "If I had the chance to vote," he once said, "I would cast a vote to pay the South for the slaves." But, he added, he would also "give something to the Negro."

It was this belief that set Price apart. No other black, save Hardin, had ever argued that blacks should have material rights. But Price was insistent. "My advice to the Negro," he once said, is "get property first. Get that before education. With property and comfortable homes for the Negro, education will follow." Then would come acceptance.

To Price, acceptance — almost as much as property — was the key to the future. And to him it came not only from the acquisition of property, but from the pride of being black. He was no hypocrite; he carried himself well, and he expected other blacks to do the same. Those who did not felt his wrath. In one notable 1879 example, when Republican Governor Frederic Pitkin appointed J.D. Anderson, a black, to the position of statehouse janitor, Price led a small palace revolt of black Republicans against the action. Anderson, said the *Rocky Mountain News*, was "an ex-penitentiary convict, a disreputable and fraudulent gambler, a trickster, a cheat in politics and otherwise of the lowest and most lascivious personal character, who not only lived in open and criminal intercourse with more than one woman, but trafficked in the services of those parties." Price agreed. Lobbying for what the *News* called an "honest and honorable colored man," he asked Pitkin — through the *Star* — to nullify the appointment. He was refused; Anderson remained and the affair ended. But the case was typical of Price. Blacks, he said to the end of his life, had to get property — true — but they also had to earn their way into the white man's world with respect. And the sins of any one of them, he insisted, set them all back. He was "terribly earnest in the matter," said the *News*, and, true to form, would "consent to no compromise." For all the battles he fought — and he lost more than he won — such was the way he lived his life.

For all his good intentions, Price failed again; after a brief and listless life, the *Star* fell, and Price's fortunes — again — fell with it. Piecing his life together the best he could, in the 1880s Price once more turned to real estate. This time he succeeded.

During the 1880s, Denver caught an upward growth curve that never seemed to stop, and Price was one of those — and the only black — who rode to its crest. During that time, buying and selling like a man possessed — which in a way he was — he became the most active single real estate man in a city teeming with them. No one matched his volume, and few matched his earnings. At one point he held title to $500,000 worth of property, most of it in the heart of Denver, and almost every day, on paper at least, the physical status of the city shifted with the disposal of Price's deeds. A daring black man in a white business did not go unnoticed. Some entrepreneurs, consumed by their prejudices, did not, would not, deal with him. But most real estate men — for the most part a breed whose admiration for daring and style transcended questions of color — accepted him, worked with him, even held him in awe. Ford had taught him well. On the frontier it was a fact: Self-made men gravitated to self-made men. In business terms at least, the fact that one of them was the color of pitch mattered little.

The key to Price's success was the fact that he invested wisely and well. But he also invested with inveterate cunning. As mindful of Hardin's advice as he was of Ford's, he approached each opportunity with a cleverness that no one else could match. To be sure, Price's hunger served him well. But so did the lessons learned from other bitter men of color in smoky barbershops on cold winter mornings. When Price dealt, he did so not as a real estate man, but as a black man. Because of this, he treated every transaction virtually as an act of war.

No one, for example, could play on white fears like Price. Like other blacks of his time, he did not understand the fears themselves or the murky reasons behind them. But he clearly understood how to convert them to his own advantage, and he did so with a vengeance. As one of his contemporaries said, Price "now has the confidence of many men of wealth to the extent that he is able to swing big deals in a way his white-skinned brothers in business would not think of."

Whenever Price needed capital — or on those days when he was motivated primarily by anger — he would buy options on white residential neighborhood lots. He would then spread the word — the kind of word whispered in Denver, not spoken — that a black church would be built on the property. The scenario that always followed was always the same: White property owners, terrified by the specter of blacks in their midst, would rush to buy the options. In a matter of days, or less, Price would double or triple his investment. Then he would donate part of his earnings to the churches. "Old-timers who knew Price," wrote a newspaperman in 1920, "agreed that he had nerve, plenty of it." Or maybe it was not nerve at all. Maybe it was simply a sense of vengeance.

There were other cases, too. In the heart of downtown Denver, for example, Price erected a four-story building — the so-called Price Block — what the *Denver Post* called "a rebuke in brick and stone to white people." In Price's eyes, at least, his building (and Ford's InterOcean) was meant to be a visual daily reminder to white men that the black man's day was close at hand. In time, a building built in 1889 on forty-dollar lots found its way into the hands of Cripple Creek millionaire Winfield Scott Stratton (who paid $285,000 for it in 1899). Stratton then demolished it. But while it stood, Price made his point.

By 1890, Lewis Price was one of Denver's wealthiest men. For ten years, riding real estate upcycles and downcycles with the skill of a tightrope artist — and with what one colleague called "unflinching courage" — he had become a genuine city institution. In 1891, with $500,000 in properties still under deed, he paid taxes on $400,000 in income.

He also lived like the black king he was. Practicing what he preached — that blacks were the equal of whites — Price bought an elegant two-story mansion at the corner of Sherman Street and Eighteenth Avenue, at the edge of a virtually all-white Capitol Hill neighborhood whose only other blacks were laborers, servants, coachmen, and bootblacks. There, in a home that rivaled any around him, he did what white families around him did. He furnished his home with antiques. He played the most beautiful Steinway grand piano in the city. He sent his daughter to an eastern finishing school. He employed white servants. And on Sunday afternoons, dressed in black suit and black top hat, with a pearl-handled cane in his grasp, he rode the Hill in his coach — pulled by white horses and attended by white coachmen — for all the world to see. He never looked to his side, they said, only straight ahead. And on his face, always, was a smile framed in bitterness.

"If Denver continues to grow," said a newspaper in 1891, Price "will become even more wealthy. Now he is sanguine that his property holdings will land him in the six-figure column. He has the capacity and the industry to do it, and above all the nerve." But two years later, in 1893, all the nerve in the world did not prevent his destruction. Caught with too many encumbered properties in the great silver crash, which demolished property values with the same suddenness it devalued silver stocks, Price was ruined. More than once before, said one account of his fall, he had been "caught short and stranded." Then, before, he had come back. But this time he did not. This time he was stranded for good.

Lewis Price spent the rest of his life dabbling in whatever real estate he could and slowly descended back into the oblivion from which he had come. As late as 1902, he made a small $500 transaction, prompting the *Denver Times* to say that "all the real estate men like Mr. Price are glad to see the indefatigable zeal with which he labors amply rewarded. Once again he is in the swim." But, in fact, he was not. There were few more $500 transactions. And a decade later he was dead. On a cold January night in 1913, penniless, without family, by then a charity case living on a cot in a back hallway of the county hospital, Price called a handful of orderlies and night nurses to his side. Softly, he sang a hymn he had learned from his mother. Then, in a voice almost inaudible, he recited a verse: "Be not wise in thy own conceit." Then he closed his eyes and, as a friend said, "fell into the sleep of peace." It was time. It may have been the only peace he had ever known.

The Denver that Lewis Price died in was vastly different from the Denver he had first arrived in. In 1870, blacks there had had few rights. In 1913, they had far more.

Until the mid-1880s, for example, blacks had largely been confined to the squalor of the lower downtown. By 1885, however, they had broken out, moving in large numbers to the northeast toward what would later be called Five Points, cutting a black swath for miles through a still-white city. Their housing remained shabby and rundown, and along the Platte far too many still lived in the shells of buildings long abandoned by whites. But for people who had never had anything at all, it was a beginning.

Education improved slightly with the slow integration of black children into white school systems (although not into white school *rooms*). For all the horror of *Plessy vs. Ferguson* in 1895, institutionalizing "separate but equal," and despite the fact that in 1900, 11 percent of Denver's blacks were still illiterate (as opposed to 0.1 percent of whites and even 4 percent of the city's foreign-born), by 1913 blacks had still progressed light years from the days of the "colored school."

In 1870, only three blacks in the entire city of Denver had owned their own businesses, but fourteen did in 1876, twenty did in 1882, and in 1890 — before the silver crash and depression ruined them — the *Denver Republican* reported that 100 blacks were worth between $500 and $10,000 each, and a few more between $20,000 and $150,000. Most blacks, still hampered by lack of education and the possession of urban job skills, and still fighting off the debilitating effects of slavery, remained rooted in menial occupations — gandy dancers, roadbed workers, porters, waiters, cooks, coachmen, bricklayers, teamsters, servants, and janitors. But for the first time, too, blacks also began to own saloons, restaurants, and boardinghouses along with barbershops, and to move into such professions as law enforcement, civil service, firefighting, pharmacy, insurance, funeral directing, journalism, and even, occasionally, medicine. Again, the evolution had not been easy. Gains were slow and often tenuous, and most blacks remained mired where they always had been — at the bottom of the economic pyramid, with no realistic hope of moving up. But at least change was in the air, and for a people still just up from slavery, the smell of it was sweet.

Finally, and most significant, blacks slowly improved their status under law. Discrimination, of course, never fully disappeared, and *Plessy vs. Ferguson* only further strengthened the segregation of blacks in public and private places. But in time, the constitutional amendments were interpreted, Colorado's state constitution — thanks to Hardin — provided for black rights, and no matter how many national civil rights laws were voided or beaten (the 1873 Civil Rights Act was killed by the Supreme Court in 1875 and an 1890 voting rights act was defeated outright), it became progressively more difficult for whites to oppress. On the day Price died, blacks could not be admitted to white restaurants or hospitals. And they sat in de facto segregated classrooms and worked in segregated workplaces. But for the first time in their lives they could own property — homes — and they could vote. And from those rights, however slowly, others would come.

At the same time, too, blacks had actively begun to participate in the government that made the laws. More and more they maneuvered for power at Republican conventions and caucuses. More and more — Ford running for the legislature in 1873, Price as a Greenbacker running for Arapahoe County commissioner — they ran for political office. And in the 1890s, when Joseph Stuart became the first black ever elected to the Colorado state legislature, it was clear, politically, that a new era had begun.

By 1913, life was not good for Denver's blacks, but it was better than it had ever been before. Between 1870 and the eve of World War I, a quiet revolution had begun in their city. And Lewis Price was witness to it all.

In retrospect, though, Price was more than a witness. He was a catalyst. He did not *cause* the revolution, nor did the other black men around him. But all of them together *did* influence it. Without Price and his brothers it would have happened. But not so soon. Without Hardin, black rights would have been years longer in coming, and without Ford, economic opportunity. But the most quietly influential force of them all may have been Price, for it was he, more than any, on a daily basis and for far longer than any other of the black champions, who gave his people respectability.

When Price died, everyone, black and white alike, agreed. He had been, wrote the *Herald*, "one of the most remarkable men of his time," and the reason was that "he had been compelled from the beginning of his life to battle against the prejudices which have existed against his race." His way of fighting was to teach his people self-respect by setting an example, by earning it himself. He had an ambition, said the *Post*, "to show white people that a Negro could outwit them. He made no secret of the inspiration behind his ambition to show the white people that, given a chance, Negro blood would accomplish big things." In his quiet, gentle way, he achieved everything he had ever set out to. He showed. And he accomplished. And in the process, he became a role model for a generation.

On the day the people of Denver put Lewis Price in the ground, they might have reflected on it all. They might have considered his life and what it meant. And they might have understood, finally, that the importance of the man they called the "Black Wizard" lay not in his business successes. It lay in his fundamental belief — as Thomas Jefferson had once said — that all men were created equal.

William Lessig

William "Billy" Lessig was a luckless man. He served his country in its bloodiest war, then helped open up a vast frontier. And though he prospered briefly for it all, it was not for long. Wealth and happiness slipped through his fingers like so much gold dust, and in the end he died with nothing but the memory of what he had once been. He was typical of the men who rode through Colorado in its golden age; some thrived in it and made their fortunes, but many more simply became its casualties.

William Lessig was a Pennsylvanian who set out early in life to become a mining engineer. In 1861, though, he interrupted his career to enlist with the 96th Pennsylvania and fight a war that seemed very remote from the rolling hills around Pottsville. He served for the duration with honor. Rising to regimental commander, then general, Lessig gained a measure of permanent fame in the Union's bloody Maryland campaign. Leading untested troops against Confederate guns at South Mound, caught between rebel fire on one hand and sheer rock outcroppings on the other, Lessig watched most of his command die in a frontal assault one April day in 1862. In a final assault of his own, Lessig charged enemy emplacements with only a handful of men, finally piercing Confederate lines almost alone. Impressed by his courage, southern officers refused to take him prisoner. Allowed to return to his own troops, Lessig finished the South Mound campaign, and the war itself, with dignity. Few people ever heard of South Mound, and fewer still ever heard of William Lessig. But on an April day in the Maryland woods — for those who *did* remember — Lessig marked himself a most uncommon man.

Ulysses S. Grant, a personal friend of Lessig's, was impressed by the man. On assuming the presidency in 1869, he named Lessig surveyor general, and in the same year the young soldier moved to Colorado to, as he put it, "advance the prosperity of the state."

For eight years Lessig served Grant — and Colorado — well. But he also served himself. Even as he advanced the interests of Colorado's mining industry, he also speculated in it himself. And he reaped a fortune. From mining he drifted into Denver real estate and the ownership of several blocks in the city's emerging core. On one California Street block (where he would die three decades later), he built his first home, then sold it for $150,000. After a tour of Europe, where he went periodically in search of antiques, Lessig returned to Denver and the elegance of Capitol Hill. There, at the corner of Ninth and Logan streets, he built one of the city's first great mansions.

The Lessig home was a five-lot, eighteen-room Denver showcase, and the man himself was a major fixture in the city's glittering society. Still young and charismatic, with silky black hair, powerful physique, dashing good looks, and a personality vibrant enough to captivate all he met, Lessig was one of Colorado's most visible leaders. On winter nights carriage after carriage delivered party-goers to the big home on the Hill where the highest of high society mingled in flower-decked rooms and drank his famous maraschino-champagne punch, laced with curacao and pure spirits of cognac. Everyone loved the tall man with the military bearing — his hospitality, his pranks and stories, his gentle friendliness. For a moment, at least, Billy Lessig stood at the top of the Hill.

Then he fell.

In 1893, the silver crash leveled Lessig like it did the other high-rollers on Capitol Hill. Plunging real estate values cost him his business blocks. His banker, David Moffat, called in Lessig's loans and lost him his credit. A man with the ability to make money almost anywhere at anything suddenly lost his golden touch. A man who spent as much as he made as fast as he made it suddenly spent no more. His fortune was gone — forever.

Maybe it was economic depression, or maybe it was some inner demons unleashed by his financial reverses, but Lessig's personality disintegrated along with his business empire. Slowly he turned inward. In 1891, his first wife, Sarah Kimberly, had died insane at the happiest time of his life. To a great extent, Lessig never recovered from her loss. In 1893, he remarried, but his second wife died almost instantly, and Lessig buried her at the same time he buried his empire. In 1894, he married a third time, to Clara Bell of Chicago, the daughter of a powerful army general and sister of Lillian Bell, an important American writer. Still, though, his once-great passion for living seemed gone.

For one fleeting moment Lessig seemed to forget his pain. For one more season — through the winter of 1893 — the old Logan Street mansion lit up and governors and statesmen again stood in warm hallways sipping the exuberant punch. Lessig told his old stories, as he had before, and Mrs. Lessig, resplendent in gowns of flowered silk, served dinners on Vienna plates once used by Louis Philippe. But for Lessig, nothing good lasted long, and misfortune soon dogged his life again.

On a July night in 1897, with his economic fortunes at ebb and the memory of two dead wives still fresh in his mind, Lessig's fabulous home was torched by what a Denver newspaper called a "desperate gang of incendiaries." Burning through every room in the home, the fire consumed priceless paintings, tapestries, fine furniture, German art needlework, and souvenirs from all over the world. Only a quick-acting bucket brigade saved anything at all. One year later the home burned again, and in January 1899, Lessig and his wife narrowly escaped suffocation in a third fire. In time the once-great mansion was left little more than a charred shell. Lessig must have wondered who could have hated him so much that they would burn his home over and over again until there was nothing left of it. But he never knew who his enemies were. Neighbors often reported suspicious men lurking in the mansion's shadows, but they were never flushed out and never caught. And because they were not, Lessig lived with a fear of fire that few of his friends could comprehend.

With his fortune gone, then his home — finally sold for a song to cover mounting debts — Lessig was left with only his wife. But she, too, was soon lost. In October 1903, in Chicago, she divorced him.

Charges against Lessig were specific and sensational. The primary charge against him was cruelty. On their wedding day, said Clara Bell, he had "displayed a temper and irritability" that were to mark their married life from then on. Instead of attending to her, she said, he spent his days with race horses, alcohol, and cards. He even insisted that she was not "too old" to work and that she should help earn income for the family. Worst of all, he kept a photograph of his first wife on his bedstand and allowed her domineering sister — who bore an eerie resemblance to the dead Sarah Kimberly — to live in the mansion as part of the family. There she taunted and harassed Clara Bell. General Bell complained that Lessig treated his daughter "shamefully" and refused her the "necessities of life." But what Lessig did actually went beyond this. By unleashing a neurotic sister-in-law on the woman he supposedly loved, Lessig — in his deepening old age and own spreading neurosis — actually waged a form of marital warfare.

There was another side, of course. Lessig's defenders said that the third Mrs. Lessig simply tired of wedlock with an old man who lived in the past. Goaded by a bitter father whom Lessig increasingly relied on for money and a jealous sister who even wrote a novel about the affair, Clara Bell simply used divorce as an excuse to change the direction of her life. No one ever knew the truth. Perhaps no one ever cared to.

Divorce marked the end of Billy Lessig's life. "I have nothing to say against my wife" was all he ever said, but old friends remarked in a Denver newspaper that divorce was a "virtual death blow" to the old man. The pain of his wife's loss, they said, "will never heal, though his pride may hide the scar." In his last years, without home, fortune, or love, William Lessig lived on thirty dollars a month at the Bell Hotel on California Street. Senator John Cullom of Illinois saw that his small pension was increased a little, and with it Lessig tried to pay back his creditors before he died. In the end, though, reported the *Rocky Mountain News*, Lessig, once as rich and powerful a man as the Rockies had ever seen, was a "wreck in body," with a mysterious paralysis slowly consuming it, and his mind "a chaos of memories of happy days gone by."

In his seventies, William Lessig died in peace, at the Bell. Old friends congregated to mourn him. Figuratively, at least, they sipped his exquisite punch one more time.

And a part of Colorado's life became history.

Enos Mills

"What is Estes Park?" an affluent British traveler to the Rocky Mountains once asked. After an extensive tour of the region, which included an ascent of Longs Peak, the traveler sat down by the dim light of an oil lamp inside a crude log cabin on a crisp October evening and put to paper the following answer: "Such as it is, Estes Park is mine. It is unsurveyed, 'no man's land,' and mine by right of love, appropriation, and appreciation; by the seizure of its peerless sunrises and sunsets, its glorious afterglow, its blazing noons, its hurricanes sharp and furious, its wild auroras, its glories of mountain and forest, of canyon, lake, and river, and the stereotyping them all in my memory." Obviously inspired, the traveler went on. "Mine too," she said, "in a better than the sportsman's sense, are the majestic wapiti, which play and fight under the pines in the early morning, as securely as fallow deer under our English oaks; its graceful 'black-tails,' swift of foot; its superb bighorns, whose noble leader is to be seen now and then with his classic head against the blue sky on the top of a colossal rock. . . . May their number never be less, in spite of the hunter who kills for food and gain, and the sportsman who kills and marauds for pastime!"

The passage was written on October 2, 1873. Its author was Isabella Bird, whose travels through Colorado Territory have

Enos Mills with his dog.
Colorado Historical Society.

become immortalized in her classic work, *A Lady's Life in the Rocky Mountains*. What is perhaps most astounding about the treatise is that today the region portrayed is very much the same as Isabella Bird described it over a century ago. In fact, wildlife numbers in some instances are actually increasing. For this wonder, we may thank a gangly, curly haired, and balding naturalist by the name of Enos Abijah Mills.

Enos Mills was born on April 22, 1870, to a Fort Scott, Kansas, farm couple who had participated in the Pikes Peak Gold Rush of 1859. The young Mills grew up on the open prairie where he suffered sporadically from a series of health maladies. At that time, Colorado was renowned throughout the world as a spa for consumptives and victims of other chronic health problems. At the urging of his parents, the fourteen-year-old Enos headed for the Rocky Mountains in 1884 to partake of the camp cure. It was eleven years since Isabella Bird had made her journey to the same area.

Arriving in Fort Collins, the youthful Mills found employment as a cowboy driving longhorns to the lands of local ranchers. On one occasion he delivered a herd to the ranch of Carlyle Lamb, the son of a pioneer Estes Park clergyman who lived at the eastern base of Longs Peak. The boy was immediately struck with awe. From that day forward, Enos Mills nurtured a life-long love affair with the majestic 14,255-foot peak.

In 1885, Mills found employment near the Lamb Ranch and began constructing a homestead cabin across a stream from Lamb's property. During that time Enos Mills climbed Longs Peak for the first time. Before his death in 1922, Mills would repeat the trip 296 more times, more than any other person with the exception of the famous Longs Peak guide, Shep Husted, who worked for Mills after the turn of the century. Beginning in 1888, Mills became a professional guide, escorting summer tourists to the summit of the great mountain.

At different times of the year, Enos Mills did many things to scrape out a living. During the winter months, he would trek to Montana to work in the mines. Some winters he worked for the Colorado Department of Engineers measuring the snow pack for the purpose of estimating amounts of spring run-off. It was during his solitary months as a snow observer that Mills probably acquired a knowledge of the flora and fauna of the region. He eventually wrote sixteen books on Colorado wildlife and lectured as a naturalist.

In 1902, Mills' savings from the mining trade enabled him to purchase the Lamb property near Longs Peak and his homestead cabin. On the property he operated Lamb's old climber's hostel which he named "Longs Peak House." The structure burned to the ground after the turn of the century. Mills rebuilt the hotel in 1906 and renamed it "The Longs Peak Inn." From that time forward he gave up guiding climbers and focused his attention on writing and operating the inn.

Beginning in 1909, Enos Mills conceived the idea of preserving his beloved mountains around Longs Peak as a national park. The venture became an obsession and evolved into a personal crusade over the next six years. During that time, Mills traversed the nation during the winter months lecturing on the need for conservation and the establishment of a national preserve in the Estes Park region.

Fortunately, the life of Enos Mills and his efforts to create a national park in Colorado coincided with an awakening consciousness in America. The frontier had suddenly vanished; perhaps nature's gifts were indeed exhaustible and should be preserved. The conservation movement after the turn of the century, however, took many forms and met much resistance. With the advance of technology and the development of the automobile, family vacations to the West mushroomed. Many Easterners, enchanted with the splendors of the West, wished to set aside vast tracts of land as their own private playgrounds. Most Westerners were against any form of conservation, believing that the right to conquer, harness, and use nature's resources was the basic ingredient of the pioneer spirit. Conservation meant government regulation with the subsequent breakdown of frontier individualism, a concept that Westerners had traditionally clung to by opposing the federal regulation of land and water usage. In the middle were those individuals like Gifford Pinchot, the first chief of the Bureau of Forestry, which had been established in 1891. Pinchot believed in "selective management" of public lands resulting in regulated use of resources while carefully keeping an eye on the potential danger of overexploiting the environment.

The conservation movement based on the selective management principle attained national impetus during the administration of President Theodore Roosevelt. He set aside 132 million acres of national forest lands which eventually included the tracts of timber adjacent to Estes Park that now bear his name. On the extreme fringes of this conservation effort were men like the charistmatic John Muir of Yosemite who organized the Sierra Club and other pressure groups for the purpose of advocating total preservation of an untouched wilderness. Enos Mills adhered to this latter philosophy.

Undoubtedly, Mills was influenced by John Muir's charismatic personality. "Go to the trees and get their good tidings," Mills advised the public in a paraphrase of Muir. More formally, Enos Mills garnered interest from Denver Attorney James G.

Rogers' effort to organize a lobbying group similar to Muir's Sierra Club. Its purpose was to promote the national park crusade. In April 1912, the first meeting of the Colorado Mountain Club convened, and the creation of "Rocky Mountain National Park" became its primary goal.

Between 1909 and 1915, Enos Mills crossed the nation many times gaining support for his cause. Historian C.W. Bucholtz calculated that during these years, Mills wrote more than 2,000 letters, drafted sixty-four newspaper and magazine articles, and gave forty-two lectures to gain support for the park. His tenacity finally brought success.

On the cool autumn day of September 4, 1915, a small group of dignitaries from Colorado and Washington, D.C. assembled in Horseshoe Park, a few miles west of the town of Estes Park. Under a silk banner which read "ROCKY MOUNTAIN NATIONAL PARK — DEDICATION, SEP. 4, 1915" they heard a few short speeches. Enos Mills stood beside Estes Park citizen F.O. Stanley, the inventor of the Stanley Steamer automobile, who had given Mills early support for his crusade.

In a sense the establishment of Rocky Mountain National Park on that September day symbolically marked the end of the frontier for Coloradoans. They had formally come to recognize that the beauty of nature known to early travelers could no longer be indiscriminately exploited. They acknowledged, perhaps grudgingly, that the mountains' majesty had to be preserved under the watchful eye of government if it were to endure into the future "for the benefit and enjoyment of the people." We can thank Enos Mills, above all others, for making them aware of that necessary relationship. Enos Mills died in 1922. It is now up to present generations to perpetuate his legacy and ensure that future generations will, like Isabella Bird, be able to go to the trees to get their good tidings.

Cornelia Baxter

On Sunday afternoons at the turn of the century, when the weather grew warm and newly mown grass flowed across the broad flanks of Capitol Hill, the powerful people of Denver appeared, like ghosts from a distant winter, ready for new seasons of exhibition. In pairs and clusters, they strutted the Hill's broad streets, women resplendent in gowns from Paris, men in the finest woolen suits that England could make. And in the day's heat, under frilled parasols, in swift carriages guided by black drivers and attended by black coachmen, they rode down Broadway as far as it went, then back, then down again, not so much to see as to be seen by others. And to be admired. Like Thanksgiving and Easter, the great spring promenade was a major Denver ritual, a kind of tribal rite.

Capitol Hill was the social crest of Colorado. Beneath the roofs of its gaudy mansions, behind its spiked fences and iron gates, beyond its green lawns and young elms, the Hill teemed with the most powerful families in the state, and some of the most powerful anywhere. Mining magnates, business tycoons, railroad giants, cattle kings, political bosses — they and their wives and children all lived there, fence to fence, shoulder to shoulder, on streets that virtually smelled of influence. In many ways, the monarchs of Capitol Hill differed from one another, but they all shared at least one thing in common: The need to acquire, maintain, and flaunt wealth as long as they lived, then to continue the process through their children when they were dead. Such dynastic mentalities, of course, were the way of the world, and Denver, for all its remoteness and its vaunted independence, was far more a part of the world than it seemed to know. Like the legendary robber barons of the Rhine, like the great robber barons of the East, the kings of Denver held to this mentality with a ferocity that bordered on obsession. Beyond the Hill's neat green lawns, beneath the leafing elms, such was the nature of life.

George Baxter was a prototype. He made and flaunted a fortune. He achieved high social status with it. And when he died, he expected his children to carry on as he had, vigorously and ostentatiously. At least one — his daughter Cornelia — did. And in so doing, she created a legacy probably unequalled anywhere in the social history of Colorado.

George Baxter, the rough-hewn son of a Tennessee judge, was a young cavalry officer when he first rode West in the early 1880s. After duty at outposts in the Dakotas and Wyoming, he bought a sprawling tract of prairie land near Cheyenne, sunk $150,000 into cattle for it, and began to operate. At various times he served as territorial governor of Wyoming (until removed by the president for illegally running cattle on federal land) and played an integral role at the state's constitutional convention. As one of Wyoming's most domineering cattle barons, he was also an instigator of the bloody Johnson County War of 1892, in which the territory's cattle dynasties attempted to destroy their smaller rivals. By the mid-1890s, Baxter, forty-one years old and a millionaire, left Cheyenne and moved to Denver. There, on the Hill — on the millionaire's row called Grant Street — he built a mansion and settled down to exhibit his power. What has been characterized as one of Wyoming's last "royal houses of cattle" now became one of the first royal houses of the Hill. At 1212 Grant Street in a huge red brick colonial house with gleaming white trim, Baxter set up court.

From the beginning, the court had a queen: Cornelia, Baxter's firstborn child. From the time of her debut in the late 1890s, she was the unrivalled darling of Denver society. And for at least the next decade of her life, no one replaced her. No society page was complete without the latest story of where she had been or what she had done, and the stories often crowded local politics and world affairs off the front page. It was little wonder. She was a dazzling beauty — tall and slim with a soft, pale face and auburn hair cascading in ringlets down her neck. In a city of beautiful women — and Hill families cultivated them like spring flowers — she may have been the most beautiful of all. Educated, gracious, and graceful, she outshone her rivals. There have been more famous society figures in Colorado's history — Louise Hill, Genevieve Chandler Phipps, Molly Brown — but none of them ruled as long as Cornelia Baxter, and none ever commanded the almost hypnotic public adulation that she did. In a world of generals and statesmen, as strange as it may have seemed, she became one of the turn of the century's most compelling public figure. She captured the fancy of a generation.

Yet, from the beginning, something was missing.

What was so singular about the story of Cornelia Baxter was its sadness. For all the happiness she seemed to have, she never seemed happy at all. And the reason seemed to be that her life — as public as any of the time — was never her own. From the very beginning of her emergence as a society queen, what the commoner got from her — or used her for — was the vicarious thrill of wealth and fame. For the masses at the gate, she was romance and escape. They cared not for her, but for the emotion she gave them. The other part of her life was her family's, particularly her father's. Every family on the hill propagated itself socially through its children, sending them to eastern finishing schools and European universities, debuting its daughters and bringing sons into partnerships.

When properly cultivated, then, the children became extensions of the families' aristocracy, carrying their visibility and influence far beyond the time it normally would have ended. Cornelia Baxter's family was no different from the rest. George Baxter was a social climber. With Guggenheims behind him on Logan Street and Boettchers across the way on Grant, he could ill afford to slide. And the rise of his daughter guaranteed that he never would. In the end, love aside, Cornelia Baxter often seemed less the daughter of a father than the simple means to his end. Surrogate nobility for those who had nothing, symbol of aristocracy for those who had everything — somewhere in the equation existed Cornelia Baxter the woman. But no one, it seemed, ever found her.

In the last decade of the nineteenth century, Baxter made her first appearance in Denver society. And over the course of several years the society pages of the city's newspapers reported every move she made. From her schooling at the Sacred Heart Finishing School in Paris to the great parties in her father's mansion, everything she did was newsworthy, and everything was reported in detail that far transcended her importance. As she came of age, her torrid love affairs, in particular, became a Denver staple. Reporting weekly on the conquests of the "ruddy blonde" with the Gibson Girl look — figure "beautifully molded in rounded contours," facial expression cold as ice — the *Rocky Mountain News* followed her with the obsession of the *Police Gazette*. Of special interest to it, and to the people who read it, was Baxter's first romance — a smoldering affair with Yale-bred attorney Gerald Hughes that became one of the great, continuing social stories of the early 1900s.

Charles J. Hughes, a Missouri-born country lawyer, was one of the richest and most respected mining and corporate attorneys in the West. Across a thin hedge, beyond a delicately manicured flower garden, his Capitol Hill mansion joined George Baxter's on the south. And from across the garden, his son Gerald loved the former governor's daughter. For months, in 1901, rumors swirled through the city of the coming union between the twenty-six-year-old Hughes, scion of one of the Hill's many socially ascending families, and the woman the *New York Journal* called one of the most beautiful in the world. In all its history Denver had never seen an affair quite like it. In great anticipation it awaited the marriage of the century, a joining of dynasties unique in Colorado's young life.

In January 1901, in the midst of the affair, Cornelia Baxter journeyed to Monterey on the California coast. For three days Hughes visited her there, then returned to Denver to await an

April wedding date. But it was not to be. In January 1901, Hugh Tevis of California also went to Monterey. He, too, carried the burden of wealth. And, like Baxter, he haunted the great watering holes from Monterey to Newport to Paris, showing the family shield and wasting his life. Forty years old, Harvard-educated, a millionaire golfer, football star, and what the press called an "all around good fellow," he too represented a massive second-generation fortune — one of the greatest on the North American continent. His father, a contemporary of George Baxter, with a life story even more compelling, had worked his way from Kentucky poverty to the California gold fields in 1849, made his first money as a local entertainer whistling songs for miners panning the streams, then struck it rich himself. With James B. Haggin and George Hearst (the father of William Randolph Hearst), Lloyd Tevis had come to control South Dakota's fabled Homestake Mine, the widest, deepest, most productive gold mine on earth — a mine so inexhaustable that it funneled through the house of Tevis a fortune almost too large for its master to calculate. When the old man died, Hugh inherited his wealth.

In Monterey, Tevis met and fell in love with Cornelia Baxter. Gerald Hughes was forgotten, and one of the bitterest inter-family feuds that Denver ever saw was born.

On a soft April morning, not far from the Pacific, Cornelia Baxter married Hugh Tevis. Radiant in white silk, flanked by great banks of Easter lilies and orange blossoms, and pale roses mounted in baskets on the steel gates of the Palace Hotel garden, she must have been as dazzling as the day. After an elegant luncheon of chicken salad, ice cream, and champagne, the bride — "smilingly indifferent" to the crowds around her, said the press, and clearly annoyed by their intrusion — left over rice-strewn floors. The wedding cake, crushed in a long ride from New York, was never cut, and those who saw omens in such things saw an omen in it all.

Denver hummed with excitement. Not since the Tabors had such a spectacular union taken place, and the city vicariously shared every moment of it. It mattered little that Cornelia Baxter's knight was Hugh Tevis, not Gerald Hughes. What mattered was the simple emotional power of the event itself. Of course, part of the intrigue revolved around the swift dissolution of the Baxter-Hughes relationship and the strain it put on two ambitious families. In lesser families the breaking of love bonds meant little to either those involved or to those who observed them, but in society circles such bonds had great significance. The public followed the actions of the jilted with the same passion it did the wedding. In the end, as the city watched, Gerald Hughes, whose diamond ring Cornelia Baxter had worn, was devastated. His father was outraged. And George Baxter, attempting to avoid a social war, prepared to sell the family mansion to Gerald Hughes and move away. But the wounds were too deep to heal. They festered for years, ever adding to the public's hypnotic fascination with the troubles of its royalty. In the midst of it all, Cornelia Baxter Tevis was almost forgotten. As angry families argued around her and hordes of strangers pressed at her gate, she said simply: "I am the happiest girl alive." Then she left on her honeymoon and whatever lay beyond.

But what Cornelia Baxter did was take a long voyage into darkness.

On June 7, 1901, not eight weeks after the wedding, George Baxter received a telegram from his daughter in Yokohama: "Hugh dead. Return to San Francisco." Two days before, while arriving in Japan, Hugh Tevis had died. Those who remembered the cake said that his death had been inevitable. But his wife, who did not believe in omens, said simply that his heart had given out. Dressed in black, she returned to America and buried her husband of two months. Then, still in mourning, and filling newspaper copy from coast to coast, she settled into the Monterey mansion she was to have shared with him.

There she seemed to change. Her face still shone from the society pages of the Sunday *Post*, and to the tens of thousands of people who had followed her life from its public beginning, her beauty and vitality seemed undiminished. But rarely now did her pictures smile. In July she inherited a half million dollars from her husband, amidst rumors that she would ultimately get $10 million more. Even sharing his estate with another —

Alice Boalt Tevis, the nine-year-old daughter of Tevis and his first wife — she became one of the wealthiest women on the continent. But, still, the nature of her life had changed.

Briefly, the widow returned to Denver. Then she left, never to return again. "I am not a Denver girl," she had once said. "I am a Southern girl." And, clearly, whatever kind of life she sought did not exist in the dusty streets of the Queen City. Before she left, she took up temporary lodging in the same apartments occupied by Gerald Hughes. "The old ashes of Mrs. Tevis' affair with Mr. Hughes were turned over," said the press, but they were, after all, only ashes, and they never blazed again. Charles Hughes married soon thereafter. Hugh Tevis' mother died a year after her son, and with the final dispersal of the Lloyd Tevis fortune — $1.5 million of it going to Cornelia and her newborn son Hugh — she left Colorado forever.

The next years of her life were an empty odyssey, filled primarily with long stays in exotic places and endless flirtations with exotic men. In the summer of 1903 she was seen driving the streets of New York City with the Countess Festetics, heiress of the Haggin fortune, on her way to the Haggin estate in New Jersey, then Newport. Radiant again and wearing the season's most stylish new clothes, said the Denver press, "she has left mourning entirely" and "has won some delightful social triumphs" in the East. A month later she was in Bar Harbor, Maine, and a year later in Paris, "thrilling the city," said the *News*, crowned the "prettiest girl" at the Grand Prix by President Loubet and "renowned as one of the beauties of the world."

Wherever she went, men followed. One was James Randolph Walker, son of John Brisben Walker, the founder of *Cosmopolitan*, who courted her in New York. In Nice, vacationing on the Riviera with Astors and Vanderbilts and the Grand Duke Michael, she was linked to Ohio millionaire Sanford Beaty, a New York-Newport dandy with railroad money and ties to the powerful Crocker Bank of California. In the fall of 1903, James Francis Harry St. Clair Erskine, the Fifth Earl of Rosslyn, took time from the gaming tables at Monte Carlo to sail across the Atlantic with Cornelia in a futile attempt to win her hand. At Bar Harbor, courted both by John Edie, a rich young officer from the *USS Indiana*, and fiery young Denver society millionaire Ernest Wiltsee, her very presence nearly precipitated a duel between the two. The affair, said the ever-present Denver press, "caused a most emphatic break in the hitherto dull season in the world of scandal." It seemed that if Cornelia Baxter was good for little else, she was still good for copy.

The pattern never changed. Her love affairs, both real and contrived, filled the pages of the Denver press, and even when she finally remarried, the event was mired in controversy. In the winter of 1903, sailing to Europe for another season, she met and fell in love with a married man, Andrew Hart McKee of Pittsburgh. After a brief tryst abroad with Tevis, McKee paid his wife $300,000 for a divorce. In a wedding at the Hotel Walton in Philadelphia, Cornelia Baxter Tevis became Cornelia Baxter Tevis McKee. Read the next day's front page headlines in the *Rocky Mountain News:* "FORMER DENVER BEAUTY, WHOSE ROMANTIC CAREER HAS EMBRACED TWO CONTINENTS, WINDS UP HER CONQUESTS BY WEDDING ANDREW HART MCKEE, EASTERN MAN DIVORCED BY HIS FORMER WIFE." "Don't worry, papa," she said to her husband's father. "I'll take good care of him."

If Cornelia McKee thought the marriage would put an end to her public life, she was wrong. She remained in the limelight until the day she died. Nothing she did, nothing that ever happened to her, was hidden from view. To both the Denver press and the city's people, she was still a good story. As the years went by, the public knew that her marriage was not a happy one. It knew that in 1912 she lost custody of her son Hugh in an almost savage divorce battle. It knew, too, that Alice Boalt Tevis died at ten of Bright's disease, and that Gerald Hughes married Mabel Yates and lived the rest of his life in peace. It knew that despite the possession of millions and millions of dollars, she lost two husbands in her lifetime, and countless lovers, and the kind of happiness that money could not buy. And maybe deep down — with the almost instinctive revulsion men in the mass often have for their masters — it was glad.

So, in newsprint and typeset, Cornelia Baxter played out her life. And in the end no one really knew her, or cared. Before their wedding in 1904, Hugh McKee called her a "clever, talented, brilliant wit," and perhaps she was. A Paris newspaper called her "the Belle of the Riviera," one of the "most popular women on the European continent," and perhaps she was this, too. Everyone who ever met her spoke of her breathtaking beauty and manners to match. She was an ideal, the kind of woman men killed for and women killed over. But, in essence, for all this, she was still never much more than a face on a paper page. For all the outward glamour of her life, to the very end of it she seemed trapped somewhere in its dark inner recesses. Pursued by the public, hounded by the press, and acutely aware, at all times, of the fact that she carried the family crest, it was never the joy of her life that made headlines, or that anyone cared about. It was the romance that mattered, the power, the men, and the scandal. And surely these things she must have known.

In the end there was no public record of her passing. It was almost as if she had never existed at all. But she did, and the shallowness of her existence — and the shallowness of the system that perpetuated and exploited her — was a graphic illustration of the nature of upper-class life in turn-of-the-century Colorado.

Preston Porter

*T*here was still light in the sky late in the afternoon on the day that Louise Frost died. Not far from the culvert where she lay, where the Big Sandy Creek cuts its channel through the land, dried sunflowers waved gently in the wind, and beyond them the prairie rolled westward toward the sun. Somewhere nearby, Preston Porter sat briefly before an open fire, warming himself against the chill. He could not have known that seven days later, in the same place that Louise Frost lay dying now, he would die, too. On that afternoon, his life and hers were connected by nothing more than the prairie around them. But before the week was done they would come together — the thirteen-year-old white girl, dying in the dirt of a Lincoln County field, and the black boy, only three years older, sitting in the dusk nearby — in one of the most horrible stories that Colorado would ever tell.[1]

It was sometime late in the afternoon of November 9 when Louise Frost hitched her buggy to the post in front of Russell Gates' store in Limon. There she bought candy, spoke to friends — and in Limon everyone knew the blonde-haired rancher's

---

[1] All quotes are from the *Rocky Mountain News*.

daughter — then left for her home near Hugo. She never arrived. Hours later, following the girl's fading trail from Limon, her father and mother found her dying in the culvert. Covered with weeds, her eyes blackened, her skull broken, her body cut and torn from the repeated stabs of a large knife, she died quietly in her mother's arms. Her last words reassured her mother that she was well: "Yes, Mama, I'm home."

On the plains, the next day was a day of rage. In turn-of-the-century Colorado, what happened near Limon simply did not happen. Indians had died there, and a generation of homesteaders, but young children — raped and murdered in the broad light of day at places like Lake Siding, where sunflowers grew and the only sound was the wind — had not. At the turn of the century, country people accepted crimes of passion that marked life in the city as part of the malignancy that came with advancing civilization. They did not accept them on the prairie. Louise Frost's death shattered the illusion that they would be safe forever. First, it stunned them, then it transformed them. First they grieved, then they took revenge. Then they wrapped the long silence of the prairie around them and returned — those who could — to what they had been before.

The day after she died, Louise Frost was buried in the same grave with her two-year-old sister. Under gray skies and soft rain, her mother and father cried silently. "We have here," said the preacher, "the bodies of two little lambs who died before they really knew the world, before they realized life. The great God will unite their spirits on the day of resurrection and make them happy in the great beyond." Said the father: "I shall never rest easy until the murder of my child is avenged." Then, with his wife, he was led away.

Even then the hounds were out. A hundred riders scoured the bluff country with them. They roamed angrily through the sandhills, prowled through sheep herds and granaries, kicked in the doors of barns and storm cellars, searching for a man they knew they would know when they found him. In Lincoln County, a man could ride a whole day without seeing another, such was the vast extent of the land. There was no cover for fugitives. But still, they found nothing.

It was not on the prairie that the hunters found their prey. It was at Market and Nineteenth streets in Denver, near a payroll office where three black men had gathered to collect wages from the Kansas Pacific Railroad. Arthur, John, and Preston Porter — a father and two sons — had come to the city from near Limon where they had spent weeks on a railroad work gang. With their money they intended to buy tickets for the train ride back to their home in Kansas. But when the train left Denver late in the afternoon of November 11, they were not on it. They sat instead in the chill of a city jail cell. Their crime was that they had been near Limon the day Louise Frost died. It was also that, in a white man's world, they were black.

Interrogation of the three began in the city jail on November 12. The father, a "respectable, hard-working colored man," was never considered the murderer. Nor was Arthur. The focus rested on Preston, a "chestnut-colored" sixteen-year-old with a reform school record — for assault on a white girl, they said — and intelligence too low to calculate. He reached only five feet and a few inches in height, and he weighed only 120 pounds, but to the dozen men who stood about him in a small basement room, he was powerful enough to have killed a child. The press — sensing a sensational story when it saw one — branded him "illiterate and dull," an "incorrigible tough never out of trouble." It made it clear — "the work is undoubtedly that of a Negro" — that there was no doubt of his guilt. And as the teenager with the "bullet" head sat among his inquisitors, the vise grew tight around him.

The circumstances of the killing were clear: A young girl in a wagon had been ambushed near the Kansas Pacific track a few miles from Limon. She had been beaten and raped, then stabbed repeatedly and left for dead in a shallow draw. Bloody tracks led from the scene of the attack to a cold fire not far away, a site where railroad gangs often gathered for coffee and warmth on winter days. The question was whether or not Preston Porter had been at the site, and the answer was that he had. All three Porters had worked in and around Hugo for years, periodically returning to their home in Lawrence, then returning to Colorado for more work when times were lean. All of them were near

Limon the day of the killing. All of them were members of a railroad gang living out of a small "cooling car" on the KP tracks, working the rails by day, periodically gathering around the fire, then returning to the car at night. All of this Preston Porter admitted. But he admitted to no killing. It mattered little. No one believed him. No one listened to him. And the system began to break him.

For two days and nights, lawmen tore at his story. While the *Rocky Mountain News* cried that "mercy for the fiend who committed the murder" was "out of the question," Denver detectives and Arapahoe County sheriff's deputies worked around the clock to weave a net of circumstantial evidence around him. His shoe fit prints at the scene, they said. A bloody knife had been found among his belongings in the car, and a bloody pair of pants and a lace handkerchief from Russell Gates' store had been found nearby. The interrogators charged that Porter had not been with the work gang on the day in question, and that he could not coherently account for his whereabouts. Slowly the pieces fell into place. With Judge Lynch stalking the streets of Limon, Preston Porter was finally tried and convicted in a Denver jail cell.

Throughout the ordeal, the frightened boy steadfastly maintained his innocence. Confused and bewildered, and often near tears, he insisted that on the killing day he had briefly sat by the fire while the road gang worked nearby, then gone to the cooling car long before dusk to sleep. He was there long before Louise Frost was dragged from her wagon. The blood on his knife, he said, was from a rabbit he had skinned and roasted over the fire. He had no bloody pants — and none were found where he lived — and he had never seen the handkerchief.

Had Porter's inquisitors been more interested in justice than in vengeance, they might have considered what he said. But they did not. Nor did they address other questions that related directly to whether he would live or die. Even among men at the scene of the crime, the feeling was that Louise Frost had been lured from her wagon by someone she knew. She had walked to the culvert voluntarily; except for some flattened sunflowers, no signs of a struggle existed there. Clearly, the girl had not known — had never seen — Preston Porter. But that fact was ignored.

Beyond this, while it was proven that the blood-stained handkerchief had been bought at Gates' store, it was never proven that it belonged to Louise Frost. Was it hers — or someone else's? If it was found *near* the cooling car, but not *in* it, what was its link to Preston Porter? Did the fact that it was examined by a doctor who was a friend of the girl's father further bias the case against Porter? Finally, witnesses in the case placed Porter in the cooling car, as he said, no *later* than 6:00 p.m. the day of the murder, one and a half hours after Louise Frost's death. If she died at 4:30, and he arrived at the car no later than 6:00, it would have meant a one-and-a-half-hour run at full tilt to get there. Again, the circumstances of the case suggested a reasonable doubt in the charges against Porter. But, like the *News* said, as long as local sentiment was that "so much of the brute and so little of the human is in evidence that one hesitates to rank him as part of the human race," all the logic in the world would not have helped.

In the end, Porter's accusers broke him with fear and lies. On the twelfth, they attempted to hypnotize him. Failing that, because of his fear, one investigator "read" his palm. "Do you see that line?" he asked. "It shows criminal assault of a recent date." When Porter replied that the investigator had drawn the line with a pencil, the police turned to his physical appearance as proof of his guilt. The "bullet head," said one, and Porter's "thick, sensual lips" were "features usually associated with those guilty of similar crimes."

Finally, late in the afternoon of November 14, after the police promised that in return for the truth he would not be sent to Limon for trial, Porter confessed to the crime. Cold and indifferent, wrote the *News*, a "fiendish smile playing around his face," sitting bolt upright, "big white eyeballs rolling uneasily in his head," he said, simply, "I am guilty." As the men around him listened, he recalled that on the morning of November 9 he had planned the crime, telling his friends that he was going hunting for rabbits, then hiding in bushes along the road he knew Louise Frost would travel. Late in the afternoon, with the sun setting in the distance, he stopped the buggy as it rolled by. "I stopped the horse and ordered the girl to get out," he said. "She was frightened and clutched her pocketbook. She couldn't run, for I held her tight by the collar." He then dragged her into the culvert, raped her, and stabbed her. "She jus' yelled and hollered 'murder.' " Stumbling to the nearby fire, he burned his bloody clothing. Then he ran.

The *News* triumphantly reported that "one of the foulest crimes in the annals of the state" had finally been solved. Porter had admitted to the truth rather than "endure another night of the torture of his own conscience, which racked his soul as he lay in his dismal cell." For the Frosts, at least, the worst was over. The child's father, "fire kindled in tear-swollen eyes" as he "battled with passions that rent his soul," tried briefly to "get Porter and tear him limb from limb." But he failed, then went home. As for Porter himself, he sat in his cell on November 14, silent and bewildered by it all. Had he confessed of his own free will? Had he been hypnotized? Had he been bullied and coerced by angry lawmen? Had he been beaten? Had he lied, finally, to deliver himself from it all? No one knew the answers to those questions. And no one of conscience seemed to care.

Confession was followed by betrayal: While angry crowds roamed the streets of Limon, Denver police made plans to transport Porter there for trial. Most knew, of course, that no trial would ever take place, that Preston Porter would never see a courtroom or be tried under law. "I will try my best to defend the man to the last," said the city's sheriff, but as well as anyone else, he knew the bloody history of western sheriffs who had stood in the way of lynch mobs. While the children of his town grieved for their classmate, and their fathers talked quietly in small groups nearby, the mother of the dead girl said that if vengeance were not taken soon, she would go insane.

The sheriff knew what was in the air. So did the townspeople, and so did the press. So, too, did a sixteen-year-old boy sitting in a jail cell, looking not so much like a killer as a frightened child. The night before he was to be taken to Limon, Preston Porter said a tearful goodbye to his father and brother. Said Arthur, "My Lord, I hope they'll either shoot or hang him, for

then I can get his body and bury him. But if they burn him. . . ."
And to his mother Preston wrote, "I wish you were here reading
the Bible and praying. I want you to pray for me."

The morning of November 16 broke clear and cold in Denver.
Fifteen minutes before noon a train left Union Station. Preston
Porter, clothed in light pants and a thin, short-sleeved shirt,
was aboard, manacled and shivering in the morning air. After
a breakfast of dry bread and black coffee — and denied a lump
of sugar for his coffee by a sullen guard — he awaited whatever
came.

It was four in the afternoon when the train approached Limon.
Like it was on the day Louise Frost died, the sun was falling
gently in the western sky, and the wind whipped persistently
through the brush. For days a large, angry mob had patrolled
the tracks there, waiting for the train it knew would come sooner
or later. One man had said at the beginning of the vigil that "if
the nigger in Denver is the man, he'll never pass here, and he'll
not die in a minute." He was right. Preston Porter did not pass.
As the train halted on the Limon track, the mob stormed the
car, overpowered the sheriff and his deputies, and pulled Porter
away. The lawmen did not fight. As one of them said later, "It
would have been fruitless to try to protect him. It would have
been criminal to shed blood in defense of a Negro."

At 4:10, Porter began his death march across the sand hills.
Only 900 people lived in Lincoln County, but 300 of them —
all of them men, most of them sheep ranchers like Frost with
their own time-honored code of law — walked and rode silently
around him. With chains on his hands and chains on his legs,
he was led with a rope around his neck to the place where
Louise Frost had died. As he walked, he read his Bible, but he
said nothing. Those who watched him wondered, even then,
if he fully understood what the night would bring.

At the culvert near Lake Siding, where the Big Sandy cut its
channel through the land, they stopped. There the 300 argued
over Porter's fate. Some wanted to mutilate him. Some wanted
the rope. But in the end, Preston Porter's executioners decided
that he would die by fire.

On the very spot where Louise Porter had died, her avengers

hammered an iron stake deep into the ground. Before it they stacked boards soaked in oil. Then they chained Porter to the stake. At 6:23 in the descending darkness, as Porter dropped his Bible and looked heavenward to the night's first stars, Louise Frost's father dropped a torch on the boards. As the fire caught the boy's trouser legs, he said nothing. Then, as the *News* reported, "the lips of the helpless wretch moved, a frightful expression changed his face, and his head tugged convulsively. 'Oh, my God, let me go. Please let me go. Oh, my God. Oh, my God.'" Slowly, his body lit up the night. As screams became whispers, and men in the mob spat epithets at him and mocked his cries, Porter's body jumped one final time. Then it was engulfed by fire. He burned slowly against the night sky, then he disappeared. In seven minutes he was unconscious; in twenty minutes he ceased to exist. At 6:43, a small pile of ashes glowed its last at the base of the stake. And the crowd — dark figures in a dark land — melted back into the night from which it had come.

The next day the prairie was silent. In Hugo the morning brought furtive glances and muted whispers, but little more. Almost as if denying what they had done, sheepmen went back to their sheep and women went back to their children. The matter was forgotten. "A great load has been lifted from me and I don't care who condemns me," said Louise Frost's father. In Lincoln County no one did.

In Denver, a historically violent town itself, with more vigilantism still in its system than it probably knew, men in the street fiercely defended the Limon mob. Wool merchant Henry Halthusen said, bluntly, "nothing that could be done to the wretch could be too bad." "Lynch law," said attorney T.J. O'Donnell, "is the court of equity of the people. The community that would not act in such a case is not worthy to exist." Even those who condemned the killers challenged not the fact that they had *killed* Preston Porter, but the fact that they had *burned* him. State representative Everett Bell of Las Animas argued that "I have not heard that the burning of rapists and murderers in Ohio and Texas has hurt either one of those states." But others, claiming that the burning was less civilized than hanging, disagreed.

"I'm in favor of plain hanging," said one man. "Roasting will do for the cannibal islands, but not for this country." Added the Reverend Daniel Rader: "The burning was a disgrace and outrage to our state. I think the Negro should have been hanged." Lost in the dialogue, of course, was the question of whether Preston Porter should have been killed *at all*. But, then, it had never been a serious question in the first place.

Within days, it seemed, the matter was forgotten. In Limon, November turned into December and snow covered the ground. And Preston Porter's ashes blew away.

The questions that should have haunted the living never did. Did Preston Porter die because he was guilty? Or did he die because he was black? Or did he die because he had the simple misfortune — black or white, guilty or not — of living in a vigilante society in a vigilante state, where the social veneer was slick and civilized, but where, beneath its surface, men still framed their existence in terms of rope and fire? No one ever knew the answers to those questions, and no one seemed to care.

Only one thing was certain: The iron stake left on the prairie to commemorate the place where a young girl died had significance far beyond her death. It also commemorated a place where the law was not law, where justice was not justice, where a human being — a black, a minor, and possibly retarded — was put to death by white men who denied his constitutional rights to trial by jury, freedom from cruel and unjust punishment, and due process of law. The stake, true enough, marked the place where a young girl died. But it also marked the place where a man was executed by a mob for a crime he may not have committed. It marked the place, finally, where, for twenty obscene minutes, two centuries of American civilization failed.

The day after his son had died, Preston Porter's father was released from jail and told to go home. He spoke softly of the boy's mother, who had recently tried to take her life. "It seems harsh," he said of the execution, "for he was a good boy." Not far away, across the prairie in Lincoln County, Louise Frost's father remarked that his wife's breath still came in sobs when she remembered her child, and that when he watched her now, all he saw was the "pitiful expression in her eyes." In retrospect, the story of Preston Porter has epic significance in the history of Colorado — an incident of racial injustice almost unparalleled in the annals of the West. And yet, when all was said and done, it was not a story of Colorado, or history, or even of injustice at all. The death of Preston Porter, and Louise Frost with him, was about two pairs of parents, one black, one white, bonded in their grief, and of two children who died before they should have.

William S. Friedman

*I*n the early days, Coloradoans called them "sky pilots" — men of God who brought religion to the wilderness. In those days they preached on mountain riverbanks in the hot summer sun. They preached in saloons in the cold dark of night. Some packed the gospel in their rucksacks and walked the high country, preaching to anyone they could find from any knoll they could climb. And in a way, wherever they went, they worked small miracles. It was said in the early years of Colorado's life that God did not exist west of Dodge City. But that was before the preachers. As they moved west, to Colorado, God moved with them. And on the new frontier, religion slowly became commonplace.

The priests and preachers of early Colorado became one of its most mellowing and civilizing influences. But for all their collective benevolence, and for all the legacy they left behind, few of them were men of particularly significant *individual* influence. For many of them, the establishment of religion in Colorado was less a quest for souls than a quest for power. Because the survival of religious sects in late-nineteenth-century America depended on the continuous development of numerical strength over other sects, and because new frontiers like Colorado offered almost unlimited opportunities for conversions,

William S. Friedman.
Western History Department,
Denver Public Library.

evangelists scattered across the region like the wind and tilled the vineyards until they dropped. But what often mattered most to them was the numbers of those proselytized. What often mattered less was the proselytized themselves.

For many of the religious leaders, too, the perimeters of religious thought often stopped abruptly at the borders of their own faiths. Rarely did men of God stray far from the teachings of their own Bibles to those of others; they knew what they knew and believed what they believed, and if the beliefs of others did not correspond to theirs, they were simply dismissed. In Colorado, the result of this attitude was predictable: From old "back-East" provincialism came new regional provincialism; from old "back-East" intolerance of one religious group for another came a new regional intolerance of the same. Colorado's men of God were not evil, but they were often myopic, and the religion they established clearly reflected the fact. They gentled and they civilized like no other group, but they also sowed seeds of parochialism, and even ignorance, that lasted for a generation.

Late in the century, though, a man appeared among them who broke the mold. His focus was people, not numbers. And his theology was as ecumenical as that of his brothers was parochial. When it came to issues of human life, he saw no limits and recognized no boundaries. And he spent his life preaching that belief. William Sterne Friedman was not just the universal Jew. He was the universal man.

On a cold spring morning in 1889, William Friedman arrived in Denver and walked to Curtis Street on the city's edge. There he stopped. Before him, on one of its corners, sat the Temple Emanuel, lumpy and forlorn in the weak spring sun, a mottled maze of slats and tarpaper nailed together in earlier years by a handful of the city's pioneer Jews. If the old building could have spoken to the young man, it would have told him much about the Jews' history in Denver and of the temple's central role in it.

Jews had come to Denver in the first wave of the gold rush, and by 1889 their roots had grown deep. Small in number but large in spirit, they had made the city their home and helped nurture it through its early years. Jacob Appel and Abraham Jacobs had built clothing stores there, along with tobacco merchant Charles Schayer and Isadore Deitsch and the Soloman brothers, Fred and Hyman. Julius Mitchell built one of Denver's first groceries, only weeks before David Kline opened his. John Elsner, a doctor, had ministered to the sick. Leopold Mayer had walked the 600 miles from Leavenworth to serve three terms on the Denver city council, and Wolfe Londoner soon would be the town's mayor. The early history of the Jews in Denver was one of great accomplishment, but, as the old temple might have whispered, there had also been trouble along the way.

Among many of the gold hunters and city builders, the Jews were suspect. The first Jews were accepted because most of them were German, and their Teutonic origins overshadowed their Jewishness. They were also accepted because of their almost passionate addiction to work on a frontier that prized the work ethic above all else, and where the god of all gods was capitalism. But for all of that, Gentile frontiersmen steeped in the ancient traditions of anti-Semitism still deeply disliked the Jews' faith. This the Jews understood. So by day they labored in the workplace with Gentiles. But by night they worshipped in darkness, behind closed doors, hiding their religion from those who would have discriminated against it.

As early as 1860, Denver's Jews met informally to bury their dead in the Hebrew Cemetery far from town, and on important holidays they congregated quietly and inconspicuously in small cabins and rented rooms. But not until 1872 — thirteen years after their arrival — did they leave the darkness and begin worshipping openly. That year they founded the Congregation Emanuel and built their first temple, on Curtis Street. In 1875, its doors opened to forty members. The *Rocky Mountain News* spoke eloquently of the "hope of the Jews for furthering the cause of the monotheism of the last 3,500 years."

For fourteen years the temple had stood, and it had seen bad times as well as good. At the heart and hub of Jewish life in Denver, the old building and its rabbis had tried desperately to keep their flock together. As the years passed, though, it had not been an easy thing to do. There were more Jews in Denver in 1889 than there had been in 1859, and rising numbers alone had triggered a corresponding rise in anti-Semitism in the Gentile population. But hatred was more than a question of numbers. It was also a question of appearance. Many of the Jews flocking to Denver in the late 1880s were southern and eastern Europeans — Yiddish, not German — men and women of little education and poor work experience, with languages and cultures almost impossible for their host society to assimilate. In a city that prized ethnic homogeneity and increasingly scorned cultures that it could not easily assimilate, they were not welcomed. Worst of all, confronted by a rising tide of Gentile anger, the Jews began to turn upon themselves. The Yiddish, bewildered by it all, made great efforts to establish themselves and become productive. But the non-Yiddish, old and settled, reasonably well accepted in a society they had worked tirelessly to condition, and afraid that anti-Yiddish antagonism would engulf them too, feared and resented them. Watching the gains of a lifetime slip away, they turned on their brothers with a savagery often unmatched even by anti-Semites. Throughout it all, no temple and no rabbi seemed able to help. Once again, the Jews wandered in a wilderness — with no one to lead them out.

It was this the temple could have told the young man. And as the temple's new rabbi — newly arrived in Denver to do what others had not — he would have to have listened.

William Friedman was born in Chicago in 1868, but at twelve he was orphaned and raised in the Cincinnati Orphans' Home. Acutely aware of his Judaism and searching for a place of his own in the Jewish family, Friedman entered the city's Hebrew Union College in 1880 and began a program of study for the ministry that spanned the next nine years. To those who knew him — bright, handsome, precocious — it was almost as if he had been born to lead. With a brilliant mind and an almost dazzling command of language, Friedman impressed all who knew him. In 1889, he graduated with high honors. And in the same year, in a world he had never heard of, he was offered the leadership of Temple Emanuel. Impatient to challenge the world with what he was and what he knew, he accepted his appointment and moved west.

What he found in Denver should have daunted him. What he faced — standing before the temple in the morning wind — was a fractured and embittered congregation. The chances of failure far outweighed those of success. On one hand he faced the Yiddish — a new generation of butchers, ragpickers, and peddlers living in squalor along the Platte, hated not only by all outsiders who knew them, but often by their own brothers as well. On the other hand, Friedman faced the Bavarians and Bohemians who had carved a place for themselves in a hostile world, who had built fine homes and prosperous businesses and educated their children in Europe, and who would fight to maintain what they had. Beyond that, Friedman faced a growing Gentile population skeptical of them all. The problem was his. As the new rabbi of Congregation Emanuel, as the new titular head of the Jews, it came with the appointment. Standing on the street, at only twenty-one, the dark young man from Ohio must have wondered if he could possibly correct the problem.

In time he did. Friedman stepped into his Denver pulpit in

1889 and did not leave it for forty-nine years, and during that half-century he became the most messianic leader that Colorado Jews ever had. He bedazzled the forty-seven families he inherited on Curtis Street, then quickly drew more. Within a decade he measured his following in the thousands, and by the early twentieth century, operating from a shining new Temple Emanuel on the crest of Capitol Hill, he was one of the most famous and distinguished rabbis in the world. More than once, big-city congregations raided Congregation Emanuel, trying to pirate Friedman away. But he never left. Almost to the end of his life his first pastorate remained his only pastorate; it was there the young man grew old, and there in spirit, at least, where he finally died. "I'll never forget my first view of the mountains," he said in his later years. "I fell under enchantment that sunny morning years ago. Denver was young, alive, and wide open. I was young and impressionable, with a wide-open heart and mind and an eagerness to get to work." And work he did until he could work no more. In 1938, haunted by illness that finally destroyed him, he left the ministry and moved to California. In gratitude for what he had done and what he had meant, his people made him rabbi emeritus. Only then did he finally slip away.

Friedman's first job was to bring peace to the Jews. To be sure, he was never completely successful. As a Reform Jew — a liberal theologian — he often antagonized the Orthodox; his rejection of the Bible as a "fetish" and the idea of the Jews' return to Zion simply never rested well among large numbers of the faithful. In particular, his rejection of Zion, the Jewish national state, earned him bitter animosity among them, particularly in years of savage eastern European pogroms. And perhaps no one — not even the great scholar-orator himself — could have completely bridged the gap between the old Germans and the new Yiddish.

In the end, though, Friedman broke down most of the Jews' divisions and brought them together by appealing to their single common denominator: Pride. He walked gently in a world of anti-Semites, and he spoke softly. But when his people were wronged, he championed them with a passion that must have seared those it touched. The result was that when Friedman fought for the Jews, the Jews then fought for each other.

Sadly, there was always much to fight about. No day passed without an incident. One Yiddish ragpicker was beaten almost daily by a gang of what Friedman called "Christian hoodlums." Layers of gunny sacks worn about his body ultimately failed to save the old man from destruction; late one morning, behind a Larimer Street pawnshop, he was beaten to death. On Christmas Day, 1905, a Gentile gang killed two Denver Jews who were loading scrap iron on a railroad car; one of the killers received a prison sentence for four years, the other seven months. In 1920, when a Gentile killed a Jew and was brought to trial, the presiding judge openly rejoiced at his acquittal. On the other hand, in 1909 a young Jew was given a sentence of nine years in the state penitentiary for fencing stolen goods. The double standard was clear: Killers of Jews went free; Jewish violators of Gentile law did not.

The main public defender the Jews had was Friedman. With each abuse, each humiliation, it was he who responded. He never ran, never retreated, never held back. "There isn't a Jewish child who lives in a block of Christian Denver who isn't taunted by Christian children and made to suffer from Christian slurs," he once said. Worse, "hatred of the Jew" was "systematically fostered in Christian Sunday schools" — then carried to the streets. The tragedy of it all, said an embittered Friedman, was that the Jews were as American as their tormentors. The Jew, he said, was a man "whose soul was knit on the soil of America. There is a rhythmic melody running through the ideals of Judaism and Americanism." With the Jews' belief in liberty and America's championship of liberty under law and democracy in constitutional government, he concluded, "no wonder the Jew in America loves the modern Canaan as the Promised Land." Ironically, it was the continuous persecution of the Jews that allowed Friedman to draw them together. Each strike against them gave him the opportunity to preach their specialness. And in time, with the temple as their fulcrum, they began to come together.

From the beginning to the end of his ministry, Friedman was

an almost uniquely successful man. His success lay in the ability not only to reach his own people, but to reach beyond them to others. Like other ministers of his time, he fiercely tended his own flock. But unlike many other ministers, he also consistently reached beyond the limits of his own faith to those of others. While others approached religion in almost purely sectarian terms, using it as a method by which to establish the supremacy of one sect over another, Friedman treated it as a vehicle by which the whole human family could be unified. "Religion is the science of human life," he said in 1899. Its purpose was to give men the "uplifting impulse to lay aside the low and attain the high." The authors of its Bible, like Shakespeare and Milton, were "moral geniuses," chronicling the "poetry of early man," who simply led the way. Rarely, even when provoked, did Friedman exalt the virtues of the Jews over others. In his world men were all the same. There were no "others."

For fifty years the universal man preached universal themes. He never talked about Jews and Catholics or Jews and Baptists. He never talked about the legitimacy of one religious sect over another. Instead he talked about social problems common to all and about social solutions. He spoke of the conflict between labor and capital and the importance of family and home. But mostly he preached the responsibility of people for other people, of society for itself.

Like many turn-of-the-century Coloradoans, Friedman believed that the nation's social problems were rooted in economics: Wealth created rich, lack of wealth created poor, and the constant quest for wealth on the part of both classes created eternal conflict. Friedman often attacked the "money microbe that breeds and blinds," and the endless pursuit of the "dead silver ducat that never satisfied a human soul or eased an aching heart." "Idolatry of the dollar," he preached, "dispels our poetry, dwarfs our literature, chills our enthusiasm, and laughs at our love. Wealth has wings and no one can master all the winds." The words were brave ones in a state built on gold and silver and overrun by new-rich capitalists, but they were also typical of Friedman, who feared the avoidance of truth far more than he did the wrath of the capitalists.

Friedman concluded that the real root of all social problems was the war that raged between capital and labor. While many reformers of his time called for arbitration to liberate labor and establish economic parity, and others advocated increased federal control of big business, Friedman rejected both — arbitration because capital could not be forced to operate at a loss in America, and federal intervention because it would force capital to seek more power than it already had. In a word, Friedman rejected all artificial means to correct the most fundamental of all human problems. Instead, he advocated educating society, particularly its economic elite, on the responsibility it had to help its own underclass.

To that end, he turned his pulpit into a crusade. From it, sometimes pleading and sometimes raging, Friedman passionately exhorted his congregation and his city to do good works. The rise of wealth, he said, continued advances in science, and the incessant displacement of man by machine was "squeezing human values to the vanishing point." Conditioned to living in comfort by scientific advances that brought man "not one whit closer to understanding the human soul," society had come to give "first regard to what is big instead of what is great and good." It had forgotten how to be its own keeper, he concluded, and only when it remembered, only when it rediscovered the importance of human commitment, would it truly prosper.

To give force to his crusade, Friedman did something no rabbi had done before him: On the Jewish Sabbath he brought Protestant and Catholic leaders to speak to the Jews, and on Christian Sundays he went to them. For the first time Jews saw others and others saw them. Barriers were broken, prejudices shattered. What emerged was a sense of brotherhood — and a sense of what brotherhood owed itself — that had not existed before. Prior to Friedman, the appearance in a Temple Emanuel pulpit of a Myron Reed or Joseph Machebeuf — the guiding spirits of the Protestant and Catholic communities — would have been tantamount to its desecration. And the feeling in Gentile churches would have been the same. More important, the idea that men and women of traditionally hostile sects could band together to help the sick and the poor would not have been a common one. But not after Friedman. This was his legacy.

During his half-century in Denver, Friedman consistently backed his words with action. He joined the two-year-old Charity Organization Society of Denver in 1889 and became such a vital force in it that he was later honored as one of its founders. From 1901 to 1923, focusing on problems of crime and imprisonment, he served on the State Board of Charities and Corrections. Between 1905 and 1907 he served as vice-president for the Colorado State Conference of Charities and Corrections, then helped found Colorado's Big Brother movement. In later years he began the Saturday and Sunday Hospital Association, providing funds for people too sick to survive illnesses without hospitalization and too proud to ask for financial help.

In a sense, the capstone of Friedman's career, and the ultimate expression of his universal religiousness, was the building of the National Jewish Hospital for consumptives. When Friedman arrived in Denver in 1889, he was appalled by the high rate of consumption existing among the city's Jews. Unable to correct the housing problems that he believed bred the condition — whole families packed into small rooms in filthy boardinghouses — he was able, at least, to help provide treatment. Working with Frances Jacobs, a Denver woman as active in humanitarian causes as he was, Friedman became the driving force behind what became one of the most advanced tuberculosis treatment centers in the world. When it was built, though, it was not just for Jews. "We never asked what nationality or faith they were," he once said of its patients — "only that they were sick and unable to pay." In a way, the hospital's first building, the William S. Friedman Building, became a perpetual memorial to the man who built it. But even more so was the hospital's legend: "None who enter pay. None who pay enter."

By involving himself so deeply in charity work, Friedman catalyzed other men of the cloth to do the same. More than any other man, with the possible exception of Myron Reed, it was Friedman who dragged religion into the social arena and clearly established its purpose there. It was certainly Friedman, constantly pushing others beyond the limits of their own sects and their own interests, who kept it there. Proud of the potent force religion became, he spoke often of the "splendid spirits" he had enlisted from faiths across the spectrum, and how they had been able to lay aside sectarianism and work together "under the banner of God as brothers and sisters." No one ever denied the power of what they did. It was the "splendid spirits," again, who gave Denver's social and charitable movements whatever force they had. This, too, was Friedman's legacy.

In 1919, recognizing his work, a grateful Temple Emanuel made Friedman "rabbi for life," with a stipend of $10,000 a year, and held to him as he served nearly twenty years more. In 1938, though, in ill health and growing old, he finally left the congregation he loved. With his wife and children he moved to California. He died in San Diego in 1944, fifty-five years from the day he had stood in the wind, on Curtis Street. On May 1 his funeral was held in the temple he had built. After recitation of Tennyson's "Crossing of the Bar," he was buried in Emanuel Cemetery. His pallbearers were clergymen of all faiths.

And what, after all, had he left behind him?

For one thing, he left behind a Jewish community more united than ever before, more at peace with itself, more confident in the knowledge of what it was, and he left it so at the right time. Watching other Jews die at Dauchau and Auschwitz, Denver's Jews needed all the identity they could muster. William Friedman was no antidote to the obscenities of Adolph Hitler. But in a small and poignant way, the Jewish pride he preached saw his people through some of the darkest days of their lives.

To non-Jews, Friedman left behind a sense of religious and human ecumenicism in a city that had never had it before, among a people who had never experienced it before. He awoke and kept ablaze the spirit of humane enlightenment, and he used religion to promote it all. In 1922, the *Rocky Mountain News* wrote that "although [Friedman] holds staunchly to the tenets of his faith, he is one of the most broad-minded and liberal-hearted leaders in religious thought today. Despite the persecution and ostracism which has been given to his people through the ages, the keen-edged bitterness of which he himself has undoubtedly felt, he still holds in his heart the spirit of unbounded good will toward all men." And he never changed. On the day he died, he still insisted that good works had to be done, that men of God had to transcend their petty differences to do them, that society had to help, and that religion — as a unifier, not a divider — had to catalyze it all. "What does the Lord require of thee but to do justly, to love mercy, and to walk humbly with thy God?" he asked. In his works, Friedman, the universal Jew, the universal man, eloquently answered his own question.

Elias Ammons

On the morning of April 20, 1914, dawn broke clear and cold over Ludlow Station near Trinidad. The day's first light bathed low-rising hills to the west in soft pink and chased away the last shadows from the tents and tar paper shacks on the desert floor. Silhouetted against the sky, heavily shawled women built small fires and hung out kettles of coffee. Children cried. And leather-faced men with loaded rifles walked in tight circles around them all. Before sundown, some of them would be dead, and their camp would be gone. And the life and political reputation of Elias Ammons would be destroyed forever, buried in the ashes of a place he had never even seen.

On the twenty-eighth day of July 1860, a year before the Civil War began, and fifty-four years before Ludlow, Elias Ammons was born to Jehu and Margaret Ammons on a small farm deep in the Blue Ridge Mountains of North Carolina. For ten years his family lived in the rushing current of Civil War and Reconstruction. Then, in 1871, Jehu Richard Ammons, whose father had fought in the Revolution and whose family had been among the first white clans on the Carolina frontier, finally moved away — to the West, to Colorado — to escape the turmoil of his home state. His new homestead, on Deer Creek in Jefferson County, supported small crops, but little more. Jehu Ammons, teaching

Elias Ammons.
Western History Department,
Denver Public Library.

school and preaching in small churches, dabbled in merchandising and lumbering to earn an income. But it was never enough. Poverty stalked his family from the day it left the Blue Ridge.

Like other frontier children, Elias Ammons became a man early. At twelve he fed spindles at a Larimer Street woolen mill, then worked as a ranch hand, teamster, and harvester at any ranch that would hire him. At thirteen, he skidded railroad ties out of high-country forests to distant rights-of-way. Then, when snow blanketed the foothills, he hauled cordwood to local lime kilns. Most of the money he made went to his family. But part of it, in a classically Lincolnesque way, he put away for books.

Between 1874 and 1880, Ammons worked his way through the Denver school system. Up before dawn, he sawed lumber and fired boilers in a Denver laundry. At night he lit lamps for

the Denver Gas Company and gathered cans to sell for their
tin. In the summers he hunted antelope and deer, then sold
them for a dollar apiece to city people hungry for fresh meat.
At the age of twenty he graduated from East Denver High
School, and he did so with honors.

The nature of his early life shaped Ammons forever. His strong
will, his sense of individualism and independence, his powerful
adherence to the belief that hard work eventually yielded rewards, all came from daily collisions with the stark reality of
the Colorado frontier. True, Ammons lived in a time that honored rugged individualism and treated Social Darwinism like a
national faith. But it was still more place than time that made
Ammons what he was. More than eastern theorists, who talked
of laissez-faire without really knowing what it meant, more,
even, than many people in Colorado, who lived on a frontier
without having to struggle with it, Ammons believed — because
of the nature of his life — that he knew what it took to survive
and succeed in the West. And, right or wrong, he never changed
his belief.

By the mid-1880s, Ammons was a cattleman, running small
herds on eighty acres of grass-thin, Douglas County prairie.
Late in the decade he married and began a family. He also
entered politics. In 1892, swept up in the Populist tide that
rolled over Colorado in years of silver crisis and agrarian discontent, Ammons went to the state house of representatives from
Douglas County. Then, as a Silver Republican, he went to the
senate. In 1912, as a Democrat, he ran for the governorship and
won. In the process he appropriated a single, powerful political
issue around which revolved the rest of his political career. And
he climbed aboard a whirlwind he rode the rest of his life.

The issue was conservation.

As the westward movement accelerated in the United States
during the last quarter of the nineteenth century and American
pioneers scattered across the prairies and mountains to take up
the land, the West's great natural resources were devastated in
the process. But few noticed, and fewer cared. The dominant
philosophy of the American nation, and especially its pioneers,
was that the soil, the minerals, the timber, water, and grasslands

of the Great West were limitless and inexhaustible. And even if they were not, they were God-given treasures to be conquered and converted to the process of creating civilization in the wilderness. It was this ethic that governed life, and in the West there was no room for any other.

As time passed, though, and the damage mounted, another ethic was born. It stressed, for the first time in the long history of America, the conservation of what was left of the nation's resources — mostly in the West — instead of their mindless destruction. The fear, emanating primarily from the East, was simple and clearly expressed: If America continued to destroy its natural heritage in the future as it had in the past, one day, arguments of limitlessness to the contrary, it would be gone.

To what end? For one thing, the nation would lose the primeval forest, the deep canyon, the sunswept plain, and their raw and timeless beauty. For the first time since the nation's birth, man would have nowhere to go to rest and think and revitalize himself emotionally or spiritually for life ahead. For another, America would no longer have a laboratory in which its unique nature could be developed. Assuming, as Frederick Jackson Turner said in the 1890s, that the frontier was the crucible in which the American character was forged, the crucible would soon be gone. Finally, the first conservationists believed, simply, that if those material things that underpinned the nation's economy — timber, grass, water, minerals — were ultimately exhausted, the economy itself would finally fail. In essence, whether arguing aesthetics, character, or economics, the conservationists concluded that if the price of progress and civilization was the permanent annihilation of the public domain, it was too high a price for the nation to pay. The pioneer ethic was dead, they argued. It was time for America to recognize the fact.

Action quickly followed theorizing. In the 1890s, Congress passed the General Revision Act, allowing presidents to lock up massive tracts of timberlands on the western public domain in national "forest reserves." In succeeding years, the government moved toward similar control of federal grasslands, mineral lands, and water power sites. Within a decade, by severely restricting public access to land and resources that had been there for the taking since the beginning of the westward movement, the government completely transformed the nature of western life. In one instant the timberlands were open to the lumberman and homesteader, the high meadows and plains to the cattleman, and mineral tracts everywhere to the miner. In the next, forest reserves were created, locked up by federal fiat, blanketed by rules and regulations, and patrolled by rangers who enforced the new order with something approaching vengeance. Beyond that, the leasing of grasslands was also advocated for the first time. Coal lands were withdrawn from public entry. Water power sites were reserved. In retrospect, the action, which took place over two tumultuous decades, was among the most positive and productive in the history of the Republic. Not only did the conservationists and their political allies enhance the lives of future generations, but they also saved the West from itself. The problem, though, was that the new policy created great hardships for the people it affected. Because it did, the West fought back furiously. At the heart of it all was Colorado, and at the heart of Colorado, riding the whirlwind, was Elias Ammons.

From the minute the conservation war began, Colorado was divided over the issues. Some Coloradoans stood with the conservationists. but many more did not. For slightly over twenty years, from approximately 1891, when Congress passed the General Revision Act, to the beginning of World War I, insurgent homesteaders, cattlemen, miners, and politicians fought the federal government with every weapon they had. In the process, they found many champions. But none stood up for them as ferociously as Ammons. Right or wrong, he was the most indomitable anticonservationist of them all.

Ammons bitterly opposed conservation, and he did so because he thought it took away the rights of the states to provide for their citizens and the right of citizens to provide for themselves. His primary contention was that the federal government had overstepped its legal and ethical bounds in dealing with that part of the public domain that lay within the boundaries of Colorado. Specifically, he charged that the government had created a vast network of forest reserves, then outlawed the use of their resources by pioneers who lived on or near them. Not content with the reservation of timberlands, said Ammons, the government had then begun formulating plans for the leasing of the nontimbered public domain. The net effect of the action was the wholesale violation of both the political and economic rights of the state and its people. Not only had Colorado's political sovereignty been undermined, he said, but its economy — always fragile anyway, riding cycles of both mining and agrarian boom and bust with dizzying consistency — had been virtually ruined.

Politically, Ammons' argument was relatively simple: He opposed the concept of federal land reservation in a sovereign state as a matter of principle. When government did reserve, he said, in effect it became a landlord — and citizens became tenants. On more than one occasion Ammons charged that the federal government had gained a "very dangerous political power" that did not exemplify "the sort of government our forefathers established." "This is a question between nation and state," he said in 1907. "It is a question of whether we are to have control of our own lands or the government is going to become a landlord and place us under a system of tenantry. Do you want it? Will you turn this land over to a system as foreign to our principles as is the government of Russia?"

He was also concerned about the economic effects of mass reservations on Colorado. What mattered to him, as it did to most pioneers, was the settlement of the state and the development of its land and resources. In that light, conservation was a very real and constant danger; the withdrawal of valuable mining, farming, and grazing land from entry — for *whatever* reason, future generations or not — discouraged settlement, which depressed economic productivity, which finally depressed the human spirit and sank Colorado back into the mire of the past. As a Democratic progressive, operating within the reform matrix of the Progressive Era, Ammons was concerned that economic retreat would damage the quality of life. Fewer settled lands meant less tax money, less tax money meant fewer services, and fewer services meant less efficient government.

To a man who had worked all his life, had been on his own all his life, who had seen the hardest of times with the best, the whole thrust of federal conservation simply made no sense.

In the 1890s, when Ammons was in the legislature and the new forest reserves (five of them in Colorado) were the main conservation issue, most of his attacks were aimed at the General Land Office, which ran the reserves, and its lock-out philosophy. Until 1897, at least, he was essentially right in what he charged: The reserves *were* outlawed to public entry and their resources *were* excluded from public use. And the effect on thousands of Colorado's public lands settler was incalculable. Even after 1897, when the government first created a code of rules and regulations providing for limited use of the reserves, Ammons still attacked the system, and he was still essentially right. Rhetoric and good intentions aside, the beginning of the twentieth century still saw the reserves effectively locked up by the federal government. When Ammons argued that conservation in Colorado was largely the work of eastern politicians and "theorists" who knew little about western land and less about western people, and who had allowed their own lands to be destroyed in the process of building up states that now dominated the Union, he was not wrong. When he argued that the regulations eastern bureaucrats applied to the West were conceived in ignorance and prejudice, he was not wrong either. When he argued that the whole process was crippling Colorado in its effort to attain equal economic footing with its eastern sisters, he was righter still.

In the early years of the new century, Ammons nailed together a powerful anticonservation platform, and from his pulpit — wherever it was — he preached all over Colorado. Forest reserve regulations were "absolutely bad," he said, made by men who "never saw the west side of the Mississippi River." Because they drove people "out of the state," they were an "everlasting nuisance" that caused massive public "suffering." When the government enacted its first forest-range grazing tax in 1906, he denounced the forces behind it as men who "do not know a ranch from a pink tea party." The head of the new Forest Service, Gifford Pinchot, was a callous "prince" and his ranger corps was bent on the "destruction of people who have gone and built homes" in the outland. The "army of range riders," he said, would "choke the state" into oblivion while subservient settlers, "whose American hearts" were "subdued with fear," cowered in "terror."

When the government first explored options to lease public grasslands — because large cattlemen were monopolizing them and large and small alike were destroying their grass — Ammons led the reaction in Colorado against it. What the government intended to do was long overdue. After wresting control of the grasslands from the barons who had controlled it for years, the government hoped to lease the land back under rigid guidelines that would stop monopoly, allow small operators to gain a share of the range, and, above all, give the badly decimated grass a chance to grow. Ammons, like others, applauded the concept, but, unlike others, he also saw its pitfalls. And with characteristic form he said so.

Part of the problem, as with the forest reserves, stemmed from the question of what rights Colorado had in the matter. Leasing, said Ammons, would "put half of this state under federal jurisdiction," creating "two systems of government." Half of Colorado's people would be governed locally and the other half would be "put under the absolute rule of some bureau in Washington." In the end, the citizen would have "no power to thwart the will of federal government." Again, Ammons also feared that widespread land leasing would impede the move-. ment of settlers into the state and delay the building of homes. Further, he believed — and he was right — that if leasing were enacted, the government would lease first and foremost to big cattlemen, not small, and that small and marginal operators already on the range would ultimately be driven off. Leasing, he concluded, was a noble idea that would not work. What Colorado needed instead of federal intrusion and the pater-nalism that went with it, was, simply, freedom. Ammons be-lieved — and here was the man from Deer Creek articulating everything he had ever felt — that the future of Colorado lay in the simple ability of the settler to settle. "The main question to me," he said more than once, "is one of the settlement of the country," the ability of the individual homesteader or stockman or miner to "put his individual brand on the land and call it home."

In the fall of 1912, Ammons was elected governor of Colorado. The platform he rode to the top was composed of many planks, but the main one was anticonservation. Ammons' insurgency, said the *Rocky Mountain News* — his opposition to federal power in Colorado — had become "a watchword and sacred trust."

As governor, Ammons never broke stride. What he had opposed before, he opposed now; what he fought for before, he fought for now. He worked diligently (and unsuccessfully) to get western insurgents placed in positions of power in Washington, and in so doing he crossed swords with presidents William Howard Taft and Woodrow Wilson. And he bitterly challenged increasing attempts on the part of federal government to lease the public domain. In 1913, when Congress began a long attempt to establish the leasing of federal grazing and mineral lands, along with water power sites on westen rivers, Ammons began what was to be the end of his odyssey.

In 1914, when the government moved to withdraw from entry all public lands suspected of bearing radium ores, Ammons called it "the most vicious thing we have had to deal with yet." Protesting to Wilson, he wrote: "I would not feel that I was doing my duty to my state government if I did not at least say a word in defense of my state's right to property within its own boundaries." Protesting to the state legislature, he raged: "The people must awake and demand their rights *now*. The present policy is damnable — the way the federal Government has held back, has retarded our growth. Do you know that Colorado has only a small portion of its land in service; that the federal Government has the balance within its mailed fist and will not turn it loose so it can serve its master, Man?"

Ammons' great fear was that if the government succeeded with radium-land leasing, a precedent would be set. The leasing of everything else would follow. Citizens again would become tenants, unable to attain "the right of trial in the courts in place of the star chamber proceedings of the bureaus," unable to enjoy "the blessings of self-government." Because of it all, the state around them would never grow. "Leasing," he said, "strikes a fatal blow at the sovereignty of the state. It is an insult to the good citizens of every one of the western public land states, a direct blow to them all. I do not believe you can go too far in resisting."

So resist he did. Mobilizing other western states to fight with him, enlisting the support of friendly congressmen and governors, traveling exhaustively between Colorado and Washington to testify in hearings, Ammons became one of the two or three most tireless anticonservationists in America. A crusade begun in 1891 was still going full tilt in 1913.

Then, on a cold spring morning in 1914, in the middle of his crusade, it ended. On the twentieth day of April, 900 coal miners and their families — on strike at the Colorado Fuel and Iron Company — were fired on by Colorado state militia sent to Ludlow to maintain order. Five miners died in the dawn ambush, and as fire raged through their camp, it killed another thirteen women and children. The nation reacted in horror. Wilson sent in troops. And Ammons, who had dispatched the militia, became one of the most reviled men in America.

By any standard, national or local, the Ludlow Massacre was one of the great tragedies of the century. Innocent people died. A state's reputation was blackened. And a governor — whose mistake of carelessness was mistaken for viciousness — was ruined. Completing his term in disgrace, abandoned by his own party, unforgiven by his people, he returned to oblivion in 1915 and was largely forgotten — except in anger.

In one respect, Ammons deserved what he got: Ludlow was a nightmare, and it might not have happened if he had been as concerned about the real dangers existing in the southern Colorado coal fields as about the perceived dangers of a leasing bill in Washington, had he paid more attention to the actual maneuverings of his own militia than to the imagined encroachment of a federal government on the rights of his state. But on the other hand, given the very nature of the Ludlow event, no one could ever say, Ammons or not, that it would not have happened anyway. Sadly for him, no one will ever know.

What cannot be forgotten, though, is the contributions that

Ammons made to Colorado before his downfall. In the strictest sense, his anticonservation war achieved nothing; forest reserves, grazing fees, rules and regulations, rangers, and the principles of leasing were as firmly entrenched in Colorado after Ammons as before. And if they had not been, Colorado would have been the worse for it.

But in a broader sense, what Ammons did was vital. Because of his own past and what he had learned from it, he articulated the fears of small pioneers in a changing time better than any other politician of his day. At the same time, no one fought harder for Colorado and the maintenance of its sovereignty in the Union. In the long run, again, Ammons was wrong in his actions; the conservation movement saved Colorado's natural environment from almost certain destruction. But in the *short* run, as a spokesman for *his* generation as opposed to the future, Ammons was an undeniably important force. The conservationists were right: Colorado needed saving. But Ammons was right, too: It also needed development. Above all, it needed to be free from the growing restraints, however well-meaning, however benevolently exercised, of federal power.

On a warm June day in 1913, addressing a roomful of delegates to the first Western Governors Conference in Salt Lake City, he launched a final, thunderous defense of his position. "Outrage?" he cried. "Yes! Who is better able to decide our fate than ourselves? We are just as brainy, just as competent as our forefathers, who said to King George, 'We are well able to govern ourselves.' That spirit helped us to gain our American independence. It is the same spirit that is causing us to demand that we be given back what is our own." It was the last great public speech he ever made. The next spring his career ended.

Who was Elias Ammons? Maybe he was a demagogue. Maybe he was a patriot. Or maybe he was simply a poor-born country boy who believed that men and states could stand on their own and through their own perseverance survive. In any event, with regard to the land, the state, and the future, Ammons forced Coloradoans to come to grips with their own values. Riding the whirlwind, the conservation conflict, it is as a catalyst, ultimately, that he will be remembered.

John Galen Locke

*I*n the autumn of 1918, when the great guns fell silent on the Western Front, the aftershock of World War I washed over America like a high tide. Peace brought intense relief to the nation and new hope for the future, but it also ushered in a decade of rage unparalleled in its history. America had seen dark times before, and it has since. But it had never seen anything like the national sickness of the early 1920s that gave rebirth to the Ku Klux Klan.

At the root of the great malaise was the nation's bitter disillusion with the war. Like the innocents they were, the children of America had marched into a conflict of such depth and fury that when it was over, they simply had not the emotional strength to cope with what had happened to them. Their goal had been to save mankind, and for this they died in numbers almost too large for them to comprehend. And when the war was over, they had saved nothing. They had destroyed Germany, only to watch Bolshevik Russia rise from the ashes; they had destroyed one kind of world totalitarianism only to create another. In 1918, pondering the graves of their dead, they resolved that it would not happen again. As 1918 became 1919, they promised that they would not again become involved in foreign conflict with foreign peoples. Nor would they any longer

John Galen Locke.
*Western History Department,
Denver Public Library.*

accept foreigners on their own soil. Embittered by the war, haunted by the rising specter of communist Russia, and disgusted by years of political liberalism and reform that they believed had brought them to it all, they hoisted the flag, asserted the glory of America, and lashed out at anything "foreign" among them. They called it patriotism. But what it was, in fact, was repression, intolerance, and bigotry unprecedented in the nation's life.

One manifestation of the new Americanism was the Ku Klux Klan, born in America in the 1870s and resurrected in Atlanta in 1915. With its emphasis on Christianity, morality, patriotism, constitutionalism, and the supremacy of the white race, it swept the nation like wildfire. By 1919, with its membership in the hundreds of thousands and rising, it attacked racial and religious minorities with abandon, condemned foreignism, exalted "100 percent Americanism," and turned national principles into a mockery. In an age of hate, it was the Klan that elevated hatred to an art form.

Colorado was fertile ground for it all. Patriotism, nativism, religious and racial animosity, and both social and political conservatism formed the bedrock upon which the state had been built. They constituted the most ancient values and traditions that it had. Because of them, blacks, Hispanics, and Eastern Europeans had suffered discrimination there for decades. At places like Sand Creek and Hop Alley, native Americans and Asians had even died. Religious bigotry had flowered the same way in the same soil. Catholics and Jews had known the hatred of the state's Protestant-Gentile majority from the days of the gold rush, and none of the progressive changes of the new century had changed circumstances. Sadly, like other rural states with rural values, Colorado was ripe for the picking. There the war created nothing new. It exacerbated something old. What it did in Colorado was unleash a kind of social virus that had lived near the surface of the state's life for generations. And for it, in the short run, at least, there was no cure.

In 1920, the Klan came to Colorado. Like fresh seed on warm ground, it grew with almost terrifying swiftness. Within two years, 50,000 Coloradoans had joined the hooded order, with countless sympathizers hiding near them in its shadows. They made Colorado the most powerful Klan enclave in the American West, and one of the most powerful in America. And all of them marched to a single drummer — the Klan's Grand Dragon, John Galen Locke.

From the beginning, there was no doubt what the Klan was. But no one knew what Locke was. In 1920, the John Galen Locke that Denver knew was a doctor, not a tyrant, a man whose life path had been marked not by the disappointments and aberrations that molded other fascist leaders of the time, but by the comforts and security that went with being the prosperous upper-middle-class family and professional man that he was. It was not difficult to understand how the 1920s created Mussolinis and Hitlers, for Europe was a crucible of chaos and discontent that bred dictators as a matter of course. But by comparison, the world that Locke lived in was still one of relative order and stability, and what was more, it always had been. In a word, no one, then or later, fully understood what brought Locke to the time and place that he finally occupied, or why he did what he did. No one understood what motivated him, or even what he believed. In retrospect, maybe Locke did not even understand it himself. Perhaps he was simply a country doctor gone astray. Or maybe he was more. In any event, as he stepped into the public arena, he became the most important Coloradoan of his time.

John Galen Locke was born in Port Henry, New York, in 1873, the son of a respected physician. His smalltown boyhood was safe and secure, and his college years as well. In 1893, at the age of twenty, he moved to Colorado with his young wife. Like his father, he took up medicine, studying at the Denver College of Physicians and Surgeons, interning at Bellevue Hospital Medical College in New York, studying briefly in London, Berlin, and Vienna with some of the most famous doctors of the time, then returning to Denver to practice with his father. During his early years in the city, he made a comfortable home for himself, contributed to leading medical journals around the nation, and gained an apparently solid reputation among colleagues everywhere as an intelligent physician and an honorable man. By 1920, absolutely nothing in either his past or his present could have possibly suggested the events of the next five years — the descent of a decent and respected doctor into the darkness of the Ku Klux Klan.

Nonetheless, in the summer of that year, recruited by national Klan officials to head their Colorado Klavern, Locke became the first, last, and only leader the order ever had there. Operating at 1345 Glenarm Street in a small brick building built by his father and still used by both men for their joint practice, Locke, wrote the *Rocky Mountain News*, "soared to an eminence never before reached by any one person in Colorado politics." In a basement hall, where only the select were allowed, in a large, plush chair on a raised platform, Locke sat, with two snarling Great Danes by his side, in judgment of those who came before him. To his enemies he was comical — a short, squat, pale-skinned man with a Van Dyke mustache, fingers circled with rings, and a roll of flesh around his waist that never got smaller. But to his followers he was a messiah. In any case, whoever he was, whatever his motivations were, from his basement empire Locke proceeded to make the Klan a Colorado institution.

His first task was to recruit and organize. His first target was Denver, overwhelmingly white, Protestant, and native-born, with a long tradition of social conservatism and intolerance in its history. A city teeming with lower- and middle-class whites fearful of "foreign" peoples and institutions in their midst was easy prey. By 1925, one of every seven people there had pledged allegiance to the Klan. Locke skillfully mobilized the countryside as well. From Longmont to Steamboat Springs to the Arkansas Valley, rural farmers quickly fell in line with their urban brothers. The army was a motley one — blue-collar clerks, mechanics, and small farmers, with a small scattering of professionals behind them. But bound together by a common ideology, the Klan was enormously effective.

With his hooded order in place, Locke swiftly marched it into action. His plan was to alter what he considered to be the social balance of power in the state, subordinating its enemies and restoring supremacy to embattled white Protestants. He hoped, then, to gain economic and political control for the same class. In an earlier time Locke — like Benito Mussolini — would have been dismissed as a buffoon. But 1920 was not an earlier time. It was a time when fascism was struggling to life all over the world, when extreme political doctrines once dismissed as harmless and foolish — and their advocates with them — simply no longer could be. A world away from Denver, Adolph Hitler was already stalking the streets of Germany, and Mussolini the country roads of Italy. In terms of class control — an elite controlling the rest — their messages, with modification, were little different from Locke's, or his from theirs. And, for all of them, the year, the time, was right.

Overnight, it seemed, the Klan appeared everywhere. In Denver thousands attended weekly Klan initiations at Cotton Mills Stadium and huge Klan picnics at Lakeside Park. Within perhaps a year, 25,000 people had taken the oath to "maintain white supremacy and the principles of pure Americanism." While klansmen marched in parades, huddled in konklaves, and burned towering crosses on Table Mountain at Golden, their women mobilized a Klan auxiliary and their children — like Hitler's — marched in a Junior Klan. In Steamboat Springs the Klan held weekly parades, marching in long, hooded lines down the town's main street. In Longmont the Klan placed an eight-foot cross in red electric lights on the town Christmas tree, and at nearby Lyons, it held the state's first Klan funeral. In Boulder, klansmen met openly and walked the streets openly, rarely even wearing their hoods, and at Indian Hills, west of Denver, they published thousands of leaflets promoting principles of "positive Christianity," "America first," and "the white race, the irreplaceable hub of the nation, of our Christian faith, and the high levels of western culture." In essence, the Klan was everywhere. In Colorado, the "Invisible Empire" was the most visible entity of all.

Behind it all sat Locke. From his basement room he orchestrated every word the Klan spoke, every move it made. It was also Locke who first pushed the Klan into terrorism. Organization came first; terrorism came next.

Nowhere in Colorado were racial, ethnic, or religious minorities free from Klan harassment. Wherever blacks lived, for example, they felt the heat of the Klan. Asserting that "the only way [black and white] races could develop their full potential" was through "racial separation," the order worked against the "high black crime rate, racial intermarriage, and the destruction of our schools" through integration. In Denver, where most of Colorado's blacks lived, the Klan attacked the National Association for the Advancement of Colored People, bullied school officials into segregating social activities, and hounded black men who courted white women (running more than one out of town with the warning that if they returned they would be killed). Jews also felt the Klan's wrath. Locke's knights used the boycott as a form of siege, ruining merchant after merchant; when and where the boycott failed, businesses were looted and burned, and their owners beaten. More insidiously, the Klan routinely disrupted the Jews' preparation for their Sabbaths, driving through their neighborhoods in noisy car caravans and burning crosses on synagogue lawns.

Catholics, the most hated of all minorities, bore the fullest brunt of the Klan's war on foreignism. In the malignant spirit of the American Protective Association, which had prospered in Colorado in the late nineteenth century, the Klan waged total war on those — mostly immigrants — they considered likely to pledge their allegiance not to the American flag but to a foreign Pope. Boycotts of Catholic businesses paralleled those of the Jews'. Catholic masses were constantly disrupted, and in Pueblo a priest performing mass was dragged from the altar of his church by unhooded klansmen, in full view of his parish, and savagely beaten. Catholics were systematically dismissed from private-sector jobs and political positions. Above all, the Klan attempted to muzzle any expression of pro-Catholicism appearing in the press. In Denver, repeated attempts were made on the life of the influential editor of the *Denver Catholic Register.* And in Longmont the Klan imported Bishop Alma White, founder of the Pillar of Fire, for a series of searing public attacks on the church. When the local newspaper objected, it was accused of being "led around the nose" by local Catholics, then it was boycotted.

In the grand scheme of things, the Klan's incursions into economic and social terrorism were but a prelude to Locke's main and final action: The acquisition of political power. It took little time to sow seeds of fear in Colorado. Then overnight, almost, its society became so preoccupied with its own paranoia that it utterly failed to understand — or even see — what happened next. But what happened next was nothing less than the most frightening political coup in the state's history. Locke simply took over Colorado's state government. No one stopped him because no one could.

Locke had no office of his own, but he needed none. Towering above the state's political stage, in the shadows where he could not be seen, he played puppetmaster to a broad and mindless array of political puppets that did his bidding without thought and without question. No community escaped them. Klansmen took over small towns, large towns, and all sizes of towns in between. They held mayorships, town councilships, and county commissionerships. They were the fireman on the corner, the policeman on the beat, the school superintendent, district attorney, city recorder, and local judge. They were everywhere, and they were everyone.

Just as European fascists organized small cells, then grew outward from their core, so did Locke's Klan. He organized the countryside politically, then moved to consolidate power both on the state level and in the vital city of Denver. In 1923, the Klan supported — and elected — Benjamin Stapleton as mayor of Denver, then worked through Stapleton to control the city's entire political infrastructure. Stapleton, who was not a klansman, but who had willingly accepted Klan support in the election, immediately filled city offices with such Locke henchmen as Rice Means (director of public safety), Clarence Morley (city attorney), William Candlish (chief of police), and others. In 1924, Stapleton, seeking to strike out on his own, repudiated the Klan. Only when faced with a recall did he recant; then, with seven of every ten voters casting ballots for him — most of them klansmen or Klan sympathizers — he beat the recall back. Marshalling a stunning show of power by his low-status blue-collar army, Locke darkly warned Stapleton that if he ever strayed again, "may God help you." Not until after 1925, with the Klan in decline, did Stapleton — one of the most powerful mayors in Denver's history — dare to try.

On the state level, Locke took dead aim at both the governorship and the legislature. The governorship fell quickly; in 1924, mobilizing the pliable, and friendly, Republican party, Locke sent Morley to the statehouse. There the former city attorney, who regarded Locke as his "master," embarked on one of the most shameful periods in the history of the office. For a full term he did everything Locke demanded of him — appointing the Grand Dragon to the boards and commissions he sought and putting klansmen in every state office that he could. By the time Morley had finished his work, the state auditor, secretary of state, attorney general, several state judges, several University of Colorado regents, and a supreme court justice — all of them klansmen — had been appointed by him. And beyond them there were more klansmen in the bureaucracy of state government than anyone could count. For all this it was Morley who got credit, or discredit. But it was Locke who masterminded it all. Morley was the governor. But Locke was the state.

Locke also set his sights on the legislature. Again working through the Republican Party, he infiltrated the body with some of the darkest personalities it ever saw. Their mission was purification, and from the outlawing of wine at the Catholic mass to the abrogation of the rights of aliens to live in the state to the establishment of "Americanism" tests for state employees, they pursued it — Locke by their side — with almost frightening zeal. The Klan controlled most of the house, part of the senate, and virtually all the proceedings.

For two years, perhaps, it all meshed. Colorado lived under Klan rule as total as anywhere in the union. Colorado became the Klan's greatest western triumph — a model, unrivaled almost anywhere else in America, of what the hooded order meant and what it could do. Then, suddenly, it all ended. The empire fell. The house that Locke built disintegrated. And when it did, it did so with the same kind of instantaneous fury with which it had been born.

In 1925 the federal government accused Locke of income tax evasion ($30,000 from 1923 and 1924) and the misapplication of Klan funds (he collected $7.50 of each $10 Klan initiation fee and $4.10 of the $6 yearly dues; the accusation against him was that he had illegally kept all the funds for himself). Although he survived the tax evasion charges, he was jailed for contempt of court long enough to allow his enemies to strike against him; for a single, fleeting moment he was vulnerable — and in that moment men and women and institutions intimidated and silent for four years swiftly massd and attacked. While Clarence Morley sat in Locke's cell, receiving instructions from him on how to run the state, the long-silent Denver press raked the Klan for what it had done, a handful of courageous men in the state legislature singlehandedly scuttled Locke's bills, and the national Klan — terrified that the Colorado scandal would unmask the national organization for what *it* was — severed all its ties with Locke's klavern. Overnight, he was left with nothing. Rather than quit, or fail, he desperately attempted to create a new group — the Minute Men of America — and to appropriate old Klan property for its use. But the Minute Men did not materialize. In the end, the Klan itself was reduced to fratricide. An era was over. The Klan was dead.

In the awful backwash of it all, most public attention focused not so much on the Klan as it did on the man who had led it. People understood the Klan itself, for it mirrored their own dark sides. But few understood the man who had led it. As the empire crumbled people finally asked the questions they never had before. Was Locke a bigot himself? Did he actually espouse the principles he had taught? Or was he simply a demagogue who had sought to manipulate the hooded order to his own selfish ends? There was no doubt that most of America's Klan leaders were part of the cloth they wore: They espoused, practiced, and enshrined hatred. But was Locke one of them? Or was he just a pretender?

One thing was certain: What truly marked Locke's life in the Klan was an almost incredible dispassion for its doctrines. Occasionally, he spoke as he was expected to — about "the evil hand of the Roman hierarchy" or about the Klan itself as "the most wonderful movement the world has ever seen." But in retrospect, for all their effectiveness, his words often seemed perfunctory and hollow. There were times when Locke explicitly (though secretly) repudiated plans formulated by his own followers for the persecution of Catholics, Jews, and blacks. Several of his closest personal friends came from those groups, and it was Locke who shielded them from harm. It was written that even at the Klan's peak, although publically ostentatious in spending his substantial personal wealth, Locke was privately charitable and gave to civic causes with great generosity. As a Denver priest recalled, "Dr. Locke did not share the racial and religious prejudice upon which the Ku Klux Klan was founded." Deep in the shadows of his own life, they seemed to say, the man was not — never had been — what he seemed to be.

If this were true, then, if the private Locke was a shy and reserved public benefactor, why was the public Locke a demon?

The answer was that Locke was a genuine enigma. Like a chameleon, he wore different colors for different times. Nonetheless, the truth of his life seemed to be that he believed only superficially in the cause that he led. To this day there is no evidence to suggest that he believed his own rhetoric, or that as a common klansman, he even would have marched to his own orders. The truth of John Galen Locke's life is that he wanted power, not purity, and that the Ku Klux Klan afforded him the opportunity to get it. To him, power, not America, was the ultimate elixir. And commanding the Klan, he breathed of it deeply.

On the first day of April 1935, Locke sat in a small waiting room in the Brown Palace Hotel, preparing to meet with mayoral candidate Charles M. Armstrong and impress his political views on him. For ten years, since his fall in 1925, Locke had fought to return to power; in 1935, growing old, and in poor health, he still lusted for it with a kind of manic energy that most common men could not have understood. In the mid-afternoon, alone in the room, Locke fell from his chair and died. He was found, face down, arms outstretched as if he had attempted to break the force of his fall, with a large roll of currency in his hand. Quietly he was taken away. Not a word was said.

Three days later Locke was buried in the family vault at Fairmount Cemetery. The simple Scottish Rite ceremony that attended his burial was almost starkly devoid of the pomp that had surrounded him in life. Strangely missing from his funeral were the public officials he had elevated to prominence, but hundreds of others cried openly as they passed his casket. Behind him police lines broke briefly against the pressure of the crowd, then formed again. And the smell of roses, sharp and sweet in the April sun, permeated the air.

The next night a small band of hooded men burned a cross at his crypt.

As Locke passed into history, Denver newspapers solemnly analyzed his life. It was power that had motivated him, they said, not hatred. Though he ruled an empire based on fanaticism, he had not been a fanatic himself; though the legions he had led had predicated their existence on hatred, neither had he hated. The Ku Klux Klan in Colorado, wrote the *Rocky Mountain News*, "brought on strife and bigotry that turned brother

against brother and made lifelong friends into bitter enemies
. . . the fiery cross that flamed across Colorado skies established
a dominion founded on prejudice." And yet, it concluded, all
the world would remember of Locke — because he did not
believe in what he led — was "a devoted friend, a man who
gave his services to those in distress."

So it was that John Galen Locke was forgiven for his sins.
But if his contemporaries forgot what he had done, history
should not. It should be recorded, always, that in the early
1920s, the Ku Klux Klan ruled Colorado with unprecedented
repression and brutality. It should be recorded that the movement collapsed only when exposed from within for what it was
— an empire of sheeted fools who turned the flag, the Constitution, the Bible, and all the principles of American civilization
into symbols of tyranny. It should be recorded that in Colorado
John Galen Locke was the heart, the brain, the muscle, and the
guts of it all. A man who one critic said had the "plump, innocent look of a Southern colonel" was in fact one of the most
malevolent American personalities of his time. And the worst
of it all, perhaps, was the fact that behind it all he had no
principles.

This, finally, was the heart of the matter. On more occasions
than it should have, history has forgiven bigots — because
bigotry, however tragic and horrible, at least involves *beliefs*.
Demagoguery does not, and John Galen Locke was a demagogue. Had he had a cause, the whole essence of his life
would have been different. But he did not, and it was not. To
the day he died, on a thin flowered carpet at the Brown Palace
Hotel, Locke was little more than a rebel without a cause, an
ideological mercenary, and it was precisely this fact that gave
his life the meaning that it had.

Lyulph Ogilvy

*O*n a cold spring night in 1895 , Lyulph Ogilvy spent the evening drinking scotch with William Cody at the Albany Hotel in Denver. Then, hell-bent for destruction, he drove a commandeered steamroller at top speed to his farm near Greeley. Under a soft April moon, he smashed mailboxes to splinters, scattered cattle like toys, sheared wooden railings off bridges, and tore the highway to ribbons. The next day it was as if a quick-striking tornado had danced along the lonely prairie road, touching down north of Denver first, then skipping away into the wheat fields south of Greeley. With the road closed for three weeks for repair, Ogilvy sourly observed that the bridges and roadbed were in need of repair anyway. There were other nights, of course, when he warmed himself at the Albany and talked of old times with Cody, the great scout. But on those nights, fortunately, history has not recorded how he found his way home.

The flat, quiet country of Weld County is not the stuff from which legends are made. Immersed in ancient pastoral traditions as colorless as the land itself, and peopled by men and women who shunned romance and glamor with the same intensity they shunned cattle kings and traveling carnivals, the land and the culture it supported have always seemed metaphysically frozen

Lyulph Ogilvy.
Western History Department,
Denver Public Library.

in time. It was not the kind of place that should have produced or sustained a Lyulph Ogilvy. But it did. Though the tall Scot with the deep brogue and lightning wit belonged to all of Colorado, he was first and foremost a man of the country. To the day he died, his roots grew deepest in the rich black soil of Weld County.

Lyulph Gilchrist Stanley Ogilvy first saw Colorado in 1879 when he rode across its northeastern prairie with his father in search of a cattle ranch to buy. As a young man, the London-born son of one Earl of Airlie and nephew of another, Ogilvy was typical of the Scots and Britons who scattered across the Colorado range in the late nineteenth century. Aristocratic and brilliantly educated, like others he was dominated by the powerful, dual instinct of adventure and profit. The cattle country of northeastern Colorado offered opportunities for both. As unruly and unbroken as the boroughs of London and Edinburgh were staid and tame, it offered adventure in spades — the chance for a young man to grow up wild with the country, to test the limits of his heart and soul in ways and places simply not possible or available in Europe. But it also held forth the simple lure of profit. Impressed by what he found, Ogilvy's father bought the SLW Ranch, then turned it over to his son to manage. Lyulph Ogilvy's adventure had begun.

The ranch did not prosper, however. By 1887, the great glory years of the Colorado cattle industry were gone. Stock prices had begun a slow, steady slide, and by the early 1890s they had skidded all the way to the bottom. The young Scot, caught in a cattle crash that rocked the West, did his best to save the faltering enterprise. Up at dawn, to bed after sunset, he rode his herds daily with the cowboys he hired. As skilled a horseman as the region had seen, and as knowledgeable about his cattle as anyone in the state, he briefly gave the old ranch new life. But not for long. In time it died. With far less money in his pocket in the mid-1890s than he had had riding the prairie with his father a half dozen years earlier, Ogilvy finally sold the SLW and moved to nearby Greeley.

He was not there for long; in the time it took to plant a field of wheat and breed a small barnful of calves, Ogilvy was gone. In 1898, responding to the outbreak of war in Cuba, he enlisted with a small Greeley cavalry detachment to fight the Spanish. Ultimately, he was attached as a corporal to Torrey's Rough Riders. There was more than a little of the warrior in the fiery Scot. As he recounted it later in his life, Ogilvys had fought the British for generations, and when they were at peace with them, they fought other Scots. But it all came to nothing in 1898. Most of Torrey's units never got beyond the American debarkation point at Tampa, Florida. Instead of fighting Spaniards, Ogilvy spent a half year of his life fighting yellow fever and the hot, lazy somnolence of central Florida.

Almost fatefully, before Ogilvy could pack away his sword and the memories of a war in which he had not fought, England went to war with the Boers in South Africa. Scot or not, he cast his lot with Britain. In 1899, with the Greeley ranch sold, Ogilvy left for the Dark Continent as an escort for mule shipments bound for British troops. Later he rode with Braban's Horse, one of the best of the Queen's cavalry units, living under sustained fire for two years. Wounded in battle and awarded the Distinguished Service Order for valor, Ogilvy rose in the field to the rank of captain. When he was finally mustered out because of wounds, he left behind memories of a soldier of significant gallantry. For a man looking for tests all his life, war brought out the best.

In 1902, at the age of forty-one, Ogilvy returned to Greeley, bought another farm, and tried yet again to settle down. He married Edith Boothroyd, a farm girl, had two children by her, and finally gave up the scotch that had warmed his soul on dreary days. But happiness continued to elude him. His wife's poor health cost him his farm — sold to pay her medical bills — and in 1908 she died despite it all. Lost and alone, Ogilvy moved to Denver while his children lived with their mother's parents. At forty-seven, he had nothing left but memories of combat on the African plain — and the scotch to which he returned with a vengeance.

One night in 1909, Harry Tammen, part owner of the *Denver Post*, stood in the dim light of a Union Station lamp and watched his circus animals board an outbound train. Nearby, a forty-eight-year-old, $1.50-a-night watchman — Lyulph Ogilvy — supervised the operation. Even in the half-light, Tammen recognized him. For almost as many years as Ogilvy had haunted the Albany with Bill Cody, he had also stood at the long brass rail of the Windsor Hotel saloon, where Tammen had tended bar. There they had briefly become friends. In the chill darkness of a Denver night, with the clatter of circus equipment in the background, the friendship was renewed. Tammen offered Ogilvy a job. In the process, he also gave him redemption.

Tammen had a purpose for the wry Scot: He was the *Post's* agricultural writer — the kind of man the newspaper did not have and desperately needed if its influence was ever to expand to the hinterland beyond Denver. As for Ogilvy, he was perfectly suited for the position. The arrangement spanned a generation: Born in 1909, it lasted until 1945 when Ogilvy died. The relationship provided the *Post* with both an intellectual credibility that it rarely got anywhere else, and a certain rakish charm that made it one of the most widely read newspapers in the West. True, Harry Tammen helped Lyulph Ogilvy at the most critical time of his life, but as the most popular and colorful character in a stable of popular and colorful characters, Ogilvy also helped the *Post*.

On the surface, what Ogilvy contributed to the newspaper (and to the people who read it) was mundane and ordinary. He wrote stock reports, commenting on everything from livestock breeding to the condition of the state's cattle market. As an expert on farming, he wrote on irrigation patterns, market trends, and everything else that went with the territory. What readers did or did not know was the fact that Ogilvy — in the words of historian Gene Fowler — possessed knowledge of his subject "second to that of no one in America." His whole life had revolved around husbandry. From his childhood days in Scotland, where his clan had lived in two castles with enormous amounts of land between them, to his ill-fated days in Greeley, Ogilvy had learned a lifetime of information simply by listening to others. From Scottish caretakers to Weld County sodbusters to horsemen in military camps from Tampa to Johannesburg, he had learned his trade well. And his wisdom — imparted through his columns — reflected it. Listening to him talk of animals and the land that sustained them, wrote Fowler, "was like listening to a reading of Homer."

In Ogilvy's expertise lay his importance to Colorado. The turn of the century was a time of profound economic transition for the state. With the crash of 1893 come and gone, Colorado's once-great mining economy was still mired in depression. Agriculture was in the process of becoming more important than it had ever been before, and Colorado sorely needed people — experts — like Ogilvy to expedite the process. In essence Ogilvy was a midwife assisting in the birth of an empire. He wrote of drought and weevils and wheat rust and riprapping, but as an architect of agrarian development, what he *really* wrote of was change. It may have been that ordinary farmers read Ogilvy's prose simply for the blunt Scottish practicality it held. But more sophisticated people, who understood that he was far more than a common flack for a Denver newspaper, appreciated the man for what he really was: An intelligent and articulate evangel for a new age.

Even with all this, though, agrarian expertise and service to the state were not what Lyulph Ogilvy was renowned for. He was know, mostly, for his color. Looking at the tall, thin-faced man in the baggy tweeds, a stranger to Colorado would never have guessed him to be anything other than the slightly disheveled country gentleman he appeared to be. But beneath Ogilvy's placid surface existed one of the purest eccentrics that Colorado has ever known. In a day and time of notable characters — Soapy Smith, Eugene Field, Ogilvy's bosses Tammen and Frederick Bonfils — Ogilvy ranked second to none. For this reason, *Post* historian Bill Hosokawa has written that "legends clustered around Ogilvy the way barnacles attach themselves to a ship's hull."

Most of the great Ogilvy stories involved either horses or scotch, or both. On more than one occasion, after a day with the bottle, Ogilvy took horses with him into his home; on at least one occasion, so the story goes, he put a huge racehorse to bed there. Another time he jumped a horse and buggy full tilt across a shallow draw, killing the horse and destroying the buggy. One memorable day in Cheyenne he galloped a six-horse rig around a sharp corner, turned the buggy over, killed a prime horse in the process, then paid the outraged owner $1,000 for the loss. Later, driving a British visitor across the prairie near Greeley, and affronted by a remark that English horses were faster than American, he stood on his wagon's seat and lashed the team out of control. When the dust had settled, the wagon lay in splinters around a shattered telephone pole and the visitor, his arm broken, was no longer critical of the speed of western horses.

If horses trembled at the sight of Ogilvy, the manager of the Windsor Hotel must have gone into shock. Proud, glossy, dignified, the very essence of western class, the Windsor was one of the finest hotels anywhere. But perhaps because it had a beautiful, well-stocked bar (tended for some years by Tammen), it also attracted Ogilvy. And when Ogilvy had leaned for some hours on its softly polished mahogany and taken his last scotch, he became another man. Once, in keeping with the horses-and-scotch pattern, he drove a team into the hotel lobby. On another occasion he took a handful of roosters into his room, and at dawn the next day their cries woke up every guest in the hotel. For a grand finale, he emptied a small cage of rats in the lobby, then unleashed a brace of hunting dogs to chase them down. The Windsor was never the same again.

There were other stories, too, all of them told and retold through the years, polished, refined, and enhanced until, like most legends, they took on a life of their own. One was the story of the midnight ride. Another was of the night Ogilvy punched the outlaw Jim Moon in a fight at the Arcade. Afraid to retaliate against the fierce Scot, so the story goes, Moon stalked out of the Arcade, shot two men on the way, and rode away to the mountains.

But the greatest story involved Ogilvy's own "funeral."

One day early in the century, Ogilvy sent notice to his friends that he was dead. True enough, flocking in sorrow to a local funeral home, his friends found him, pale as ice and clearly dead, lying in a coffin flanked by elaborate sprays of carnations and roses. The next day, halfway through the funeral procession, as the coffin was solemnly borne toward Riverside Cemetery, Ogilvy lifted the top of the casket, raised a mostly empty bottle of scotch in salute to himself, and leaped to the ground as the hearse rolled on. At the cemetery a small barrel of yet more scotch was hoisted from Ogilvy's unoccupied grave, setting off a celebration the likes of which Riverside surely never saw again.

So ran the course of Ogilvy's life. When World War I broke out in 1914, he enlisted in the Scottish Horse and served as a fifty-three-year-old lieutenant buying cavalry horses for the British army and running a training depot in London. After the war was over, he returned to the *Post*, and there he spent the rest of his life. Abandoning his home in Denver — for some years a small Boothroyd cottage on Twelfth Avenue in Capitol

Hill, in other years a smaller home he called "Hardscrabble" off South Broadway — he moved to "Three Waters," a quiet ranch on the Big Thompson River near Loveland. By that time there was little left of his life but the *Post*. His wife and daughter were dead (his daughter dying while he was away at war). So he dedicated the years he had left to the paper.

In his last years Ogilvy became one of the most beloved and widely recognized public characters in Colorado. As time went by, as the world changed around him, Ogilvy himself changed little at all. The tall, stooped man of 1940 was little different from the tall, stooped man of 1907. Perhaps the angle of the body was a little different, its forward bend a little sharper, the thin frame a bit more skeletal, and perhaps the clothes were a little more worn. Perhaps the mind was not as incisive either. But the spirit, passionate and independent to the end, never changed.

Dividing his time between the *Post*, where he wrote stories as he always had, and his Loveland ranch, where at last he was able to raise horses and a few head of cattle, Ogilvy lived out the last years of his life in the best of both worlds. Then, in a Boulder nursing home, on April 5, 1947, he died. The spike-bearded Scot who once had "made champagne pour around him like a river," as one author has written, was history. And this time he did not disrupt his own funeral.

With Ogilvy gone, the tales of his life grew in stature. And in stories of the old man told and retold at country granges on Saturday nights, he was remembered by all with love. He was "blessed with the highest type of human fire and daring," wrote Gene Fowler in what would have made a lovely epitaph. His legend was "a glamorous and honorable one." Fowler, like others, was entitled to his opinion. But Ogilvy, alone among his peers, probably would have disagreed.

Spencer Penrose

Spencer Penrose once commented satirically that his Broadmoor Hotel in Colorado Springs was nothing but a "monument to a damned fool." This flippant pronouncement, made no doubt during the late stages of one of his incessant cocktail parties, in actuality foretold of changing attitudes among many Coloradoans regarding the nature of tourism in the Centennial State. Ever since the gold rush era, tourism in one way or another has been a fixture in Colorado's economy. Such booster literature as Samuel Bowles' *The Switzerland of America*, published in 1869, and Isabella Bird's *A Lady's Life in the Rocky Mountains*, published in 1879, accurately predicted a bright future for tourism in the Rocky Mountain region. With the advent of the railroads in the 1870s and 1880s, that prediction became reality.

Aside from the spectacular grandeur of its majestic mountains and its natural wonders, Colorado very quickly became a mecca for health seekers. The restorative mineral waters of Glenwood Springs on the Western Slope and Eldorado Springs near Boulder elegantly catered to wealthy Victorians from the East. More important, the high altitude and fresh air attracted thousands of tuberculosis victims. Rich and poor alike, these unfortunates swarmed to the mountains beginning in the 1870s to partake of what was called the "camp cure." Many stayed only through

Spencer Penrose.
Western History Department,
Denver Public Library.

the summer season. But many more became so enchanted with the tranquil forests and snow-covered peaks that they stayed for the remainder of their lives. Such figures as Denver's dynamic mayor Robert W. Speer and author Helen Hunt Jackson were among the consumptives who made Colorado their new home. By the 1880s, close to one-third of the state's population consisted of individuals recovering from tuberculosis or other maladies.

Resorts and spas sprang up on the plains and in the mountains to accommodate every taste and bank account. Colorado Springs became the hub of it all. William Jackson Palmer, head of the Rio Grande Railway, had founded the town in 1871 on the belief that eastern vacationers as well as tuberculosis patients could be lured by the thousands from their fashionable Victorian spas at Saratoga Springs, Newport, or the Virginia coast to the base of Pikes Peak. He was right. After 1871, lavish, gothic hotels were constructed complete with theaters, medical treatment facilities, and even polo fields. Easterners by the scores flocked to the new resort town in the "Wild West." Europeans, especially from the British Isles, had always been attracted to Colorado from the days of the first gold strikes. These Englishmen, proclaimed historian Marshall Sprague, "taught the easterners how to behave genteely, and that is how the town got its nickname, Little London."

Tourism was well on its way to becoming Colorado's most important industry when the strikingly handsome Spencer Penrose stepped off the train at the Santa Fe depot in Colorado Springs and viewed Pikes Peak and the mighty Rampart Range for the first time. It was December 10, 1892, and the twenty-seven-year-old Philadelphian was hungry and broke when he met his old friend Charles Tutt at the station. Within a few short years, Spencer Penrose would amass one of the greatest fortunes in America. And Colorado Springs would never be the same again.

Spencer Penrose was born in Philadelphia on November 2, 1865, to a cultured, well-to-do family with impeccable credentials. On his father's side he was directly descended from William Penn and on his mother's side he could trace his ancestry to William Hubbard — Harvard class of 1642. From the seventeenth century forward, Penroses attended either Harvard or Yale. Princeton, Columbia, and Dartmouth were beneath them. It was said that Penroses married Drexels, Biddles, or Chews, at the least, and in one way or another the family was related to every other blue blood the City of Brotherly Love had turned out over the preceding two centuries. Sometime during his prep school breeding, Penrose acquired the innocuous nickname "Spec," supposedly a cute truncation of Spencer. One of his older brothers, Boies Penrose, served in the United States Senate and became one of the most autocratic political bosses in American history. Like all of his successful elder brothers, Spec attended Harvard. Barely graduating, Spec's only distinction at the former seminary for Puritan clergy was that he consumed a whole gallon of beer in thirty-seven seconds, a new school record.

Somewhat of a black sheep, Spencer Penrose went to New Mexico after college to find fame and fortune. Spec was certainly not the only wealthy easterner ever to come west. Neither was he the first Penrose. President Thomas Jefferson had appointed his great-grandfather commissioner of Louisiana Territory in 1804. A cousin, General William Henry Penrose, founded Fort Lyon, Colorado Territory, in the 1860s. Like most easterners who colonized the West, to exploit the landscape and the resources, Spencer Penrose had a burning desire to get rich quick. Writes Marshall Sprague: "He wanted to get rich as quickly as possible. He did not just have a vague idea about it. With him, the desire to get rich — very, very rich — was burning and fundamental, an overwhelming urge which had been accruing in his rather complicated psyche from earliest childhood."

Unfortunately for Penrose, however, he squandered his savings in Santa Fe, and that is why he was stone broke when friend Charles Tutt met him at the train in Colorado Springs on that December day in 1892. To make things even worse, after asking Tutt for a job, Penrose distinguished himself once again by smashing up the Cheyenne Mountain Country Club and the organization's star polo player along with it. This episode occurred during his very first week in Colorado Springs. Nevertheless, Tutt offered Penrose a partnership in his real estate company located in the new boom town of Cripple Creek. Penrose accepted the offer, and during the next three years he made quite a bit of money selling mining claims and pouring profits into the C.O.D. Mine and a newly established gold mill.

During his days as a mill operator, one of his employees interested him in a scheme to process low-grade copper ore in Utah. Penrose soon helped incorporate the Utah Copper Company, and with it, he compiled one of the greatest (and quickest) fortunes in the history of the West. After the company opened its open pit copper mine at Bingham Canyon near Salt Lake City, Penrose found himself earning in excess of $200,000 per month while concurrently creating one of the most hideous scars to be found anywhere on the face of the North American continent.

Now a wealthy man, Spencer Penrose courted a pert, bubbly

Detroit widow by the name of Julie Villers Lewis McMillan. Her husband had died in Colorado Springs. Spec and Julie were married in London on April 26, 1906. The happy couple honeymooned through the chateau country of France in a motor car that broke down every few miles. After returning to Colorado Springs, Penrose and his bride settled down to a life of luxury. By 1923 he had sold his Utah Copper interests to Kennecott Copper Company. A multimillionaire, he was listed in *Who's Who* along with his father and brothers.

Even before the sale of the copper company, Spencer Penrose had begun to make his mark in Colorado Springs by entering the tourist business. Always enchanted with the lavish resorts in and around the Springs, especially the opulent Antlers Hotel, Penrose simply decided to outdo them all. He acquired property around lovely Broadmoor Lake in the shadow of Pikes Peak. Included on the property was a casino and a modest hotel. After removing the old hostelry, Penrose sold stock, sunk $700,000 of his own money into a construction company, and began building what is today the Broadmoor Hotel. From that point forward until his death in 1939, there was always some sort of construction taking place at the eclectic, pink stucco edifice. His goal was to make the resort the most ostentatiously lavish resort in the Rockies. For many years he kept a construction crew of 300 workers on the payroll. He built a zoo on the property and a riding ring because he liked the smell of horses.

The architects for the project were the firm of Warren and Wetmore, who had designed the Ritz and Biltmore hotels in New York. They told Penrose the project would cost $1 million. By the time it was finished, the bill reached in excess of $3 million. Only the very best would do. He imported Italian artisans to reproduce European frescos and bas reliefs. Marble floors and gold-leaf chandeliers adorned the interior. Reflecting pools and flower gardens graced the immaculate lawns. There was a billiard room, a squash court, and even a fleet of boats on the lake. For a price, America's wealthy classes could vacation in splendor to their heart's content at the base of the Rampart Range.

The resort officially opened in 1918. The cuisine at the grand opening gala was the finest available, as was the 1858 Napoleon Brandy and the Chateau Lafitte Rothschild. Among the first guests was John D. Rockefeller, Jr. After spending only a few minutes in the lavish suite prepared for him, however, this baron of Wall Street sent Penrose a message proclaiming that the smell of fresh paint made him sick. He promptly went down the street and registered at the Antlers Hotel. So much for the guest of honor.

During his lifetime, the Broadmoor Hotel never turned a profit for Spencer Penrose. But it was not for any lack of effort. To popularize his brainchild, Penrose splattered the region with everything imaginable. There were miles of bridle paths, a cooking club on Cheyenne Mountain, a skating rink, greenhouses, tennis courts, Turkish baths, and a golf course. The Penrose home at El Pomar was almost as elegant as the hotel itself. Perhaps his most outlandish promotion, however, was the annual Pikes Peak Hill Climb, an automobile race to the top of the famous mountain. Begun before the completion of the hotel as a means to stimulate a sagging tourist economy, the race became an annual event. Starting in 1915, Spencer Penrose spent $3 million improving the old carriage road up Pikes Peak despite reservations among Forest Service officials that the project was a waste of money. On August 11, 1916, Fred Junk, driving a wire-wheeled Chalmers, won the opening day's heat of the first Pikes Peak Hill Climb. Rea Litz won the second day's race in an eight-cylinder Romano. Celebrity Barney Oldfield only managed to finish in twelfth place driving a French Delage. In little more than a century after its official discovery, automobiles had raced up the great peak that Lieutenant Zebulon Pike had predicted would remain a wilderness. Thus it was that Spencer Penrose gained the distinction of building the highest auto road in the world — even if it cost him a fortune.

If publicity over the Pikes Peak highway could not stimulate sufficient revenues for the Broadmoor, the advent of prohibition made things even worse. On New Year's Day in 1916, Colorado closed its saloons. If there was ever a man who opposed prohibition to the point of outright obsession, it was Spencer Penrose. It is believed that between 1916 and 1933, when prohibition finally ended, Penrose donated hundreds of thousands of dollars to anti-prohibitionist groups. A conservative Republican all his life, Penrose jumped party lines to vote for Democratic presidential candidate Al Smith when Republican Herbert Hoover ran on a "dry" platform. Just before the saloon doors closed, Penrose purchased an estimated 24,000 cases of liquor and stored them in rooms at New York's sedate University Club. The liquor was brought in by a fleet of trucks and stacked to the ceilings. The spirits remained there for fifteen years, during which time Penrose paid out more than $28,000 in rent. The liquor itself had cost him a quarter of a million dollars. When the University Club requested that he move his property, Penrose responded by sending in masons to brick up the rooms containing the booze. Even more cases were brought to his El Pomar home at Broadmoor. After the repeal of prohibition, Penrose had his New York supply, along with hundreds of cases he inherited after the death of his brother Dick, shipped to Colorado Springs in two boxcars. It was stored at El Pomar, and he hired a watchman to guard it.

In 1937, two years before his death, Spencer Penrose became a philanthropist. Having been diagnosed as having cancer, he set up the charitable El Pomar Foundation. The Kennecott Copper Company became a major contributor. On December 7, 1939, Spencer Penrose died at El Pomar. He was buried in the vaults at the $250,000 granite shrine he built to honor his friend, Will Rogers, on the heights overlooking his tourist empire. After his death, his $40 million estate formed the base of the El Pomar Foundation. A subsidiary of the foundation owns the Broadmoor Hotel today. Through the years the foundation has sponsored such activities as the Colorado Springs Symphony, Boys Club of America, zoos, arts centers, and community chests. The City of Colorado Springs is indeed richer for its activities.

During his lifetime Spencer Penrose was somewhat of an eccentric man. He would tend his zoo and pet elephants while dressed in safari clothes. For many years he heralded his arrivals to local fund drives by riding a sulky pulled by a llama. He enjoyed the company of artists and playboys. Physically, he was the picture of an athlete. At heart he was a showman and a romantic. But Spencer Penrose was more than this. Behind the facade was one of the most ruthlessly conservative businessmen in the history of Colorado. A classic Social Darwinist, Penrose continuously opposed any form of government interference or regulation of what he considered to be traditional American values. Much of his later life was devoted to protesting what he felt was the overt erosion of American freedoms by the government. In no other case was this feeling more obvious than in his blatant denunciations of prohibition.

He built a monument to his concept of man's right to flaunt wealth and pleasure in a chiefly material sense — the Broadmoor Hotel. Costs be damned. The critics be damned. But the critics were, and still are, ever present. Born to the nineteenth century, and its definition of unrestricted freedom to build and exploit, Spencer Penrose, perhaps, did not foresee future trends in reasoning among many westerners during the twentieth century. Open pit mining and auto roads to the summits of great peaks are now anathema to many people. Today, Spencer Penrose's concept of recreation and tourism is, perhaps, the greatest anachronism of all. Although glamorous resorts are still well patronized throughout America, the type of recreational experience offered by such establishments as the Broadmoor Hotel is to many westerners counterproductive to the type of image they would like to project for Colorado.

At the very time that Spencer Penrose was constructing the Pikes Peak Highway and starting construction on the Broadmoor Hotel, another man, Enos Mills, who came to Colorado for health reasons, was working equally hard to secure legislation that would set aside Rocky Mountain National Park. In this respect Mills foresaw the day when tourists would be able to enjoy the grandeur of the mountains in a more pristine, natural state, unencumbered by man's exploitive building. Eventually, the federal government set aside over 12 million acres of forest land in Colorado under the Forest Reserve Act to further protect much of the state's beauty under federal use regulations.

Inspired by the writings of John Muir, Enos Mills, Aldo Leopold, and others, conservation groups like the Sierra Club and the Colorado Mountain Club redefined the concept of recreation and tourism for many Americans after the turn of the century. By the 1960s, the recreational experience which harmoniously couples man with the physical environment in a more natural, nonexploitive fashion has appealed to more and more residents of the western states, including Colorado. Even the concept of the elegant ski resorts which scar the land in places, at least, assumes some degree of direct, natural appreciation and interaction between the tourist and his natural surroundings. To a large extent the wilderness itself, only minimally enhanced by man's handiwork, has become the major tourist attraction. What is now termed the "elemental vacation" or the "wilderness experience" is in vogue.

By contrast, Spencer Penrose's concept of tourism centered on building monuments to man's materialistic instincts and his conspicuous consumption. It is doubtful that he would be an advocate of the elemental values of the 1980s. To many westerners, the vacation experience advocated by Spencer Penrose belongs to an earlier age when exploitation and progress were thought to be synonymous. This belief is no longer acceptable given the fragile and threatened nature of the physical environment in the Rocky Mountain West. In addition, contrived vacation experiences offered by glamorous resorts with their numerous planned, indoor activities, many believe, belong to states which have less to offer than Colorado. According to the new wilderness ethic, such conspicuous resorts are indeed monuments to damned fools.

William Harrison (Jack) Dempsey

On a bleak winter day in 1904, a disheveled little eight-year-old boy sat crying on the hard oak passenger seat of a lumbering Denver and Rio Grande train. Outside the window, surrounded by the mountain fastness, it was snowing relentlessly. Visibility was down to almost zero. The train was still hours out of Denver. In the aisle of the passenger car the boy's destitute mother was pleading an apparently hopeless case with a scowling, brass-buttoned conductor. "Sorry, ma'am," the conductor said. "Can't help you. Rules are rules, and I stick to 'em. You either pay the fare for the boy or he's put off at the next stop. I'll be back."

While this emotional scene was taking place, the boy's eyes wandered across the aisle to a dandy-looking cowboy who was taking in the entire argument between the conductor and the poor woman. The cowboy was attired in his finest regalia — hand-tooled leather boots, fancy spurs, and a pair of pearl-handled pistols. Once the conductor was out of sight, the cowboy motioned to the young boy. "Tell your ma to stop worrying," he told the child. "If it comes to a showdown, I'll pay your fare, sonny. But I don't think it'll come to that; I think he's bluffing. Don't worry about a thing, pardner." The cowboy was right — the conductor was bluffing. But the boy was ashamed and

William Harrison
"Jack" Dempsey.
*Western History Department,
Denver Public Library.*

humiliated. He was, of course, touched by the cowboy's gesture.
His eyes once again brimmed with tears. He later recalled that
the humiliation stuck like a pitchfork in his belly. It made him
realize for the first time how poor his family really was. How
they had come west from the hill country of Kentucky in search
of the promise of the frontier. And how, like so many others
had discovered, the dream of the West had turned out to be
the great myth of America.

From that very moment the child vowed that no similar inci-
dents would happen to him when he grew up. "One day," he
recalled, "I would have enough money to pay for as many fares
as I wanted. One day I would be grand, just like the cowboy."
And so he became grand. Two decades after that humiliating
scene on the Denver and Rio Grande Railroad, William Harrison
(Jack) Dempsey became one of the most widely admired heroes
in the history of professional sports.

Jack Dempsey lived during an age of heroes. With the settling
of the American frontier and the war with Spain in 1898, the

United States came as a proud and virile world power into the community of nations. Then in 1917, American armies marched off to Europe to "save the world for democracy." In 1919, the soldiers came marching home to return to normalcy, whatever that meant. To some people it meant 100 percent Americanism, a return to rural values, and a contempt for anything foreign or anti-American. The Red Scare of the early 1920s sent seemingly respectable citizens out on veritable witch hunts to find subversive communists. Others revived the Ku Klux Klan. Such hate groups took Colorado by storm. To others it meant a great awakening of evangelism which witnessed Sister Aimee McPherson gather throngs of thousands for her impassioned sermons in the open air.

But to still others it meant the dawning of a new age for the adoration of American heroes. Gone were the chivalrous mountain men, Santa Fe traders, drovers, frontier soldiers, and stout pioneer farmers of the great adventuresome West. The doughboys from the vermin-infested French trenches had come home to run clean shops and farms. The gaudy Wild West shows of Buffalo Bill Cody and Pawnee Bill, which painted a mythical picture of a more romantic age, were fading into memory. The nation wanted a new generation of heroes and the revolutionary media of radio and celluloid film provided them in every town and city across the nation. Through the exciting new technology, an immigrant youth whose only ambition may have been to become a farmer could change his name from Rudolfo d'Antonguolla to Rudolph Valentino and quickly become the greatest male symbol of passionate romance to ever emerge from the American dream factory.

To flaunt independence by tossing down an illegal cocktail in the titillatingly wicked speakeasy replaced the allure of the wide open western saloon. Treasury agents like Izzy and Moe became surrogates for western lawmen of old when they attempted to enforce prohibition and were scoffed at by the middle-class majority. Perhaps for most, however, the dashing vaqueros and cavalier mountain men of the past were replaced in the mind of the new urban American by the dashing sports figures of a more mechanical age. Through the miracle of the home radio set, Babe Ruth and Red Grange came alive. And they were every bit as captivating as Buffalo Bill had once been to the imaginations of hero-worshipping Americans. So, too, was a once-dirt-poor hard-rock miner from Manassa, Colorado, by the name of William Harrison Dempsey.

William was the ninth of what became a total of thirteen children born to Hyrum and Celia Dempsey. He came into the world on June 24, 1895, in the crude log cabin the family had built in the San Luis Valley town of Manassa. Celia had converted to Mormonism during the 1880s, and the family followed the American dream from Kentucky to this isolated Mormon community during the decade. Almost immediately, the Dempseys came face to face with abject poverty. With few skills to his credit, Hyrum tried his hand at many trades, including mining and farming. He failed at all of them. The family was frequently on the move. Uncompahgre, Creede, Leadville, Cripple Creek, Steamboat Springs, Montrose, in fact, most of the rugged Western Slope mining towns saw the Dempseys trying to alter their misfortunes. Hyrum was seldom able to hold down a job for very long. He was sending eight-year-old William and his mother to Denver to live with an older sister on that memorable day in 1904 when the conductor threatened to throw little William off the train because the family could not afford the fare.

Frequently, Hyrum Dempsey was forced to take work far from home while his wife was left behind to raise her brood. In the rough Colorado mining camps, she took in laundry and even cooked for the miners in an attempt to make enough money to feed her clan. Celia Dempsey was a determined mother. Described as being a tough, wiry little woman who always knew what she wanted, she also possessed the virtue of an unselfish soul. It was said that when she smiled, she could melt even the hardest heart. She frequently took in and fed hobos and busted miners who had nowhere to spend a cold winter night. Once a grateful vagabond insisted that she take one of the few possessions he carried in his weathered carpet bag when allowed the warmth of the Dempsey fireplace during a mountain blizzard.

For some reason, Celia took an interest in a ragged old book entitled *Life of a 19th Century Gladiator* by John L. Sullivan. She reread the story of the legendary prize fighter so many times that she decided her son William would grow up to be just like the great John L. Sullivan.

It is not at all surprising that Celia Dempsey became so enchanted with the sport of boxing. Any perusal of archives which describe recreational pursuits in the western mining communities reveals that the manly art of self-defense (for money) was very popular. Indeed, among the working class it was the great sport of the nineteenth century. Contests which matched opponents' virility were well rooted in frontier tradition by the early years of the twentieth century. Awakening before dawn to trudge miles through the cold and snow to spend twelve hours in the confines of dangerous mines was not a pleasant existence for the hard-rock miner. From cradle to grave the miner could find himself at the mercy of the company. He shopped at the company store, attended company physicians, indebted himself to the company at the company bank. And he was eventually buried in the company coffin at the company graveyard. Strikes for adequate wages or safe working conditions (the death toll in Colorado mines was the highest in the world) was usually met with federal troops and frequent bloodshed. It was natural that during his time off, the miner frequently vented his frustrations through either alcohol or brawling or both. Professional prize fights became a surrogate way to release tension. And successful prize fighters became heroes.

For young William Harrison Dempsey, the sport of boxing became a way out of poverty and squalor. It became a means to secure the elusive promise of the West his parents so ardently sought but could not attain. Leaving school at an early age, William, like his brothers, turned to mining to help support the large family. During his spare time, however, the lanky youth trained to become a prize fighter. Often he would make believe that he was the world champion but told no one for fear they would laugh at him. William's older brother, Bernie, got him his first serious job mining when he was sixteen years old. The boys left home for Utah, where the eccentric Colorado Springs financier, Spencer Penrose, had helped finance the opening of a huge copper mine in Bingham Canyon near Salt Lake City.

William was a mucker, that is, the lowest member of the mine crew. He worked only when the other miners had quit for the day, loading the ore into small carts. Then he wheeled the carts to the mine shaft, where they were hoisted to the surface. On his very first day, an ore car jumped the tracks, cutting the lights and leaving William in pitch darkness 3,000 feet below ground. For this job he was paid three dollars per day. When the two boys were finally able to put aside a little extra cash, they leased a mine in Cripple Creek, Colorado. According to Dempsey: "We worked like dogs, without helpers or machinery, doing everything ourselves. We sweated like pigs, we turned on each other, we collapsed in the sun, but we kept right on working that mine. The experience was one of my most unforgettable. . . . Ore? We found none."

During their spare time, which was infrequent, both William and Bernie trained for the ring. Bernie taught his younger brother the techniques of the sport. At one of their many homes in Lakeview, Colorado, the boys used a dilapidated chicken coop for a gymnasium. The two boys threw an old mattress on the floor for tumbling. They made a cloth bag stuffed with sawdust for a punching bag. They would sprint against the horses in the town. During his teenage years, William was somewhat frail. Bernie taught him how to chew pine gum right from the tree to strengthen his jaw, then he tested the results by throwing a surprise left hook to his brother's chin. William bathed his face in beef blood mixed with water to toughen his skin. Only through hard work and days in the mine did the slender youth build up his body. By this time the future champion was called Harry by his family, and on occasion, Kid Blackie. "You don't want them to stop a fight because of a little cut, Harry," Bernie would taunt as he rubbed more beef brine on his brother's face.

By 1914, Harry and Bernie had begun taking on prize fights when mining jobs were scarce, which was often due to continued labor unrest in the Colorado mines and the overall collapse of the industry. The boys rode the rods, that is to say, they used handkerchiefs to tie themselves to the undercarriages of speeding trains to get from town to town. Harry could get fights by walking into saloons in the mining towns and announcing: "I can't sing and I can't dance, but I'll lick anyone in the house!" Much of the time he was not taken seriously because of his high-pitched voice. Consequently, Harry would pass the hat making the first bet himself. He rarely lost a fight. Occasionally, he would make a deal with a bartender to get rid of the local bully by baiting him into a fight, giving the bartender a percentage of the purse if he won. Immediately upon collection of his share of the winnings, however, Harry would streak out of town before the saloon patrons found out they had been hustled by a tough fighter with a sissy voice.

Occasionally, Harry and Bernie would get legitimate fights. Bernie took the name Jack Dempsey in deference to a great nineteenth-century Irish fighter of that name, but one day Bernie could not make a match in Cripple Creek with George Copeland and sent his brother Harry instead. Since no one in the town knew either boy, Harry simply announced that he was Jack Dempsey. He won the fight and from that day forward he kept the name. By 1916, Jack Dempsey had fought and defeated a lot of men. Traveling from mine to mine, he would challenge the local champion and then move on. Soon he built up something of a local reputation. He hired a manager and had numerous fights especially in the slums of Salt Lake City, where Hardy Downing's Boxing Club was a proving ground for local fighters from the mines. Eventually, Jack defeated all the local competition.

By late 1916, it was apparent that Jack Dempsey was ready for bigger and better things. That meant he had to leave his beloved Rocky Mountains in search of new opportunity. There was really only one place he could go, a city where working-class dollars were available in abundance to support the fight game at the level Dempsey was beginning to reach — New York. The thought of it excited the twenty-one-year-old fighter. But as he was soon to find out, New York was not what its aficionados claimed it to be. The people seemed strange to Dempsey. Billed as a fashion-conscious city, the residents, Dempsey found out, threw fashion to the wind when it came to dressing warmly in winter — something a self-respecting westerner would never think of doing. Pueblo newspaperman Damon Runyon warned Jack, "New York never wants you — it's you that wants New York." Many years later a retired Jack Dempsey admitted that Runyon was absolutely right.

Nevertheless, under the astute guidance of expert managers and ballyhoo promoters, Jack Dempsey rose to unprecedented fame within the next three years. Finally, on July 4, 1919, on a steamy hot day in Toledo, Ohio, Jack Dempsey knocked out Jess Willard to become the heavyweight champion of the world. America had marched home from the great war and a modern hero from the American West was born on the Fourth of July. From that day until he retired in 1932, the life and career of Jack Dempsey became a legend. He defended his title many times against such opponents as Georges Carpentier, Luis Angel Firpo (the Wild Bull of the Pampas), Tommy Gibbons, and Jack Sharkey. In September 1927, he finally lost his world championship in a controversial fight with Gene Tunney in Chicago. He never regained the title. But during the 1920s, Jack Dempsey was a symbol of the new genre. It was said that he fought with a tenacity unequalled in the history of the sport. *New York Tribune* sports writer Paul Gallico called him "The Manassa Mauler," a skinny kid from the Colorado mining camps who carried into the ring the hopes and dreams of every working class youth in America each time he defended his title.

Jack Dempsey's life after retirement was wrought with controversy, frustration, and four marriages along with champagne-toasting success. His friends and associates included presidents and mobsters, including underworld chief, Al Capone. But none of them did he treasure more dearly than his old Colorado companions, especially journalists Gene Fowler and Damon Runyon, who had helped him through the bad times as well as the good. From his landmark restaurant on New York's Broadway he often reminsced about his old days in the mines, his mother who lived to see him become champion, and of course his mentor, brother Bernie. Most importantly, he knew that in the sum total of it all, he was really just a symbol of an era; a transitory symbol to be sure, but one which characterized the new American hero in a time when men like Buffalo Bill were starting to slip from memory. Jack Dempsey knew the myth of the West, the myth of America. Very few ever make it big. And those who do, many times become make-believe symbols for a host of others. Such was the illusion of normalcy which characterized life during the 1920s, but even after it all came tumbling down with the Great Depression of the 1930s, the dreams of working-class kids were not much different from those of older kids who believed in the myth of the Old West. If you can't make it to the top yourself, then you do so vicariously through your heroes, and your will to make believe.

Josephine Roche

Josephine Roche was a woman for all seasons, and her seasons spanned almost the entire social and political life of twentieth-century Colorado. Progressive, New Dealer, laborite — her politics ran like a long, bright thread through the sometimes dark years, and so did her sense of social justice. Josephine Roche was one of Colorado's most brilliant businesswomen and one of its most potent social activists, and she fused the two entities into one of the state's most remarkable personalities. She was, simply, a woman of great grace who believed in the most fundamental of human tenets: That the sanctity of the human spirit was the most important thing in life. In twentieth-century Colorado, using her politics and business acumen as weaponry against those who did not agree, she waged an almost singular one-woman thirty-year war to help those who could not help themselves.

Josephine Roche was not born a social crusader, nor was she born in the house of one. She was born in Omaha in 1886, the daughter of a banker who dabbled in cattle and attracted money like most men attracted debt. As young western women with family money did, she went east for her education — to Vassar, then Columbia — then returned, refined and cultured, to her prairie home. At some point in her early life — no one knew

Josephine Roche.
Colorado Historical Society.

when, not even Roche herself — she developed an almost classic sense of noblesse oblige. As early as her Columbia years, working on a degree in social work, she studied the link between delinquency, prostitution, and economic depression in New York, then followed with in-depth studies of child labor practices. She never forgot what she found, or what she saw, and when she returned to the West, she carried in her baggage a new, deep, and restless social conscience.

In 1908, Roche's family moved to Denver, where her father owned and managed the Rocky Mountain Fuel Company. For two years Josephine commuted between Denver and New York, finally completing her work at Columbia in 1910. When she finished, it took little effort to find a place to apply her skills. The place was Denver.

In 1910, Denver was a city with as many serious social, political, and economic problems as any city its size in the Union. The Queen City that outsiders saw was economically rich and physically beautiful, an elegant young metropolis of graceful homes and hard-driving businesses, and churches and schools to match. But what insiders saw was a still-frontier city with old frontier problems — rundown homes in decaying neighborhoods, class stratification, racial and religious hatred, an economic imbalance that enriched mining kings and merchant princes over all others, and political domination by bosses and rings as complete as anywhere in the nation. The city's reform mayor, Robert Speer, had bloodied himself attacking the malaise; since 1904 he had fought against it, and on some fronts he had won. But the 1910 Denver that Josephine Roche found was still a city with acute problems. Worse, it was caught in a bitter crossfire between Speer, a pragmatic progressive who catered to the city's political and economic rulers even as he tried to control them, and a rising group of progressive purists who rejected his tactics no matter what their success. It was into this hornet's nest that Josephine Roche walked.

Sometime in 1912, Roche was recruited by George Creel, the *Rocky Mountain News* journalist and city police commissioner, to join a small band of progressive insurgents in its efforts to clean up Denver, turn out Speer, and muzzle "the Beast" — progressive activist Benjamin Lindsey's term for the city's powerful capitalists. She did. At twenty-four, a small, slim, brown-haired beauty with a voice that barely carried beyond where she spoke, Josephine Roche became the first policewoman in Denver's history.

Roche's job was to patrol Denver's "entertainment district" — theaters, saloons, gambling dens, and brothels — from Arapahoe Street to the Platte, and, in Creel's mind, to destroy the area's vice by neutralizing its prostitution base. Armed more with a sense of moral outrage than anything else — like Carrie Nation smashing up a saloon — Roche quickly became an effective officer of the law.

Roche condemned a society that nurtured cribs and venereal sickness and violence against women — many of them still children — and the almost incessant cycle of suicide by morphine or cyanide that formed an integral part of the prostitute's life. She raided, arrested, preached, and sheltered until prostitution in the district was essentially gone. In the process, however, she created controversy. To some extent a city comfortable with the status quo was not comfortable with moral crusaders. But the real fact was that stripping the entertainment district of its entertainment — sordid and tragic as it might have been — damaged its business. Inevitably, business complained of harassment, and just as inevitably, politicians (many of whom patronized the prostitutes) responded. In the end, Josephine Roche, whose only crime had been to protect women protected by no one else, was ousted from her position. Some said the reason was that as a woman in a department of men, and hired outside of regular channels at that, Roche simply had caused too much dissention around her.

Roche's life hardly stopped with the setback. She simply looked elsewhere for causes. Primary among them were women. Motivated in particular by the Triangle Shirtwaist Company fire in New York in 1911 — which left 147 women dead in the ashes of a giant sweatshop — she never lost an opportunity to attack the exploitation of women in the workplace. She also continued to fight prostitution, working as before to get women out of the cribs and streets and back to their families. Some called her shrill and militant, and she was. But if she erred, it was on the side of compassion. Even her enemies conceded that.

Roche also championed children. Joining with Lindsey, Denver's celebrated "childrens' judge," she became a probation officer and worked with juvenile offenders with the same furious diligence she gave women of the night. In the mid-1920s, working with the United States Children's Bureau against the exploitation of child labor, Roche became a national expert on the existence of environmental links between juvenile delinquency and poverty. What she knew she had learned at Lindsey's side. Lindsey became a legend in the progressive era, and he should have. No one much noticed Josephine Roche, but she was there, too.

Slowly, Roche became an important figure in Denver's progressive movement. On one side of her stood Creel and Lindsey, the journalist and the judge. On the other side stood Edward Costigan, a fiery southern-born attorney, and Thomas Patterson of the *Rocky Mountain News*, who galvanized them all. For at least a half dozen years it was largely this quartet that challenged the city's political and social status quo. The battles they fought — this "rare company," as one newspaperman called them — were relentless. Women and children were part of their war: Behind the slogan, "industrial justice," they continued to fight for child labor laws and for the rights of women in the work force. They also warred on the corporation — the banks, railroads, smelters, and utilities that had held Denver in a condition of economic bondage most the days of its life. And always, in the whorehouses and sweatshops, in the statehouse and in the press, they fought the politicians. The state legislature — big-money, corporation-fronting Republicans — despised them. So did the city's venal bosses, the small gangs of political predators Creel labeled the "Big Mitt." So, too, did Speer, whom the Creel group hounded until Speer's death in 1918.

In 1914, after several years of working together, the group disintegrated. Disagreements over the presidential candidacies of Woodrow Wilson and Theodore Roosevelt in 1912 became open wounds two years later; friends though they were, and allies in a singular cause, they could not heal the rift, and finally they disbanded. What they had achieved was hard to evaluate; only time and history would really tell. But certainly they had achieved something. In 1946, writing about "that heroic little group" and its lonely charge against "Things The Way They Were," *News* columnist Lee Casey argued that in crusading for women's and children's rights, utilities control, and collective bargaining, they had participated in one of the great liberal reform movements in American history. More important, though, for Denver and Colorado, they made the unthinkable of 1912 the commonplace of 1946. As for Roche, said Casey, "she never gave up, not even when it seemed almost hopeless. The beatings she took hurt her, but she helped us win that fight."

Then, suddenly, there were no more fights. The Great War crippled progressivism and the postwar killed it. Reformers like Roche found themselves stranded on the almost endless shoals of America's new conservatism. Roche never lost her ideals, but, momentarily at least, she lost an arena in which to practice them. In 1925, after service in Washington during the war, Roche returned to Denver. Two years later, when her father died, she inherited his stock in the Rocky Mountain Fuel Company, the second-largest coal corporation in the state. In 1928, she became the company's president. She may not have realized it, but she had found a new arena.

From the day she took over the company, Roche ran it in a way unprecedented in the annals of western mining: Applying the principles of progressivism to company management, stressing the importance of men over product, she evolved a kind of hybrid form of welfare capitalism probably unique in the West. All of her adult life Roche had argued the value of people in social, political, and economic systems. Before, her arguments had been largely abstract; social workers and policewomen, after all, rarely effected real change. But in 1928, operating from a cramped office on the sixth floor of the Patterson Building at Seventeenth and Welton streets, Roche finally possessed an *instrument* of change — a company. So for the first time, she was able to translate the abstract into the concrete. In the process, of course, she triggered a great storm. But then, storms had never bothered her before.

In the mid-1920s, the Colorado coal industry was a theater of confrontation, violence, and almost stultifying inefficiency, and it had been so for years. As far back as coal had been dug in the state, controversy had been dug with it. For a generation, as they had made their own fortunes, Colorado's coal barons and the big coal companies had slowly raised the exploitation of their workers to an art form. Inhuman working conditions, miserable living conditions, low pay, no benefits, company towns, and company stores — while the barons lived in splendor, their workers lived in poverty, contracted black lung, then died. To be sure, they did not die peacefully. For decades they had battled the coal capitalists with unions and strikes. But in Colorado, as everywhere else in America, power begat power and weakness remained constant. Busting unions, smashing strikes, the barons only got stronger and the workers got weaker.

Serious confrontations first began in 1903. When Josephine Roche was seventeen and packing for Vassar, the United Mine

Workers first organized in Colorado and struck the state's southern fields. Their primary targets were those companies (including Rocky Mountain Fuel) that supplied the Colorado Fuel and Iron Company of John D. Rockefeller. In 1910, a second wave of strikes swept the same fields, again engulfing Rocky Mountain Fuel. Josephine Roche learned much at her father's side. Hard-bitten, union-hating, and completely insensitive to the misery of his workers' lives, he treated them with annoyance and contempt. In one trip to the fields his child asked to go into a mine. When Roche refused on the grounds that it was "too dangerous," she then asked how the men she saw around her could be sent there. It was a question with no answer, and it haunted her for years.

The coal wars culminated in 1914 with the Ludlow Massacre. In a bloody showdown between the U.M.W. and C.F. & I., state militiamen torched the miners' camp at Ludlow, killed women and children in the process, drove the U.M.W. from the state, and finally destroyed whatever power the miners had. Only one more spasm followed. In 1927, six miners died in a hail of state police bullets at Rocky Mountain Fuel's Columbine Mine in Weld County. Then, at last, came quiet.

It was into this world that Josephine Roche stepped in 1928 — a world of sullen miners, intransigent companies refusing to deal with them, and falling returns for all. She could do little about other companies. But she could, and did, do something about her own. Drawing deeply on old progressive principles, declaring that "capital and labor have equal rights" and that the old days of machine-gun justice were finally over, she initiated a program to help coal miners just as she had helped women and children before them.

Her actions were almost painfully simple. First, she invited the U.M.W. back to Colorado, back to her mines, where it was allowed to unionize, unimpeded. Then she instituted the highest wages in the coal industry (seven dollars a day) and reestablished collective bargaining. She even donated the surface of her coal lands to her workers so they might farm during months of low coal production. Above all, she became the miners' friend, learning their names, visiting their homes, sharing — as a person, not as a manager — their pain and their dreams. The heart of Roche's philosophy was that her company should be run for the benefit of those who dug its coal, not for the owners and stockholders who mined its profits. And in Colorado, in the mining industry, and in the nation, this tack marked an almost incredible reversal of a generation of paternalism, hatred, and industrial warfare.

Change, of course, did not come easily. Roche faced bitter antagonism from rival coal companies and the almost savage animosity of John D. Rockefeller, Jr. Like ancient manor lords controlled their serfs by keeping them on the land, the West's coal lords, particularly Rockefeller, suppressed theirs by miring them in company towns, indebting them to company stores, then shackling them to the lowest wage scale in the industrial world. When Roche shattered this tradition, she also shattered the solidarity that had made the coal combines so potent. Her action, in fact, threatened their very existence. For what Roche did, she was reviled by the coal men as a dangerous social-experimenting industrial radical and a traitor to their cause. Then they set out to destroy her.

To undercut Rocky Mountain Fuel and bring down Josephine Roche, C.F. & I. slashed coal prices (and its workers' wages with them), then watched the ripple effect run its course. Rocky Mountain Fuel was hurt immediately. Trapped between high wages on the one hand and falling coal prices on the other (caused mainly by the growing substitution of fuel oil for coal), the company nearly collapsed. But Rockefeller had underestimated not only Roche, but her workers as well. In the fall of 1931, Roche's miners loaned her half of their own wages — $80,000 — to keep the company afloat. For the moment, at least, the strategy worked. For the moment, at least, Roche had done what scores of men before her had not: She had survived the Rockefellers.

By 1932, with the nation falling deeper into the Great Depression, Rocky Mountain Fuel was in trouble again. And this time it did not get out of it. In desperation, Roche finally dropped company wages to $5.25 a day — then spent all of her days helping her workers survive the cut. She still gave them land to farm, gave them credit at her company store, devoted building materials to them for the weatherization of their homes. And still, as in the past, she visited their families and learned the names of their children. Her actions did little to alleviate the condition of the company, but they did catch the attention of Eleanor Roosevelt. One of the greatest humanitarians America ever produced called Roche one of the greatest humanitarians of her time.

In 1934, Roche ran for the governorship of Colorado against the Roosevelt-baiting, New Deal-hating Edwin C. Johnson, a vitriolic conservative Democrat with a record of anti-Washington political intransigence virtually unmatched in the Rockies. As an old progressive steeped in the Square Deal-New Nationalism of Theodore Roosevelt and in the laissez-faire liberalism of Woodrow Wilson, Roche firmly believed that in an age of depression, state reliance on federal government was the only option to human destruction. In that light, dismissing Johnson as the demagogue he sometimes was, and running on the slogan, "Roosevelt, Roche, and Recovery," she challenged him in a bitter primary. But she lost. Backed by the *Rocky Mountain News*, which said she had "already accomplished more than most Coloradans in government," and by her old friend Edward Costigan, who declared that "her candidacy is regarded everywhere as an event of national importance," Roche's always-controversial ideas of federal-state cooperation and government humanitarianism simply did not root. Unemployment insurance, old-age pensions, and the graduated income tax were simply issues of no great interest. It was the state's loss. "Her administration would mark a new era in our history," Costigan had said. But, sadly, it was a history never written.

In defeat, Roche still salvaged something. Among others, President Franklin D. Roosevelt had noticed that Roche was "the very embodiment of the New Deal in Colorado," as one columnist expressed it. More than anyone else in the state, she had sought industrial stability in unstable times; she had effectively applied the philosophy of the National Recovery Administration to her own industrial world and had saved the state millions of dollars in the process. Impressed by her record of humanity and convinced that what Colorado did not appreciate, the nation would, in November 1934, Roosevelt named Josephine Roche his assistant secretary of the treasury.

In a sense, the new position marked the culmination of Roche's public life. Asserting that "among our objectives I place the security of men, women, and children of this nation first," Roche, only the second woman ever to hold even a subcabinet rank in federal government, led 56,000 federal workers in an all-out battle against depression poverty. As head of the Public Health Service, Roche's primary job was to take Americans out of poorhouses and soup and bread lines and put them in programs with at least a semblance of economic security. In what she herself called a personal war against "human and economic waste," she achieved much. Then suddenly, it all ended.

When Roche went to Washington in 1934, she left the Rocky Mountain Fuel Company in a condition of accelerated deterioration. And over the years, the condition did not improve. What falling coal prices did not do to it on the one hand, the steadily increasing use of natural gas did on the other. Reluctantly, in the fall of 1937, Roche resigned her job in Washington to return to Denver to salvage what she could. Roosevelt, deeply disappointed by her loss, held her position open in the hope that she would return. But she did not. Although her crusades were not yet over — in 1938 she headed a national commission studying health care for the poor — the rest of the 1930s belonged to the coal company and its employees. For their part, Roche's workers finally returned the favor she had done them in 1928: By 1941, the U.M.W. had pledged $450,000 to her company in hopes of keeping it alive. In the end, though, it did no good. In 1944, Rocky Mountain Fuel filed for bankruptcy. The great social experiment was over.

As an entity, the company existed for many years (many of them in receivership) beyond the Great Depression. But Roche never actively ran it again. In the late 1940s, she became director of the U.M.W.'s pension fund, designed to "recognize human need and allay squalor and poverty," a position she considered "the highest privilege" she had ever had. Years later she retired to Washington, where she spent the rest of her life. In a 1975 interview with the *Rocky Mountain News*, Roche appeared as a tiny, ninety-year-old "wisp of a woman" whose face mirrored "an everchanging series of moods." She lived in the present and loathed the past, read the interview — a curious thing for a woman who had "made more history than most people read in a lifetime." Then, a year later her life ended in a nursing home in Bethesda, Maryland.

In the wake of her death, people remembered Josephine Roche as one of two persons — as the pragmatic businesswoman who sustained Rocky Mountain Fuel as a force in the mining industry long after its time had passed, and as the progressive humanitarian who wore causes like the buttons on her sleeves. In reality, of course, the two persons were always one, and it was the fusion of the two that made Roche as unique as she was. On the one hand she *was*, like Eleanor Roosevelt, the universal humanitarian, honored by Chi Omega in 1935 for her outstanding contributions to the "culture of the world," and living the principles of the award every day of her life. But she was also the brilliant businesswoman who focused, as one newspaper wrote, "not on what was wrong with sales, but what was wrong with the working conditions of men." In so doing, she came to typify a more hopeful future where business leaders might seek "to make the earth a safe place for humans as well as stocks and bonds." Roche "has studied men first and business second," concluded the paper, "and all businessmen could profit from the method."

In 1946, *Rocky Mountain News* editor Lee Casey wrote of Roche that "she knows what it's like to give one's self to a cause — the cause not only of aiding those less fortunate, but of trying to aid the less fortunate to help themselves. She set out to do it thirty years ago. She hasn't done it yet, and won't until her last trump is played, but she's made major strides because of her courage and loyalty and great common sense." Thirty years later, when she died, she still had not played the trump. But time and again she had tried. And those who knew "Josephine," and remembered her, did not forget.

Florence Rena Sabin

 O n February 26, 1959, a statue of Dr. Florence Rena Sabin was presented to the nation. Executed by sculptor Joy Buba of New York, the statue was Colorado's first contribution to the National Statuary Hall in the nation's capitol, where each state is entitled to two sculptures of its most honored citizens. It is both fitting and proper for Colorado, the second state in the nation (after Wyoming) to provide for political equality between the sexes, that its first contribution to grace this national parthenon honors a woman. It is also highly unfortunate that almost thirty years since the statue's dedication, few citizens know of the contributions that this dynamic physician made toward improving the quality of life in the Centennial State during the middle years of the twentieth century.

Like many members of pioneer families in Colorado, Florence Rena Sabin could trace her roots to the mining camps of the Rocky Mountains. Born on November 9, 1871, Florence was the second daughter of a Central City miner named George Sabin and his wife Serena. In 1875, the family moved to Denver. Serena Sabin died in childbirth three years later. Sometime after her mother's death, Florence and her sister Mary were sent east to live temporarily with their uncle in Chicago while father George got back on his feet. Apparently, their father's financial ventures

Florence Sabin.
Western History Department,
Denver Public Library.

were insufficient to raise the girls properly in frontier Denver, for they eventually wound up moving in with their grandparents in Vermont. While residing in New England, Florence and her sister demonstrated strong academic aptitudes early in their lives. Mary soon returned to Denver and began a long career as a mathematics teacher in the Denver public schools. Florence attended Smith College in Massachusetts, where she graduated Phi Beta Kappa in 1893.

While attending Smith, Florence Sabin became engrossed in science and research. Upon graduation she decided to pursue a medical career. Unfortunately, she soon came face to face with the discriminatory admission policies which characterized higher education during the Gilded Age. Few women were admitted to medical school. She returned to Denver, waiting for a chance. For three years Florence taught school at the city's Wolfe Hall Academy, a profession more socially acceptable for women of that generation. She would not give up her dream, however, and in 1896 she finally got her opportunity. Aided by a woman philanthropist and benefactor whose endowment stipulated that a certain number of young women would be admitted to medical school on an equal basis with men, Florence was accepted at Johns Hopkins University in Baltimore. There, she proved to be a top student despite numerous attempts by male professors to discourage their female students. During a concentrated obstetrics course which lasted two months, she was required to deliver nine infants. As a part of a research project, Florence Sabin developed a model of an infant's brain which was used in medical schools for many years thereafter. Despite the many barriers, she graduated with distinction from Johns Hopkins.

After her graduation in 1900, Sabin went on to a distinguished career in medical research. Although she had to fight continually against sexual discrimination within the profession, she won many honors. She was one of the first doctors in the country to extensively research the lymphatic system, blood cells, and tuberculosis. Her tuberculosis research provided a rethinking of how to deal with the terrible disease. She published a long-used textbook, *Atlas of the Medulla and Mid-Brain.* And her research findings were published in respected medical journals throughout the world.

Honors followed. In 1923, Florence Sabin was honored as the first woman elected to the National Academy of Sciences. She was the first woman president of the American Association of Anatomists and the first woman to serve on the staff of New York's prestigious Rockefeller Institute of Medical Research. She received honorary degrees from at least fifteen universities. *Pictorial Review* awarded her a cash prize in 1925 for "the most distinctive contribution made by an American woman to American life." In 1931, *Good Housekeeping* named her as one of twelve of America's greatest women (from 2,786 nominations). Among the other twelve were Jane Addams and Helen Keller. Dr. Simon Flexner, the head of the Rockefeller Institute, called her the "leading woman scientist in the world."

At the age of sixty-seven, Florence Sabin retired and moved back to Denver. She had never married. Although she fully intended to enjoy the mountains during her late years, it was not to be. Her career had already succeeded beyond the hopes and dreams of most people by the time of World War II. But it was not enough for Florence Rena Sabin. During the 1940s, she began what has been called her second career. The people of Colorado benefit today because of it.

Toward the end of World War II, Governor John Vivian appointed a series of state committees for postwar revitalization. Vowing that the State of Colorado must make ready for returning war veterans, Vivian appointed a host of prominent men to the new positions. *Denver Post* reporter Frances Wayne noticed, however, that Vivian had appointed no women to head up any of the new committees. One day she approached the Republican governor and demanded an explanation. Tutored in the prudent style of the political campaigner, Vivian blandly asked Wayne whom she might suggest for one of the offices. Wayne informed the governor that one of the most prominent women in America was currently living in retirement in Denver — Florence Sabin. It is doubtful that Governor Vivian was aware of Dr. Sabin's accomplishments, if indeed, he even knew who she was. Nevertheless, Vivian appointed Florence Sabin to head the new state health subcommittee, certain that a seventy-three-year-old retired woman would not make any political waves. He was wrong.

Florence Sabin took her new position seriously. She crossed the state at her own expense investigating health conditions in both urban and rural areas. The findings were appalling. Though long known as a refuge for invalids, Colorado of the early 1940s was one of the unhealthiest states in the union. It had one of the highest infant mortality rates. It was fifth in the nation in incidence of diphtheria. Only two other states ranked lower than Colorado in the rate of deaths caused by scarlet fever. Worst of all, there were no regulations providing for the uniform pasteurization of milk. It seemed that the Department of Health was nothing more than a dumping ground for political hacks, loyal party members appointed by appreciative, victorious governors; the staff had little aptitude or training in health or medicine. In fact, most of the state's health laws had been passed in 1876 at the time of statehood. They had never been modified or updated.

Florence Rena Sabin immediatley set out to make sweeping changes. Utilizing her own money, she again canvassed the state, gaining support for a new health program. She turned her subcommittee into a political action group under the slogan "Health to Match Our Mountains." Usually prefacing her speeches with the words, "We think of our state as a health resort, yet we're dying faster than people in most states," Florence Sabin demanded sweeping reform in Colorado's primitive health codes. She advocated eight measures that became popularly known as the Sabin health laws; they included removal of the health department from politics, required pasteurization of all milk, sewage control, public health education, and the establishfment of local health boards throughout the state. Although some interest groups like dairy farmers and religious fundamentalists objected, Florence Sabin met any and all opposition with a determined front. Politically, her measures were popular and those who opposed her reform ideas usually went down to defeat.

Among the groups that found themselves out of favor (and out of the statehouse) in 1946 was the conservative state Republican Party. Due in part to his support of Sabin's crusade, Democratic gubernatorial candidate Lee Knous won an upset victory that year. By April 1947, even the Republican-controlled General Assembly had seen the light and narrowly passed the Sabin health program into law. At the age of seventy-five, Florence Sabin had won the most important battle of her illustrious career. Although she declined the new governor's appointment as head of the reorganized Board of Health, Florence remained active in politics. In May 1947, she endorsed Quigg Newton for mayor of Denver when he promised to take the city health department out of politics. When he won election, he appointed Florence Sabin manager of the Denver Department of Health and Charities. She accepted.

Once again the aging physician pushed her causes. She dedicated herself to instituting a city-wide X-ray program to check for tuberculosis. The abundance of rats in the city bothered her.

In a series of speeches she vividly described the vermin-infested trash dumps and filthy streets in the city's inner core. Soon Florence Sabin became a force to reckon with in Denver. She called for increases in vocational training for the poor. Only by insuring that people did not wind up on welfare, she believed, would they remain healthy. Poverty, believed Florence Sabin, bred filth, unsanitary conditions, and a lowered health standard. If her Department of Health and Charities was to fulfill its mission to the fullest, the level of education in Denver had to be raised.

Finally, in 1951, at age eighty, Florence Sabin retired for the last time. Two years later, on October 3, 1953, she suffered a heart attack and died during the seventh inning stretch of the World Series game she was watching on television. (She had become an avid baseball fan during her younger days in medical school at Johns Hopkins.)

During her second career, Florence Rena Sabin did her job very well. Today the automobile, rather then infectious disease, is the chief health culprit. The brown cloud of carbon monoxide along Colorado's front range is second only to Los Angeles in creating public health problems. Combined with a higher than desirable number of toxic waste dumps and nuclear facilities near populated areas, these environmental hazards of the 1980s are once again casting a shadow on Colorado's historic reputation as a health resort. Nevertheless, the state's rate of communicable disease is among the lowest in the nation. All things considered, the state's population has increased at alarming rates during the past three decades despite efforts to limit unchecked growth. Every day new arrivals see the Rocky Mountains on the horizon and set down their roots. And they give thanks for a chance to live in a region which possesses, in their estimation, a quality of life superior to that found in overcrowded eastern cities or along the West Coast. In no small margin was that quality of life enhanced by a whirlwind humanitarian who is now referred to as Colorado's "woman of the century"— Dr. Florence Rena Sabin.

Wayne Aspinall

Wayne Aspinall, author Philip Fradkin has written, was a man who "did not know when to quit." When he died in 1983, this might have been his epitaph.

On April 3, 1896, on a small farm near Middleburg, Ohio, Jessie Aspinall gave birth to a son. She and her husband Mack named him Wayne Norviel, then watched him grow, season by season, alongside their crops. When the boy was eight, the family moved to Colorado. It settled in Palisade, where the north slope of the Grand Mesa bottomed out and the Colorado River flowed by below it. Beneath the ribbed white shale cliffs that gave Palisade its name, Mack Aspinall nurtured his orchards, and his son went to school. Hunting the high country in fall, fishing Plateau Creek in summer, the young man developed a deep love for the place. Watching the Colorado ebb at his feet, watching the land bathed in afternoon sun, he could not have imagined then how inextricably bound his own existence would be with them.

In 1915, Wayne Aspinall enrolled at the University of Denver. Four years later he graduated with a bachelor of arts degree; ten years later in 1924, he received a bachelor of laws. In between degrees he taught school in Palisade, and when he was admitted to the bar, it was to Palisade that he returned to practice. Slowly,

Wayne Aspinall.
Western History Department,
Denver Public Library.

he became immersed in the civic life of the country town. At twenty-four he chaired the Mount Lincoln School Board and served as town trustee. Then, slowly — as talented small-town country lawyers have done for generations — he drifted into local politics. Moving swiftly up through the ranks of Mesa County Democrats, Aspinall was elected to the Colorado state house of representatives in 1930 and served there for eight years (two of them as speaker). In November 1938 he moved to the senate, where he served a decade more as both majority and minority leader and as an expert member of the senate's committees on agriculture and irrigation. By the end of his eighteenth year on Capitol Hill, Aspinall was still a thin, gawky countryman with the twentieth-century look of an eighteenth-century Ichabod Crane. But he was also one of Colorado's shrewdest and most efficient legislators. In that year, 1948, Fourth District

Democrats chose him over Thomas Matthews of Grand Junction to run for Congress. On election day he beat Republican Robert Rockwell of Paonia. In 1949, as he packed his bags for the trip east, Aspinall could not have known it, but he would not see the white cliffs of Palisade again — except for visits — for the next quarter century.

From the beginning, Washington was business to Aspinall, not romance. There was no doubt that the man from Palisade was awed by what he found there — a Congress so steeped in tradition that its members still wore tailed coats and top hats, yet a body so legislatively powerful that the whole world watched it. But if Aspinall was awed, he was not intimidated. At fifty-three, he was not naive. Pushed by a fierce desire to work, and armed with the experience of eighteen years of legislative combat in Colorado to go with it, Aspinall settled in. Given a position on the House Reclamation Subcommittee, he becan to carve a deep niche for himself in a city and a system as far removed from western Colorado as an alien planet.

Aspinall's primary responsibility was to serve his Fourth District — twenty-four counties strewn over 43,000 square miles, holding 150,000 people from Grand County to the Four Corners. In some ways service was difficult. Size and space alone created serious problems, and the sharp divergence of the district's three Eastern Slope counties (Park, Lake, and Chaffee) from those on the Western Slope compounded them. But on the other hand, Aspinall also had the advantage of dealing with a section in which only two issues — land and water — were paramount. In the end, size and space and regional fractiousness were all incidental; the overriding questions of land and water, and what to do with them, created a common interest among almost all the citizens of the district that neutralized everything else. All Aspinall had to do was understand what the common will was, then act on it.

In 1949, the public will was easily defined. Most people in Aspinall's district felt generally the same about the land they inhabited and the rivers that washed it: The land existed to be developed and the rivers existed to be dammed. The ethic was as old as the country itself, stretching as far back into time as its holders could remember. Natural resources, they believed, were for use, not contemplation. "You can't eat mountains," they used to say, and in 1949 they still said it. And the same was true with water. There may have been some among them who disagreed, but not many. Conservation may have been a part of life in other parts of America, even other parts of the West, but it was not a part of life in the Fourth Congressional District of Colorado.

Nothing, of course, affected the daily life of the region like the great river that bisected it. In a land where water was the essence of life, the Colorado was the king of waters. With it the land bloomed. Without it, and others like it, the land withered and died. Because of this, a fact of life in the desert West as old as the West itself, the damming of the Colorado and the storage of its waters was as vital to the people along its path as anything else in existence.

It was this ageless condition that shaped an ageless philosophy. The people of the Fourth District may have understood little else, but they understood water law. They understood that since the Colorado River Compact of 1922 — which "split" the river at Lee's Ferry, Arizona, and allocated its flow equally to clusters of states both below and above the line — they received only a certain portion each year of the river that began in their own state. They also understood that Colorado, Wyoming, Utah, and New Mexico then split the split. And they knew that under the doctrine of "use it or lose it," upstream states that failed to put their allocations to "beneficial use" stood to lose their legal rights to downstream states that did. When Wayne Aspinall went to Washington, the mood of western Colorado was that the state should catch, dam, and store every drop of the Colorado that it could. If it could hold it, and put it to beneficial use, none of the state's precious allotment would ever flow downstream. And with it, the land, as Brigham Young had once said, would "blossom like the rose."

In effect, then, like the land around it, the river had to be mined.

In 1949, the year that Aspinall took his congressional seat, the lower Colorado had been in the process of development for twenty years. In 1935, Hoover Dam had ushered in a whole new era of multipurpose western water projects — dams accompanied by reservoirs — some of them providing hydroelectric power and flood control, and all of them storing water for "beneficial use." By 1949, the lower river was studded with big dams, and huge reservoirs behind them, with more in the planning stage and all of them ready to store not only lower basin water, but upper basin water as well should upstream states forfeit it. But if the lower Colorado was being dammed, the upper river was not — and to western Colorado this was a catastrophe in the making. Operating on the ageless assumption that western Colorado would die if the river were not dammed and used, Aspinall, in his influential position on the House Reclamation Subcommittee, began to act.

With his "mandate" from Colorado, Aspinall quickly became the primary congressional force behind upper Colorado development. But in his first eight years he achieved little. Despite his best efforts to bring a comprehensive upper Colorado bill to the House floor, he was stopped again and again by the Eisenhower administration and its congressional allies. "The West will get lots of talk about reclamation," said a bitter Aspinall, "but can expect little in the way of dams. Not since Theodore Roosevelt has the Republican party wholeheartedly supported reclamation." Sometime in the early 1950s, Aspinall made a choice: He could peacefully coexist with Republicans or he could hound them. The choice was made. Ascending to the chairmanship of the House Interior and Insular Affairs Committee — one of the most powerful positions in American government — he began to push.

As much because of Aspinall's relentless pursuit as any other single factor, work on the upper Colorado finally began in 1956. Within a few years, massive Glen Canyon Dam appeared near the Arizona border, eventually backing up 27 million acre feet of precious water in Lake Powell. The spectacular Flaming Gorge Dam followed in northeast Utah, then Blue Mesa Dam on the Gunnison River in Colorado and Navajo Dam in northern New Mexico. And beyond them forty more projects spread across the planning board. In the process of transforming the upper

Colorado, no one stood out in more vivid relief than Aspinall. There were dozens of other western legislators in the movement, of course, all of them influential and some of them legendary. But none of them had the importance of Aspinall. And none of them realized it like he did. Running for reelection in 1960, he asked his constituents for three more terms (to 1966) until the Colorado River storage program was in its completion stages. Then, his job done, he hoped to rest.

Aspinall was returned to Washington in 1960, then again in 1962. In that year he began working toward implementation of Colorado's Fryingpan-Arkansas Project, one of the most significant in the state's history, on the grounds that if it were not undertaken, "we'll be going downhill with the whole Colorado reclamation program." Promising a "do or die" charge at one of the most ambitious transmontane diversion projects in America's history, Aspinall passionately argued — in the midst of almost incredible controversy — that if the project failed, others would fail with it, and "the whole reclamation program of the West" would falter and "development of our great natural resources" would suffer a "terrible blow." If it failed, he concluded, "nothing else of consequence will happen again." As the chief overseer of the nation's water projects, he saw to it that it did not fail. In 1962, Congress approved the Fryingpan-Arkansas Project, a $180 million development to divert water from the Western Slope's Fryingpan River (a Colorado tributary) through a tunnel under the Continental Divide to the Arkansas River basin in the east. In the arid West's long battle to harness the Colorado, it was one of the most significant of all victories.

By the tail end of the 1960s — reelected in 1966 and 1968 and moving inexorably toward the end of his career — Aspinall was the most powerful public water broker in America. And he believed still more development to be necessary. In 1968, in what turned out to be his swan song, Aspinall forced the inclusion of five final upper Colorado River projects — Animas-La Plata, Dolores, Dallas Creek, San Miguel, and West Divide, all of them in his home district — into a bill authorizing the lower Colorado Central Arizona Project. To the bitter end, Aspinall the Interior chair was also Aspinall the horsetrader: In return for his support of Arizona's project, he forced Arizona to write the Colorado projects into its own bill.

Then he rested.

Throughout the years of Colorado River development, for all of Aspinall's participation in it, he was hardly a one-dimensional man. He was not so partly because his position as Interior chair never allowed him to be. But he also was not because his interests — again mainly with reference to western Colorado — extended far beyond the river. Almost as important to him, for what they were and were not, were the public lands that embraced it.

Aspinall believed that if the river had to be mined, so did the land beyond it, particularly the vast, untapped expanses of public lands which his committee oversaw. It was not an idle belief; with Aspinall it was an article of faith. In 1966, criticized by a young state legislator, Richard Lamm, for his views on resource use, Aspinall replied, "I have always believed the Creator placed natural resources to be used as well as viewed, and to be used by the people generally." Candid and blunt perhaps to a fault, Aspinall pursued this canon for twenty-four years, just as he did the principle of water storage. In the process, he came to demonstrate the ethic of resource development more clearly than any public figure in the West.

Aspinall's belief — consistent with that of most other westerners in the 1950s and at least the early 1960s — was that the development of western land and resources was vital both for the economic benefits it brought to the developed regions and for the economic stability of the nation that used them. Fallow land, to him, was useless land. It contributed no strategic metals to the nation's stockpile or fuel for its energy needs. It offered no timber for harvest or even grass for cattle. Its very uselessness eroded the stability of both region and nation. Conversely, productive land — land that yielded mineral or lumber or grass — was the heart of life. Aspinall appreciated beauty and the lay of the land. But he did not appreciate, and could not tolerate, its idleness.

To that end, and in the belief that as America's storehouse it was the West's particular mission to supply the nation with raw materials, Aspinall led a twenty-four-year crusade to open up the western public domain to maximum use. On one front, he was one of the first to push for shale oil recovery in western Colorado. He doggedly supported mining, lumbering, and large cattle interests in their efforts to develop and utilize the public domain. Most important, he consistently used his position as chair of the House Interior Committee to promote legislation that encouraged development and to kill legislation that did not. In that context, too, he became one of the most potent forces in Congress battling the 1960s movement toward wilderness preservation.

If the upper Colorado storage program was the pinnacle of Aspinall's water development plan, his 1964 attempt to create a Public Lands Review Commission to codify all public land laws and reclassify the public lands they covered marked the high point of the comprehensive resource development plan he had chased since 1949. Remarking that "I vigorously challenge those who say all the present federal lands should remain in federal ownership," Aspinall insisted that it was "imperative for the economic and political advancement of the West that big blocks of uncommitted acreage be made available for private development under the free enterprise system." To that end he fought for the legislative establishment of a committee that would review all public land laws, clearly define developable and undevelopable lands and separate them, then invite their private development so that the "natural resource harvest" would continue. In the end the commission was formed, and for five years it worked (with Aspinall its chair) on a final recommendation to set before the Congress. But while Congress finally accepted its massive report, it did not act on it. That it did not adopt the commission's land disposal formula marked one of the bitterest disappointments of Aspinall's life.

Up to 1964 or 1965, Wayne Aspinall remained the House kingpin of western land and water affairs, imperial and unchallenged, the kind of politician who looked like he could rule forever. But even at the peak of his power, life was changing around him — changing slowly, to be sure, but changing nonetheless. Nationally, attitudes were beginning to change about public lands disposal, and the change was deep, profound, and lasting. Attitudes about water projects were also beginning to shift in the same subtle way. Whether or not Aspinall ever understood this was never clear. In 1966, he faced a major challenge from Republican Jim Johnson in the Fourth District, then won and shook it off. In dismissing the election's closeness, however, he made a fatal mistake. A steamroller was bearing down on Aspinall, and all indications were that he never saw it coming.

By the late 1960s, much of Aspinall's water development policy was finally returning to haunt him. As early as 1960, for example, he had come under criticism in his own district for advocating the diversion of Western Slope water to the east, and in 1962 Fourth District Republicans asked each registered voter in the district to contribute to a fund to retire the congressman — principally because of his support for the Fryingpan-Arkansas Project. More and more, too, people began to blame Aspinall for the overallocation of Colorado River water and the widespread damage that had begun to result from it. Whether the issue was salinity, the overappropriation of water rights to coal and shale oil interests, or the physical desecration of the river itself, the Colorado system's problems all came to rest on Aspinall's doorstep. The charge had been made before, but it was made more openly and more caustically now: Aspinall was no longer "Mr. Water." He was "Mr. Boondoggle," the last of a dying Washington breed more interested in pork for his district — to which he had given $1 billion in water projects — than in progress for the nation.

More ominous for Aspinall than changing attitudes about water storage and big dams were sharply changing ideas — even in his own district — about land use. The 1960s marked the apex of a national conservation movement that had been born with Theodore Roosevelt and John Muir and had roared unchecked through the twentieth century. Over the course of six decades, once-cavalier attitudes about the land and its meaning in the life of the nation had undergone almost incredible transformation, even in the West. There were those, to be sure, who still believed that the land was to be used first and saved second. But there were also those, more and more, who believed that its beauty was more important to society than the money its resources fetched at market. As their numbers grew, so did their influence. But this fact Aspinall apparently never understood or accepted.

The new environmentalists disliked Aspinall, and some of them loathed him. Part of their attitude stemmed from his water policies — his attempt, for example, to build dams in the Grand Canyon, and similar support for the Echo Park Dam on the Green River near Dinosaur National Monument. They also opposed his catering to large mining, shale oil, lumbering, and cattle interests that either bought or leased large parcels of the public domain for what their enemies considered dubious purposes. Aspinall's 1965 effort to give 4 million acres of public domain shale land to oil companies, his 1966 fight against creation of Redwood National Park in California (delaying Interior hearings on it while it was badly overlumbered), his fight against Lyndon Johnson's 7.6 million-acre national park withdrawals, his similar fight against amendments to the Clean Air Act, his efforts to cripple the National Environmental Policy Act, and his successful strategies to keep grazing fees low and antiquated mining laws on the books simply no longer set well with growing numbers of people.

Aspinall's nadir may have been his fight against the 1964 Wilderness Act, a measure first proposed in 1957, which eventually placed 15 million acres of pristine forest wilderness in the protective custody of the federal government and outlawed virtually all forms of development on them. In 1963, despite personal pleas from President John F. Kennedy that he release it, Aspinall bottled up the bill (which had passed the Senate in 1961) until he received assurances that mining would be allowed in withdrawn wilderness territory. When he received the assurances, he released the bill from committee. On September 3, 1964, the law passed, by all odds one of the most important pieces of legislation in American history. When it did, Aspinall had played a key role in its passage.

But while the bill had not died, Aspinall had played a key role in its near death. An intransigent Aspinall insisted, conservation or not, wilderness or not, that public lands still had to be disposed of to "provide the maximum benefit for the general public." "To remain silent and take no action," he concluded, constituted "consent to the limitation of further development." Little wonder it was, then, that Aspinall was named to the "Dirty Dozen" of Washington-based Environmental Action and targeted with other anti-environmentalists for defeat in the election of 1972.

In 1970, the clock ticked down for Wayne Aspinall. Forced into the first primary of his career, he narrowly beat University of Northern Colorado political science professor Richard Perchlik for the Fourth District congressional seat. Then he narrowly beat Republican rancher William Gossard of Craig in the general election. Among his opponents were rising numbers of environmentalists whom he dismissed as "McGovernites" and "wilderness zealots," who considered him to be, finally, out of step with his times. In 1972, the bell tolled: Forced into yet another primary by Alan Merson, a young law professor at the University of Denver, Aspinall was finally beaten. Only 1,635 votes separated the thirty-eight-year-old newcomer from the seventy-six-year-old warhorse. But it might as well have been a million. A career had ended. And so had an era.

Wayne Aspinall returned to private life and lived for ten more years. In October 1983, at the age of eighty-seven, he died of cancer at his Palisade home. Not far away the Colorado rolled silently by. "The river means the West to me," he had once said. "It is the heart of my West." It was the river, probably, and the land that stretched beyond it, that were the last things he ever saw.

When the old man died, he was mourned by all who knew him. In the small mining and farming towns of the Western Slope, where Aspinall's jowly face had been as familiar as summer sun, people remembered what he had done in taming the desert and stimulating the economy. "Crusty," they called him. "Arbitrary" and "unmovable." But above all they called him beneficial to Colorado. He had been a "giant of a man," said Senator Gary Hart, whose record and achievements would be "permanently imprinted on the West." Added sometime critic

Governor Richard Lamm: "He exemplified all the virtues of the state. He was tough. He was honest. He had a total dedication to preserving the beauty of our mountains and plains and a full appreciation of our natural wealth. Any good history book will recount his contributions."

Along the Potomac his colleagues shared the view. Honest, fair, thorough, knowledgeable, trustworthy they called him, the kind of man who checked in at dawn and worked until dusk. The kind of man, they remembered, who rode to work not with the House speaker but with the House doorkeeper, and who shunned formal affairs because he hated formal dress. The kind of man so awed by his office, in fact, that he opened and answered his own mail. All who knew him understood that he had wielded almost unprecedented power and that he had come as close as any man alive to actually governing the public lands and waters of the American West. But they also knew that he had wielded his power with fairness and that he had never sacrificed honesty for a deal. And they knew, most of all, that for all the baggage he carried as the quintessential dam-building, wilderness-busting western politico, he was never really that at all.

So what crime had he committed to lose his office? None. He had committed no crime. But he had become an anachronism.

"Water?" he once said. "No person has been a leader like I have." And even Richard Lamm agreed: "We shouldn't be able to take a drink of water in Colorado without remembering him." Resource use? To the bitter end, railing against "ecology freaks" and "well-intentioned zealots who cause the nation to lose its chance to continue to be a strong power," he insisted that he was more of a conservationist than any of them.

There was truth in what he said, but by 1972, it was largely irrelevant. The problem was that if Aspinall had been in step in the past, he was not in step anymore. In an age where big dams and big water projects were no longer politically acceptable or economically feasible, Aspinall continued to push for them as if nothing had ever changed. That made him anachronistic — not evil, but anachronistic. And in an era of increasing environmental consciousness, his blistering tirades against ecological "faddists" and their "emotional environmental binges" and "near hysteria" illustrated the same condition. Aspinall was right when he said that "people cannot exist without using the crust of the earth." But his charges that the "ecology group wanted all the public lands to play on" and "wanted to lick them all up as wilderness" and "keep others out so they can use it themselves" hurt him badly. "The rest of us are realists," he concluded. "We know we wouldn't be here if we weren't using nature's bounty." But in the end it was the realist who was the most unrealistic of all.

In 1983, when Aspinall died, former governor John Vanderhoof composed what might have been his epitaph. "He'll go down in history as one of the great leaders of the West," said Vanderhoof. "He created monuments that were not static. They will be used for generations and generations. Thank God there was a man of his caliber to do the work when it needed to be done." It was a fitting tribute to a true man of the West, but it might have included two other thoughts: That there was no middle ground on a battleground, and that no one could outrun change forever.

Not even Wayne Aspinall.

Bibliographical Notes

JUAN BAUTISTA DE ANZA

An overview of Anza's role in the Southwest may be found in Herbert E. Bolton, *Coronado: Knight of the Pueblos and Plains* (Albuquerque: The University of New Mexico Press, 1949), and C.H. Haring, *The Spanish Empire in America* (New York: Harcourt, Brace & World, 1963). For a good description of the San Carlos community, see Carl Ubbelohde, Maxine Benson, and Duane Smith, *A Colorado History* (Boulder, CO: Pruett Publishing Company, 1982). An excellent sketch of Anza in Colorado is Walter R. Borneman, "He Walked in Step with the Future," *Denver Post: Empire Magazine*, September 2, 1979.

SUSAN SHELBY MAGOFFIN

The diary of Susan Shelby Magoffin, *Down the Santa Fe Trail and into Mexico* (Lincoln, NE: University of Nebraska Press, 1982) is the classic account of this young woman's trek across the prairie of Kansas and Colorado. Other sources include Ray Allen Billington and Martin Ridge, *Western Expansion: A History of the American Frontier*, 5th edition (New York and London: Macmillan Publishing Company, 1982); Colorado Historical Society, *Bent's*

Old Fort (Denver: State Historical Society of Colorado, 1979); Josiah Gregg, *Commerce of the Prairies* (Lincoln, NE: University of Nebraska Press, 1957; first published, 1826); Kate Gregg, ed., *The Road to Santa Fe: The Journal and Diaries of George Champlain Sibley* (Albuquerque: University of New Mexico Press, 1952); and Sandra Myres, *Westering Women and the Frontier Experience, 1800-1915* (Albuquerque: University of New Mexico Press, 1982).

ALEXANDER MAJORS

Although somewhat biased, the most complete account of the life and times of Alexander Majors is Raymond W. and Mary L. Settle, *War Drums and Wagon Wheels: The Story of Russell, Majors, and Waddell* (Lincoln, NE: University of Nebraska Press, 1966). Other material is in Billington and Ridge, *Westward Expansion, A History of the American Frontier*, 5th edition (New York and London: Macmillan Publishing Company, 1982); and Martin Ridge and Ray Allen Billington, eds., *America's Frontier Story: A Documentary History of Westward Expansion* (New York: Holt, Rinehart & Winston, 1969).

BLACK KETTLE

For Chief Black Kettle, see Frank Hall, *A History of the State of Colorado*, Vol. 1 (Chicago: Rocky Mountain Historical Company, 1889); Stan Hoig's definitive *Sand Creek Massacre* (Norman: University of Oklahoma Press, 1961); and William K. Powers, *Indians of the Northern Plains* (New York: Capricorn Books, G.P. Putnam & Sons, 1973). For articles, see John O'Leary, "Black Kettle: A Brief Profile," *American Indian Crafts and Culture*, Vol. 7, No. 9, November 1973; George Rawlins, "Old Times Corral," *True West*, Vol. 4, No. 4, April 1957; Colin W. Rickards, "Black Kettle: The West's Most Ill-Fated Indian," *Westerner's Brand Book*, English Corral, Vol. 6, Nos. 2 and 3, December 1957 - January 1958; and Gary L. Roberts, "A Message from Black Kettle," *American West*, Vol. 9, No. 3, May 1972.

JACK STILLWELL and SIG SCHLESINGER

There are some stirring accounts of the Battle of Beecher Island. The unique material pertaining to the Stillwell-Schlesinger relationship can be found in Cyrus Townsend Brady, *Indian Fights and Fighters* (Lincoln, NE: University of Nebraska Press, 1971; first published, 1904). Also see George Bird Grinnell, *The Fighting Cheyennes* (Norman: University of Oklahoma Press, 1966; first published, 1915); William H. Leckie, *The Military Conquest of the Southern Plains* (Norman: University of Oklahoma Press, 1963); and Paul I. Wellman, *The Indian Wars of the West* (New York and Garden City: Doubleday Company, 1947).

CERAN ST. VRAIN

For material on Ceran St. Vrain, see Edward Broadhead, *Ceran St. Vrain, 1802-1870* (Pueblo, CO: Pueblo County Historical Society, 1982); Harold H. Dunham, *Mountain Men and Fur Traders of the Far West*, LeRoy Hafen, ed. (Lincoln, NE: University of Nebraska Press, 1982); Michael McNierney, ed., *Taos 1847: The Revolt in Contemporary Accounts* (Boulder, CO: Johnson Publishing Company, 1982); Nolie Mumey, "Black Beard," *Denver Westerners Monthly Roundup*, Vol. XIV, No. 1, January 1958; and David Lavender, "Adobe Empire," *Denver Post: Empire Magazine*, December 5, 1954. Lavender's book, *Bent's Fort* (New York and Garden City: Dolphin Books, 1954) remains one of the most interesting accounts of the trading post.

GEORGE GRIFFITH

Material for George Griffith can be found in Sandra Dallas, *Colorado Ghost Towns and Mining Camps* (Norman: University of Oklahoma Press, 1985); Liston Leyendecker, *Georgetown: Colorado's Silver Queen, 1859-1876* (Fort Collins, CO: Centennial Publications, 1977); Rodman Wilson Paul, *Mining Frontiers of the Far West, 1848-1880* (Albuquerque: University of New Mexico Press,

1974); and Muriel Sibell Wolle, *Stampede to Timberline* (Denver: Sage Books, 1962).

"POKER ALICE" TUBBS

Material on the cigar-smoking "Poker Alice" Tubbs can be found in Kay Reynolds Blair, *Ladies of the Lamplight* (Leadville, CO: Timberline Books, 1971); the *Denver Post*, February 19, 1950; and the *Omaha World Herald*, March 29, 1919. The quote by Steckmesser is from Kent Ladd Steckmesser, *The Westward Movement: A Short History* (New York: McGraw-Hill Book Company, 1969).

DAVID DAY

David Day's life can be reconstructed from an extensive set of newspaper clippings from the *Denver Post*; the *Rocky Mountain News*; Ouray, Colorado's *Solid Muldoon* and *Inter Ocean*.

CHIN LIN SOU

Accounts of the life and times of Chin Lin Sou are scarce. An excellent early account of his life in Black Hawk, Colorado, is in *Field and Farm*, June 21, 1919. Other sources include the *Denver Post*, July 15, 1973, and Francis Melrose, "Rocky Mountain Memories," *Rocky Mountain News*, May 20, 1984. A good interpretation of Denver's anti-Chinese riots in 1880 can be found in Lyle W. Dorsett and Michael McCarthy, *The Queen City: A History of Denver*, 2nd edition (Boulder, CO: Pruett Publishing Company, 1986).

OTTO MEARS

An interesting original source for the Mears' story is Sidney Jocknick, *Early Days on the Western Slope of Colorado and Campfire Chats with Otto Mears, the Pathfinder, from 1870 to 1883, Inclusive* (Glorietta, NM: Rio Grande Press, 1968; first published, 1913). Other sources are Ervan F. Kushner, *Otto Mears: His Life and Times with Notes on the Alferd Packer Case* (Frederick, CO: Jende-Hagen Book Corp./Platte N Press, 1979); David Lavender, *The Great Divide* (New York and Garden City: Doubleday Company, 1948); and Lavender's story on Otto Mears in the *Denver Post: Empire Magazine*, November 21, 1948.

NICHOLAS CREEDE

The Creede story is relatively obscure. Much undated material can be found in the Lute Johnson Scrapbook in the Western History Department of the Denver Public Library. A good analysis of Creede and David Moffat is an editorial written by Cy Warman in the *Denver Times*, July 27, 1902. Other newspaper sources included the *Creede Candle*, March 5, 1904; the *Denver Post*, July 2, 1910; the *Denver Republican*, July 13 and 14, 1897; the *Denver Times*, November 8, 1899, July 7, and November 23, 1900; and the *Rocky Mountain News*, March 12 and 24, 1892, January 18 and August 10, 1897, May 25, June 13, and November 15, 1899.

ALFERD PACKER

Sources for Alferd Packer included Alice Polk Hill, *Tales of the Colorado Pioneers* (Glorietta, NM: Rio Grande Press, 1964; first published, 1884); Sidney Jocknick, *Early Days on the Western Slope* (Glorietta, NM: Rio Grande Press, 1968; first published, 1913); Robert Fenwick, "Alferd Packer: The True Story of the Colorado Man-Eater," *Denver Post: Empire Magazine*, April 21, April 28, May 5, 1963; and Duane Vandenbusche, *Early Days in the Gunni-*

son Country (Gunnison, CO: B. & B. Printers, 1974). The quote by Ruxton is in George F. Ruxton, *Adventures in Mexico and the Rocky Mountains* (London: Privately published, 1849).

FRANCES JACOBS

For the life of Frances Jacobs, see Elinor Bluemel, *One Hundred Years of Colorado Women* (Denver: Williamson-Hoffner Company, 1914); *The Trail*, Vol. 5, No. 12 (May 1913); a series of reports in the *Rocky Mountain News* for November 1900; and undated newspaper reports from the *Rocky Mountain News* and the *Denver Post* in the Western History Department of the Denver Public Library.

TOM HORN

For material on the controversial Horn case, see Dane Coolidge, *Fighting Men of the West* (Freeport and New York: Books for Libraries Press, 1960); Tom Horn, *Life of Tom Horn: Government Scout and Interpreter with an Introduction by Dan Krakel* (Norman: University of Oklahoma Press, 1964; first published, 1904); T.A. Larson, *History of Wyoming* (Lincoln, NE: University of Nebraska Press, 1965); and the *Rocky Mountain News*, August 10 and 21, 1903.

ANN BASSETT

Fine material for Ann Bassett can be found in Ann Bassett Willis, "Queen Ann of Brown's Park," *Colorado Magazine*, April 1952; Mary Ellen Barber, "The Queen of Brown's Park," *Denver Post: Empire Magazine*, August 17, 1980; and Frances Melrose, "Big Cattlemen Force Ann to Fight Back," *Rocky Mountain News*, December 20, 1984.

SOAPY SMITH

For Soapy Smith's colorful story, see William R. Collier and Edwin V. Westrate, *The Reign of Old Soapy Smith: Monarch of Misrule in the Last Days of the Old West and the Klondike Gold Rush* (New York and Garden City: Doubleday Company, 1935); Leland Feitz, *Soapy Smith's Creede* (Colorado Springs: Little London Press, 1973); and Bull Hemingway, "Soapy Smith: King of the Colorado Con Men," *Denver Post: Empire Magazine*, July 2, 1978.

CASIMIRO BARELA

Information on the life of Casimiro Barela can be found in the *Denver Times*, March 13, 1899, and April 2 and 10, 1902. Other material is Inez Hunt, *The Barela Brand* (Colorado Springs: Division of Instructional Services, Colorado Springs Public Schools, 1971). Information on the modern chicano movement may be found in Carl Abbott, Stephen J. Leonard, and David McComb, *Colorado: A History of the Centennial State* (Boulder, CO: Colorado Associated University Press, 1982); an excellent interpretation of Federico Peña's election as mayor of Denver can be found in Dorsett and McCarthy, *The Queen City: A History of Denver*, 2nd edition (Boulder, CO: Pruett Publishing Company, 1986).

WALTER VON RICHTHOFEN

For material on the eccentric Walter von Richthofen, see newspaper clippings from the *Denver Republican*, the *Denver Times*, the *Denver Post*, and the *Rocky Mountain News*. An excellent history of the Montclair experiment and the condition of historic residences in the Montclair neighborhood is Thomas J. Noel, *Richthofen's Montclair* (Boulder, CO: Pruett Publishing Company, 1976). Other useful material is in Edith Kohl, *Denver's Historic Mansions* (Denver: Sage Books, 1957).

LEWIS PRICE

For material on Lewis Price, see newspaper articles from March 1890 to January 1920 in the *Denver Herald, Denver Post, Denver Times,* and the *Rocky Mountain News.*

WILLIAM LESSIG

The troubled life of William Lessig can be reconstructed from an extensive series of nineteenth-century *Rocky Mountain News* clippings housed in the Western History Department of the Denver Public Library.

ENOS MILLS

The introductory quote for the Enos Mill's story is found in Isabella Bird, *A Lady's Life in the Rocky Mountains* (Norman: University of Oklahoma Press, 1960; first published, 1879). Material on Enos Mills can be found in C.W. Buchholtz, *Rocky Mountain National Park: A History* (Boulder: Colorado Associated University Press, 1983); Enos Mills, *The Story of Estes Park* (Privately published, 1980); Enos Mills, *Early Estes Park* (Estes Park: Privately published, 1972); Ruth Stauffer, *This Was Estes Park: Historical Vignettes of the Early Days, 1915-1965* (Estes Park: Estes Park Area Historical Museum, 1979); and Peter Wild, *Enos Mills* (Boise: ID: Boise State University, 1979).

CORNELIA BAXTER

Extensive sets of articles and society columns from the *Denver Post* and *Rocky Mountain News* portray the life of Cornelia Baxter.

PRESTON PORTER

The convoluted events leading to the tragic death of Preston Porter are reported in the *Rocky Mountain News* throughout November 1900.

WILLIAM FRIEDMAN

Material on William Friedman can be found in Ida Uchill, *Pioneers, Peddlers and Tsadikim* (Denver: Sage Books, 1957); *The Glory That Was Gold* for 1934; and extensive news articles from the *Denver Post, Denver Republican, Denver Times,* and *Rocky Mountain News.*

ELIAS AMMONS

Sources for Elias Ammons include G. Michael McCarthy, "Elias Ammons and the Anticonservative Impulse," unpublished M.A. thesis, University of Denver, 1962, and G. Michael McCarthy, "Insurgency in Colorado: Elias Ammons and the Conservative Impulse," *Colorado Magazine*, Winter 1977. For an extensively documented volume on the conservation history of Colorado, see G. Michael McCarthy, *Hour of Trial: The Conservation Conflict in Colorado and the West* (Norman: University of Oklahoma Press, 1977).

JOHN GALEN LOCKE

An excellent source book on the Ku Klux Klan during the 1920s is David Chalmers, *Hooded Americanism* (New York: Oxford Press, 1967). Other sources include Robert Goldberg, *The Ku Klux Klan in Colorado* (Urbana: University of Illinois Press, 1981); Lyle W. Dorsett and Michael McCarthy, *The Queen City: A History of Denver*, 2nd edition (Boulder, CO: Pruett Publishing Company, 1986); Jon Kolomitz, "The Influence of the Ku Klux Klan in

Colorado Politics," unpublished M.A. thesis, University of Colorado, 1962; James H. Davis, "Colorado Under the Klan," *Colorado Magazine*, Vol. 42, Spring 1965; and numerous newspaper items from the *Denver Post, Rocky Mountain News,* and *Longmont Times-Call.*

LYULPH OGILVY

A lively account of the history of the *Denver Post* and early Colorado journalists in general is Gene Fowler, *Timberline* (Sausalito, CA: Comstock Editions, 1974). Ogilvy's humorous activities are also described in Forbes Parkhill, *The Wildest of the West* (New York: Henry Holt & Company, 1951); and J.D.A. Ogilvy, "Lyulph Ogilvy and His Friends," *Denver Post: Empire Magazine,* May 23, 1977.

SPENCER PENROSE

The best source on Penrose and early Colorado Springs is Marshall Sprague, *Newport in the Rockies: The Life and Times of Colorado Springs,* 3rd edition (Athens, OH: Swallow Press, 1980). Other sources for the eccentric Penrose include Helen Geiger, *The Broadmoor Story* (Denver: A.B. Hirschfeld Press, 1968; revised, 1979); Frances Melrose, "The Broadmoor Empire," *Rocky Mountain News,* March 31, 1946; and Marshall Sprague, "Mr. Broadmoor," *Denver Post: Empire Magazine,* February 22 and March 1, 1953.

JACK DEMPSEY

By far the most compelling story of the Manassa Mauler is his autobiography with Barbara Piatelli Dempsey, *Dempsey* (New York: Harper & Row, 1977). Other sources include Frank M. and Marie L. Fahey, eds., "The Will to Make Believe," *Chapters from the American Experience, Vol. II* (Englewood Cliffs, NJ: Prentice-

Hall, Inc., 1971); Randy Roberts, *Jack Dempsey: The Manassa Mauler* (Baton Rouge: Louisiana State University Press, 1979); the *Denver Post*, June 6, 1960, March 18, 1964, May 5, 1965; and the *Rocky Mountain News*, April 10, 1977 and June 23, 1985.

JOSEPHINE ROCHE

For material on Josephine Roche, see the brief profile in *Cervi's Journal*, June 9, 1965; Lyle W. Dorsett and Michael McCarthy, *The Queen City: A History of Denver*, 2nd edition (Boulder, CO: Pruett Publishing Company, 1986); Marjorie Hornbein, "Josephine Roche: Social Worker and Coal Operator," *Colorado Magazine*, Spring 1976; Marion Castle, "Josephine Roche," *Forum and Century*, August 1934; Josephine Roche, "Mines and Men," *Survey*, Vol. 61, December 15, 1928; and Frank L. Palmer, "War in Colorado," *Nation*, Vol. 125, December 7, 1927.

FLORENCE SABIN

Sources for Dr. Florence Rena Sabin include the Denver *City Edition*, March 4, 1984; the *Denver Post*, July 23, 1947 and December 15, 1985; Mike Flanagan, "Florence Sabin," *Denver Post: Empire Magazine;* and the *Denver Times*, April 23, 1903. Florence Sabin's complete life story is found in Elinor Bluemel, *Florence Sabin: Colorado Woman of the Century* (Boulder: University of Colorado Press, 1959).

WAYNE ASPINALL

A good overview of Aspinall's accomplishments is found in Philip Fradkin, *A River No More* (New York: Alfred Knopf, 1981). News reports are found in *Business Week*, September 23, 1972; *U.S. News and World Report*, November 9, 1972, and extensive items over the extent of his career in the *Denver Post* and *Rocky Mountain News*.

About the Authors

John H. Monnett has taught Western history at colleges in Arizona, Missouri, and Colorado, and was formerly the administrator for continuing education at Community College of Denver. He currently teaches Colorado and Western history at Metropolitan State College in Denver. He is the author of numerous articles on the history of the frontier movement and the Indian wars.

Michael McCarthy, a native of Pueblo, Colorado, teaches history at Community College of Denver and was formerly Director of Student Academic Services at Regis College in Denver. He is the author of *Hour of Trial: The Conservation Conflict in Colorado and the West, 1891-1907* and is co-author of *The Angry West: A Vulnerable Land and Its Future* with former Colorado governor Richard D. Lamm.

Index

Other History Titles from Cordillera Press

BLICKENSDERFER: Images of the West
Edited by Rutherford W. Witthus
160 pp., 64 duotones, (8½ x 11), ISBN: 0-917895-09-6, $35.00, hardcover.
Special Limited Edition: $75.00

GUIDE TO THE GEORGETOWN-SILVER PLUME HISTORIC DISTRICT
48 pp., photos, maps, (7½ x 9 oblong), ISBN: 0-917895-08-8, $4.95, softcover.

GUIDE TO HISTORIC CENTRAL CITY AND BLACK HAWK
Sarah J. Pearce and Christine Pfaff
48 pp., photos, maps, (7½ x 9 oblong), ISBN: 0-917895-15-0, $4.95, softcover.

ROOF OF THE ROCKIES: A History of Colorado Mountaineering
William M. Bueler
264 pp., photos, maps, (5½ x 8½), ISBN: 0-917895-06-1, $12.95, softcover.

SKI TRACKS IN THE ROCKIES: A Century of Colorado Skiing
Abbott Fay
100 pp., photos, (8½ x 10½ oblong), ISBN: 0-917895-02-9, $10.95, softcover.

A CLIMBER'S CLIMBER: On the Trail with Carl Blaurock
Edited by Barbara J. Euser; Foreword by David Lavender
100 pp., 175 photos, (8½ x 10½ oblong), ISBN: 0-917895-01-0, $12.95, softcover.